WOMAN
TO
WOMAN

WOMAN TO WOMAN

From Sabotage to Support

Judith Briles

NEW HORIZON PRESS
Far Hills, New Jersey

Library of Congress Cataloging-in-Publication Data

Briles, Judith
  Woman to woman

  Bibliography: p.
  1. Women—Psychology.   2. Interpersonal relations.
I. Title.
HQ1206.B76   1987   305.4'2   87-21977
ISBN 0-88282-032-X

Acknowledgement:

Woman to Woman is a book of perseverance, commitment, belief. Its genesis began many years ago. Its final birth is credited to many, many friends and thousands of women I met in my travels as a professional speaker. Without their encouragement, it would have been easy to throw in the towel numerous times.

It owes a great deal to the assistance of Alan Leavens, Ginny Foat, Marjorie and Ken Blanchard, Barbara Mackoff, Wendy Rue, Carolyn Morris, Linda Rogers, Lucy Hillestad, Pat Marriott, Shirley Brooks, Sheila Murray Bethel, Patricia Fripp, Susan RoAne, Ruth Ross, Nicole Schapiro, Jef Blum, Gart Sutton, John Maling, Aurora Elia, Sunny Merik, Shelley Briles, Sheryl Briles, Mitzi Mathews, Michael Katz, Susan Strecker, Carole Hyatt, Tom Kelley, Barbara Pletcher, Chris Preimsberger, Luann Lindquist, Gail Schatten Fisher, Vicky O'Brien, Diane Zuckerman, Tom Fryer, Kathie Vreda, Josie Graham, Leslie Smith, Marilyn Murray, Wendy Reid Crisp, Rita Lavelle, and Gini Scott. I especially want to thank Phyllis Chesler who has given me much good advice and support. Hundreds of women and men generously gave their time in participating in my original survey and follow-up interviews. Many have become friends, and I use this opportunity to express my appreciation.

Without my two right hands, it would have been impossible. Louie Ward and Jo Hanley make the impossible possible. Thank you.

I thank Joan Dunphy, Editor-in-Chief of New Horizon Press, and Margaret Russell, Executive Editor, for their guidance through the final phases.

Thank you to John Kenneth Anderson for his generosity and permission to use portions of Maxwell Anderson's *Mary of Scotland*. Bill Wall, Ron Greenwood, and Steve Achterhagen offered expert guidance through my dissertation, and the myriad research, in this book. Thank you.

A thank you is very appropriate for Jacques de Spoelberch, my former agent, for his caring and understanding and to Mel Berger, my current agent, who is making me reach.

Contents

INTRODUCTION

THE MARY QUEEN OF SCOTS STORY RELIVED

Maxwell Anderson's *Mary of Scotland** was written over fifty years ago and depicts historical events that occurred over four hundred years ago. But is it an old story? Is it merely a reminder of outdated values? Does it simply call to mind archaic tactics no longer practiced? Is Elizabeth's duplicity and treachery an anachronism today? Would idealistic Mary be a laughable caricature now? Or are the ethics, values, and naiveté practiced by woman to woman all too familiar to all too many of us?

In the play, the Catholic Mary Stuart has returned from France to rule Scotland despite the fact that her cousin Elizabeth, a Protestant, has determined that this would not happen. The Earl of Bothwell, Mary's friend and supporter (though a Protestant himself), urged war against the Protestants as the

---

*Maxwell Anderson, *Mary of Scotland* (New York: Anderson House, 1933, copyright renewed in 1960 by Gilda Anderson). All subsequent references are to this text.

xii   Introduction

only way of ensuring control for Mary. Idealistic Mary, however, insisted that she "will win, but . . . in a woman's way, not by the sword."

Meanwhile, Elizabeth had also concluded that outright war was the least desirable method of keeping Mary off the throne. But Elizabeth chose cunning and ruthlessness as her weapons and declared that "We are not what we are, but what is said of us and what we read in others' eyes . . . It is necessary . . . to undermine her (Mary) with her own subjects." Then Elizabeth set out to turn Mary's supporters against her. Mary, who had vowed "to rule gently," gradually fell into Elizabeth's trap.

Spurred by vicious rumors against her, as well as by her own husband's betrayal, Mary's earls rebelled. Her faithful secretary was murdered, the Scottish armies attacked, and she was finally imprisoned.

Undaunted by Elizabeth's duplicity, Mary continued to insist that "thrones fall that are built with blood and craft," and "What I am will be known. What's false will wash out in the rain." Finally, however, she could no longer deny her cousin's treachery and lamented that "In all this kingdom I can trust only five, and one's myself, and we're women, all of us." Beaten, she broke down and cried, "Oh God, this vice of women, crying and tears. To weep, weep now when I need my anger!"

Finally, when the two women came face to face in Mary's prison cell, Elizabeth demanded Mary's abdication and Mary refused, preferring lifelong imprisonment. The two women's diverse philosophies, values, and beliefs were most apparent:

> *Mary:* But does this mean you can lend no hand to me . . .?
>
> *Elizabeth:* I say it recalling how I came to my throne as you did . . . beset as you were with angry factions . . . This was many centuries since, or seems so to me, I'm so old by now in shuffling tricks and the huckstering of souls for lands and pensions. I learned to play it young, must learn it or die. It's thus if you would rule; Give up good faith, the

word that goes with the heart, the heart that clings where it loves. Give these up, and love where your interest lies, and should your interest change, let your love follow it quickly. This is queen's porridge, and however little stomach she has for it a queen must eat it . . . You have too loving a heart, I fear, and too bright a face to be a queen . . . I am all women I must be. One's a young girl, young and harrowed as you are—one who could weep to see you here—and one's a bitterness at what I have lost and can never have, and one's the basilisk you saw. This last stands guard and I obey it. Lady, you came to Scotland a fixed and subtle enemy, more dangerous to me than you've ever known. This could not be borne, and I set myself to cull you out and down, and down you are.

Mary: When was I your enemy?

Elizabeth: Your life was a threat to mine, your throne to my throne, your policy a threat . . . It was you or I. Do you know that? The one of us must win and I must always win.

Mary: This trespass against God's right will be known. The nations will know it . . . They will see you as I see you and pull you down . . . Win now, take your triumph now, for I'll win men's hearts in the end—though the sifting takes this hundred years—or a thousand.

Elizabeth: Child, child . . . it's not what happens that matters, no, not even what happens that's true, but what men believe to have happened. They will believe the worst of you, the best of me . . . all history is forged!

Mary: This crooked track you've drawn me on, cover it, let it not be believed that a woman was a fiend.

The treachery practiced by Elizabeth toward Mary is still alive and operative today. Some women are still spreading scandals and dealing in half truths. Others are still the naive, incredulous victims of more envious "sisters." Even though there are victims and perpetrators, both types of women are at risk. And to a very great extent, both are the victims of the rivalry between them.

Today's "Marys" suffer frustration, anger, and resentment and all too often have a need for revenge that is as self-defeating to them as to their intended victims.

And what of the "Elizabeths?" Often their successes are not as sweet as they might have hoped. Sometimes the deceit and sabotage that won them early victories deter them from the very goals for which they aim in the long run. Today the old adage, "United we stand, divided we fall," applies to women's actions toward each other with frightening frequency.

WOMAN TO WOMAN addresses women's relationships with each other. It is a book of exploration—into the history and present consequences of women's dealings with one another. It is a book of confrontation—with women's fears, motivations, and reactions. It is a book of evaluation—of what is wrong with the way women deal with each other, of how and why it differs from the way they deal with men, and of how they can improve their relationships with one another. Finally and most importantly, WOMAN TO WOMAN shows that women's motives, ethics, goals and efforts can further improve, and that this transition can evolve from sabotage to support.

Chapter 1

Ms. Quote

ARE WOMEN REALLY BARRACUDAS?

"This crooked track/You've drawn me on, cover it,
let it not be believed/That a woman was a fiend."
Mary to Elizabeth
Act Three

It had been a good year, a beautiful day, a fine meal, and an animated reunion of friends who, we all agreed, never got together often enough: five professional women—"sisters," if you will—who had known, supported, goaded, and otherwise interacted with each other over a period of several years.

One heads a famous advertising firm; another is a highly visible political figure; the third is a top executive in a prestigious Silicon Valley company; the fourth is the successful owner of a company specializing in investment and financial education. We were almost heady when we talked about our many successes.

We had, inspired by the goals of the Women's Movement, conquered the rigid barriers which had once held women back from achieving their full potential.

Both men and women had supported our successes. At times, they had been heralded by the media and professional women's

1

groups. With pride we congratulated each other and toasted the achievements of those women pioneers who had forged the territory and made our achievements possible.

In comparing the successes and the failures, all of us acknowledged the support of other women and men—they were critical components of our success. Our failures had different elements. In those which involved women, it turned out that the women with whom we were involved had lied, sabotaged, spread rumors, and gossiped. As we sat talking, it became clear that my friends still carried the pain of their experiences with them. We explored them together.

Charlotte is a brilliant financier. She coordinated, developed, and presented a major financing strategy which was to lead one of the Fortune 500 companies to the forefront of American business. That kind of visibility and leadership attracts the attention of others. She soon had several offers to become a principal in other companies; she accepted the post of CEO of a start-up company in the Silicon Valley. Since that time she has started another company and is recognized as a leading and innovative management consultant.

Charlotte's biggest failure centered on money. She was duped by a woman who verbally, publicly, and visibly purported to support other women, and sabotaged them instead. Charlotte was just one of many victims. The magnitude of the problem surfaced when one of Charlotte's colleagues began to recheck references—not an easy task since multiple references were given, even different resumes for different purposes were held by several women that Charlotte knew. The total cost to Charlotte was in excess of $150,000.00. Charlotte could not conceive that one woman—especially one who was a sponsor of major feminist events that included many well-known and successful women on the East Coast—would openly lie, betray, and steal from another. Charlotte let her guard down and didn't fully check the background of the culprit.

Charlotte was just one of many victims taken in by an unethical woman. Today, she no longer assumes that because there's a woman on the other side of the table sisterhood is automatic.

Then Linda spoke. She is a successful entrepreneur who heads her own advertising agency. She claimed that her biggest failure came from the non-support of other women within a company that was well known in the Silicon Valley for its innovations, its support of its employees, its caring—at least today it enjoys that reputation. Linda was in the forefront of consciousness-raising within the corporate structure, aiding women who had been sexually harassed and discriminated against in the form of job promotions. Many women came to her asking for her support, her help, her advice. Their complaints became so overwhelming that she felt that some action needed to be taken.

Meeting with her coworkers led to understanding, segregating, and identifying the various complaints. Approximately twenty-five women vowed to unite against these injustices, protest the sexual harassment and discrimination, until the unfair employment practices were changed and some women received comparable and equal pay.

Energy levels were high—Linda's coworkers asked her to act as spokesperson. Linda felt they were united in purposefulness. Then a rude awakening occurred; she discovered she was the only one out on the limb.

For a variety of reasons, they all dropped out. They were worried about their jobs; they were worried about rocking the boat; they were too busy. Linda, who had become visible and vocal about the company's unfair practices, was fired. She sued. After some time, the company reached a financial settlement with her. Today, in her capacity as head of one of the innovative ad agencies within the Silicon Valley, she is amused that the company which fired her now actively seeks her advice and pays handsomely for it. She's delighted to take their checks. She is also quite firm in her statement that she will never stick her neck out again as she initially did. Ten years have passed and she still feels the hurt that was produced when she gave freely of herself to aid other women.

It was Laura's turn. Laura was the mayor of a wealthy community. She and her husband had built a very successful business. Laura was well liked, publicly acknowledged, respected within the community, the state, and even the nation. She was eventually done in by her political mentor—a woman who became so envious of Laura's power and her unwillingness to act as a puppet that she initiated the subsequent series of events that led to Laura's withdrawal from community, state, and potential national politics—and her indictment for bribery and fraud. Three hundred fifty thousand dollars in defense fees later, the state conceded that they didn't, nor did they ever, have a case. The case was dismissed, but the two years of trauma Laura and her family went through is still causing her pain.

Tracy conceded that her failures were not as glaring as the rest of ours, but they were nagging and subtle. Tracy is a project manager for a large Silicon Valley company. Her expertise is employed worldwide. Her negative experiences involved sabotage at the times she was being considered for other jobs: it was always a woman who gave the final thumbs down. The reason given her for the job denials was that she was either overqualified or that she wouldn't fit in with the team already in place. Today, she runs many of these teams. Tracy feels that the primary components of the sabotage that she experienced for years were envy, power, fear, and insecurity.

All of us had experienced professional and personal trauma; my own was no exception; the trauma extended to my family, my friends, and my business. It involved trust—the violation of it; money—the misappropriation of it; friendships—their termination; talk—the spreading of rumors and malicious gossip.

I was a partner with another woman who was the spokesperson in a venture in Berkeley, California. The managing partners were the developers, and future managers, of a small hotel. Their previous successes had been impressive, their credentials enviable. Through a mutual attorney I had raised over five hundred thousand dollars to buy the property and augment the construction loan from a major bank.

Two years into the project, after an extensive search through the company's books, we realized everything was in trouble—big trouble. A large amount of money had disappeared, almost four hundred fifty thousand dollars. At this point, the woman who was my copartner left. The managing partners were thrown out by the other investors who asked me to take over. I felt obligated—I had referred many of the investors; if I could attain the know-how, perhaps it could be saved.

We managed to save our investment for the time being. But in the process of saving it, I filed for bankruptcy to protect the hotel from the scads of creditors, filed a lawsuit againt the bank, and literally shut down my own business.

How did it work out? Since my former partners all filed for bankruptcy once they were no longer executives of the company, that left me holding the bag. All the creditors got one hundred percent plus interest, plus attorney fees; the bank settled the suit; I was forced to sell all my assets—home, cars, investments, and the remaining assets of my business—to settle the claims. After the creditors were paid, the attorneys got the rest. The court, the attorneys, and the creditors considered it a successful bankruptcy. To me it was a colossal failure.

Whether I will ever rebuild the approximately one million dollars I had in material assets in 1981 I do not know. I do, though, have my health, my family and friends, some old, many new, who understand and support me in both good times and bad. The woman who was the spokesperson for the developing partners and my ex-partner is doing just fine today. After walking away from the problems her group created, she remarried and built another small hotel.

It was late when I finished my own story. I said good night to my friends and fell into my chair to let my adrenalin subside. What I found, however, was that the hormone seemed to be increasing in my system. My heart was pounding and I had an unsettling, anxious feeling in the pit of my stomach. Reliving the night's conversation, I recognized a sort of sad irony in the events of that evening. I had just spent several hours in the company of some of my best friends. We had laughed, talked, bragged, revealed and extracted secrets. In short, we had engaged in one of the most enjoyable pleasures of "sisterhood." But the last part of the conversation and its subsequent revelations about sabotage, duplicity, and unethical behavior had left me distracted and upset.

I had always valued my relationships with my "sisters"— those women I had met and grown to like, admire, and trust in both professional and personal settings. But as I reviewed my professional "failures" and reflected on the failure stories of my friends that evening, a disturbing question surfaced. Could genuine sisterhood be a myth?

To answer that question, I felt the best method was to formulate a survey of hundreds of women and men from the business community. A random sampling was used of women drawn from the 1984 edition of "Who's Who of American Women" and men from the 1984 "Who's Who in Finance and Industry" (at the time of the survey, there was no "Who's Who of American Men"). Originally, two thousand questionnaires were sent out, and the replies represented a response rate of seventeen percent by the computer analysis cutoff date. An additional five percent was received after the cutoff date. Analysis of these revealed basically the same type of responses as the surveys received prior to the cutoff date.

Those who responded represented a broad cross section of business people all over the United States: the West Coast, the Midwest, and the East Coast. Two-thirds of the participants were women, one-third were men. Most were thirty or older, and the majority were over forty. Typically, they were in top business and professional jobs. Included were CEOs, VPs, and chief financial officers of corporations; administrators, managers, and supervisors; teachers, engineers, and scientists; people who were self-employed, professionals, or in sales and marketing.

They also represented different kinds of work situations, ranging from small companies to large corporations to social service and government positions. About a third owned their own businesses, with emphasis in professional consulting, followed by financial services, marketing, and real estate.

The respondents also can be considered quite knowledgeable about what goes on in the business world—two-thirds had been in the business environment for more than ten years, and half of these were there for more than twenty years.

Incomes of the participants ranged from under $30,000.00 to more than $100,000.00, with approximately one-third earning more than $50,000.00, one-third between $30,000.00 and $50,000.00, and the rest less than $30,000.00

THE FINDINGS

About sixty-five percent of all respondents reported that they had been unethically treated by a man; forty-seven percent reported unethical treatment by a woman. This was determined by the key question: "In your opinion, have you been treated unethically by a man or woman in a business situation?" Ethics is defined by Webster's II New Riverside University edition as:

> 1. A principle of right or good behavior. 2. A system of moral principles or values.

Business was defined as anything outside of being a homemaker in which actual payment for work was received.

We discovered that fifty-three percent of the women said other women had treated them unethically. Thirty-five percent of the men blamed women for unethical treatment. The difference between women who reported women treating women unethically and men who reported women treating men unethically reflects a fifty-one percent increase. There are similar reportings of men, only with a lesser spread—ten percent. Men seem to experience more unethical behavior from other men (sixty-nine percent) than what women report about men (sixty-three percent).

Why should this be? Two key words summarize the findings: *opportunity* and *power*. Men generally have more power in the workplace, so they have more opportunity to behave unethically in the struggle to get ahead. Women are more likely to sabotage each other simply because women are more likely to work together and because they are viewed as weaker due to their lack of experience, not knowing the rules, or being naive.

However, as women move up the occupational ladder or are more likely to work with other women, they tend to encounter more unethical behavior. Why? Again, *opportunity* and *power*. As women move up, they have more power to do something unethical. And when the woman moving up is more likely to work with other women, the victim of her unethical behavior is most likely to be another woman. For instance, the women who reported the most unethical behavior from other women were those in the higher job positions, earning more than $100,000.00 a year (thirteen percent of all female respondents)—or those in the lower-paying jobs, earning less than $30,000.00 a year (twenty-three percent of total female respondents); they were also women who owned their own businesses or who had been in the business world for more than twenty-one years.

Subsequent interviews with many of these women seemed to indicate that as women move up the ladder they feel more threatened and isolated. Top positions are limited, so many women are put in a situation of battling with other women for the new choice spots at the top.

Women who own their own businesses are typically in small businesses and are likely to work with women in other small businesses. Sometimes they take unethical shortcuts in order to get ahead.

The situation is similar for men who move up the occupational ladder, start their own businesses, or greatly change position in the working world: they're more likely to run into unethical behavior, especially from other men with whom they are more likely to work.

In addition to power and opportunity, the ramifications of fear, jealousy, envy, and low self-esteem surfaced in our interviews. Titles usually carry a form of power—some earned, some assumed. If a man or woman is in a notch of power but has a low self-esteem, it's improbable that subordinates or coworkers are going to be treated fairly. If a person doesn't feel good about who he or she is or have confidence in what he or she is doing, then those feelings will permeate the work environment.

The question arises: do most women follow the same style of sabotaging that has been traditional in the male-dominated business world? That question becomes particularly important now, since women are already at a distinct disadvantage getting ahead in the business world because of years of prior discrimination and prejudice. If additional barriers are added by women to restrict other women, the resulting blockades become almost insurmountable.

ETHICAL DIFFERENCES BETWEEN WOMEN AND MEN

The findings of my survey indicated that women are more likely to behave unethically to other women than they are to men. And unprincipled men and women have different styles: women have a more covert, indirect style when it comes to behaving unethically, while men are more characteristically assertive and direct.

It also appeared that women were more likely to be motivated to act unethically out of fear, which usually can be traced to the power imbalance of men and women. Women are more fearful, more threatened because generally they are further down the power ladder. The most common reasons why many women commit unethical acts were that they were jealous, envious, or even afraid someone was after their jobs. Fourteen percent of the participants in our survey said a woman acted unethically for these reasons; only four percent accused a man of behaving in these ways.

Men, on the other hand, were more likely to do something unethical to build up their egos, reflecting this traditional male push to be assertive. Men, much more so than women, failed to give someone else credit for their work or misrepresented it as theirs: twenty-three percent of the survey respondents blamed men for this; only fourteen percent accused women. Then, too, men were usually the ones accused of sexism or sexual harassment: forty-four percent of the respondents accused men of both these actions, but only about five percent accused women.

However, women can be just as unethical for power reasons as men. Women's power is more generally over other women; if there is unethical behavior, the recipient is more likely to be another woman. Almost sixteen percent of all female survey respondents claimed that they had experienced a woman failing to give credit or taking credit for work completed by others. None of the male respondents reported this experience in their dealings with women. It's not always clear if their actions were intentional, although ninety-one percent of the respondents who were treated unethically believed the women did this intentionally.

WHAT ARE THE COSTS?

Significantly, men and women not only have different styles of unethical behavior, but the results of their action also are different. Male and female victims have different experiences. It's as if the men and women are playing in different ballgames; not only are the rules and players different, but so are the strikes and fouls.

How? When men act unethically toward an individual the effects are usually fairly straightforward—a loss of money or a lost promotion. In our survey, forty-four percent of the respondents said a man's actions cost them money; twenty-three percent of them said it cost them a promotion. But women's unethical behavior is somewhat less likely to cause their victims to lose money (only thirty-five percent of the respondents) or a promotion (fourteen percent reported this). Instead, women are much more likely to be guilty of other less tangible costs, including causing their victims embarrassment or damaged reputations.

Why such differences? Again, it probably goes back to the different agendas of men and women and what is more important to each. Men tend to be pragmatically oriented: when they decide to do someone in, they do so for what appears to be more practical reasons—to get more money or to get the other's job. They are, likewise, more sensitive to losing money themselves when they are the victims. Women focused more on emotional factors, and, to a greater extent than did men, caused their victims to suffer other losses, such as embarrassment and damaged reputations. Many women who are unethical leave their victims in financial binds or cause the loss of jobs. But after such a loss, the victim is more likely to feel other types of devastation than he or she would if betrayed by a man.

When it comes to damaging a company, however, men are more successful. When we asked the survey participants about the various categories of damage their companies experienced, the participants were more likely to accuse males. Men, it seems, are more likely to cause companies to lose money or business. They are more likely to start legal action. And they are more likely to embarrass their companies.

Why? Presumably because men simply have more power to do major harm to a company. They are in higher positions or are in charge of their own companies, so they can take on the company as a whole. Many women, stuck lower down in the work hierarchy, strike out at other individuals but have less clout when it comes to doing company-wide damage.

Also significant are the different perceptions of men and women about the nature of this damage. While both men and women generally agree that men do more damage, they seem to be watching a different ballgame when it comes to describing the damage. Men are more likely to mention money as the major cost, no matter who gets it by behaving unethically. In our study, fifty-one percent of the men compared to twenty-three percent of the women blamed a man for doing their company out of money; forty-two percent of the men compared to eighteen percent of the women accused a woman of a similar act. Also, the men in the survey were likely to accuse other men of causing their companies to lose business or to embroil their companies in legal action, while the women talked about a company suffering embarrassment or a loss of visibility.

There are two major explanations for these differences. First, since they tend to occupy different power positions in the company, men and women simply observe unethical behavior from different perspectives; since men are more typically in higher executive positions, they are privy to knowing when a company has monetary problems or is losing business. Secondly, men and women may perceive what happens in different terms because of their different orientations. Since men are more pragmatically oriented, they may be sensitive to any losses of money or business by the company. Many women are more emotionally oriented so that they are more sensitive to costs to the company in terms of embarrassment or a loss of visibility.

WHAT ARE THE GAINS?

The person who targets another individual for downfall does so to gain certain ends. As to the reasons for such behavior, the views of the men and women surveyed differed notably. Both men and women agreed on basic motivations for a man or woman acting unethically toward an individual. Most of the time they believed the man or woman wanted more money or a better reputation.

The big difference was that the men surveyed were much more likely to think the individual acted to gain money. About forty percent of men indicated this reasoning, whereas only twenty-four percent of the women did. Conversely, many more women than men thought the motivation for unethical behavior was a better reputation, especially when a woman sabotaged another woman. Twenty-seven percent of the women felt this to be the case, compared to only four percent of the men.

The difference appears to relate to the different success agendas men and women have. Men are more likely to be concerned about money, and they think other men are, also.

Women traditionally have been concerned about their images to others, so reputation is high on their agendas.

Likewise, male and female participants in the survey had different opinions about what the person's company would achieve through his or her unethical behavior. Overwhelmingly, the men argued that the main company gain would be money. Seventy-five percent of the men thought the company would benefit by getting more money when another man treated them unethically; only twenty-seven percent of the women thought this. On the other hand, more women than men believed a woman acted unethically to gain visibility or a better reputation for her company.

Many of these findings about costs and gains supported much of the observed comments we received from both male and female colleagues that women and men have quite disparate agendas and perceptions when they enter the business world. As a result, they act differently and also perceive others' actions discrepantly.

These sharp differences suggest that men and women are coming to the workplace with dissimilar rules and motivations that affect how they act and what is important to them. For men, the main goals of business success center around bottom-line factors. Most men have been traditionally brought up to measure success in material terms and this credo shows in the reasons why some men are unethical to others and the losses men experience when they become victims themselves. There are other issues that come up for men, of course, when unethical behavior surfaces, but men in the survey repeatedly mentioned money.

In contrast, for women, who have been spectators or second-string players in the business game, the crucial elements of the game are quite different. Money may be central for some, but there are many other important factors which motivate their unethical behavior, since they are outside the main arena. Issues such as personal esteem, reputation, and embarrassment seem especially significant for most women.

In a way, what has happened with these women is what

happens to those participating in sports in a spectator or second-ary role. The players on the field are the ones who do the scoring, so their focus is on the score itself: increasing it for themselves and keeping others from making gains. In compari-son, the spectators and the supporting players, since they don't have the same focus on scoring, become interested in more tangential things. For instance, spectators may gain satisfaction from seeing or interacting with other spectators, while the supporting players may be especially interested in being noticed and building up their own reputations so they can be chosen to play more in the game.

In the business world, men for the most part are still the main players, so scoring—or, making money—is their central con-cern. At present, women are more likely to have less important executive positions, so they stand on the sidelines or are sup-porting players, so tangential issues, such as gaining reputation, suffering embarrassment, and seeking more personal esteem, become more important.

Thus, there are some very good reasons why men and women play the business game differently, and consequently engage in and experience unethical behavior differently.

DOES IT MATTER WHO
THE VICTIM IS?

The survey also elicited information as to whether men and women differ in whom they choose to treat unethically. Does it matter whether their victim is a woman or a man?

There appears to be a big difference of opinion between most men and most women on this point. Most of the women in our survey believed that when a man treated them unethically he was taking advantage of them because they were women, and, as already mentioned, many of the women accused men of sexism and sexual harassment. However, the men didn't think their sex had anything to do with it. They believed that those who acted unethically toward them did so because of other reasons.

Regarding unethical behavior by women, both the women and the men in our survey made clear statements as to whether their own sex mattered or not. Sixty percent of all respondents thought there was a relationship between what happened and their own sex. Ironically, sixty-two percent of the women and forty-eight percent of the men felt there was such a relationship involved in unethical treatment by a woman. Eighty percent of the women and fifteen percent of the men felt such a relationship when treated unethically by a man.

Why the differences? It may tie into the fact that women are the new kids on the block in the business world. Although a majority in number, they are a minority in power. When anything happens to them, whether a woman or man is the "bad guy," they may conclude that the person acted badly out of sexism. On the other hand, men, more secure in their positions, are more likely to think there was no relationship between their sex and what happened. They may be rather blasé and even accepting and forgiving when a man is involved.

THE RELATIONSHIP
BETWEEN HELP AND
HARM

The flip side of hurting someone in the workplace is helping someone. In our survey we looked for a connection between who helps and who harms whom, since those who have the power to behave unethically also have the power to help people.

We found that, indeed, helpful and harmful behavior seemed to go very much together, and the underlying glue was power. Reflecting the lyrics of the old song, "You Always Hurt the One You Love," it often appeared that the people who were doing the harming were also offering help.

The survey revealed that the men who were most likely to hurt some people, regardless of sex, were also somewhat more likely to provide assistance to other people. Seventy-six percent of the survey participants were helped by a man, sixty-eight percent by a woman. More than likely the slight percentile differential between the sexes reflects men's greater power, and their concomitant capacity for helping—and harming—more people.

It also indicated that members of the same sex not only were more likely to treat each other unethically than they would members of the opposite sex, but were also more likely to help each other. The majority of women reported they received help from both women and men—seventy-three percent and seventy-seven percent, respectively. The men claimed they received more help from other men than they did from women—seventy-two percent and fifty-seven percent, respectively.

In the special situations where people claimed more—or less—help from others, this relationship seemed even more frequent. The respondents working in the social services and government agencies were more likely than those in other work settings to be helped by a woman than by a man, presumably because the women there have more power. By the same token, the participants who were most likely to be helped or treated unethically by a woman were those earning under $30,000.00 a year.

Even the types of help offered reflect the twin themes of power and opportunity. There were certain types of help acknowledged by both men and women: personal advice, counseling and encouragement, obtaining information and experiences for more visibility and growth, gaining help from a mentor, and receiving client referrals and sales leads. But when it came to receiving assistance in getting a job or a promotion, our survey showed that women were more likely to get help from another woman, while the men were more likely to get that assistance through another man.

However, when it came to getting help for a business, all of the participants reported they were more likely to gain a job or more business for their company from a man. Why? Power. Men have higher executive positions in most companies, and thus more power.

The same kind of differences described earlier between men's pragmatic orientation and women's feelings-oriented approach surfaced again in the kind of help each reported. More women than men reported that through the help of others their company gained more visibility. The men were more likely to claim that their companies benefited by gaining more money. Again, this difference shows the same sort of split described earlier, relating to how men differ in their reactions to unethical behavior. The women were more likely to complain about damages to appearances; the men were more likely to say they had lost money.

OTHER CONNECTIONS

Are there any other connections? If there is so much unethical activity out there, who is most likely to get hurt, the innocent victim or the unethical person? What about preferences? If the people who work together tend to both help and sabotage each other more, do people who prefer to work with one sex or the other differ from those who don't in their experiences with unethical behavior? And finally, do the reasons people have for choosing to work with others have anything to do with what happens to them ethically?

The results of our survey showed that to some extent unethical behavior begat more unethical behavior. In other words, if sabotaged, a person most often fights back by sabotage. Not many of the respondents said they had been accused of doing anything unethical themselves: only fourteen percent of the respondents said so, and the vast majority of these—eighty-seven percent—said there was no basis for the accusation. As it turned out, those who were accused of sabotage were more likely to report that someone else treated them unethically. For example, only two percent of the respondents who said no one treated them unethically were accused of acting unethically themselves, but around fifteen percent of those who said they had been treated unethically by a man or woman were accused of unethical behavior themselves. And when it came to who was treated unethically by both sexes, twenty-four percent reported they had been accused.

Is there a kind of tit-for-tat in unethical behavior going on in the business world? Possibly. The more people experience unethical behavior from others, the more they are likely to be accused themselves, justifiably or not. Men are twice as likely to be accused as women. Thirty-eight percent of the men who reported unethical treatment by both men and women claimed they were accused themselves; only twenty percent of the women admitted an accusation. This difference may be telling. It suggests that men may be better able to strike back and do— or at least others perceive they do. In contrast, women who are less powerful are less likely to be accused of action directed at men. Others are less likely to perceive them in the aggressor role. When many women react to unethical behavior, they do so covertly, as opposed to the male's overt posture, and others are then less apt to see them do it.

To look at this relationship in another way, those who were accused of acting unethically were much more likely to report that someone else, especially of the same sex, treated them unethically. For instance, sixty-two percent of those so accused thought a woman treated them unethically, versus only thirty-five percent of those who weren't accused; eighty percent of the accused thought a man unethical, versus only fifty-four percent of the unaccused. The percentages for the accused dealing with their own sex were even higher. Nearly three-quarters of the women who were accused felt a woman treated them unethically; ninety-four percent of the accused men felt another man was unethical.

When preferences were explored, there didn't seem to be much connection between those with whom people like to work and their experience of being treated unethically. Only a small percentage of men and women expressed a preference in either direction. Approximately twelve percent preferred working only with a woman or a man. While it is true that the women in the survey were more likely than the men to want to work with a woman (sixteen percent to two percent), this is still a very small number. Then, too, in their reports of unethical treatment by men or women, there was relatively little difference between those who did have a preference and those who didn't. The only major difference that emerged was that those who had experienced unethical treatment by women were much more likely to prefer working with men (about twenty-eight percent of the women reporting and forty percent of the men). Those who preferred doing business with men were slightly more likely to believe that women had done them in than those with no preference (forty-eight percent versus thirty percent), and the same was true of those who preferred working with women: they were slightly more likely to think a man had done them wrong (sixty-five percent versus fifty-one percent).

Apart from these slight differences, personal preferences seemed to have little impact. Perhaps this is because people look on unethical behavior as part of the game in doing business; it's one of those things people have come to tolerate if not accept; therefore, they have no strong preferences influencing their opinions about whether they think people are unethical.

But there was a much stronger connection between helpfulness and preferences. Those who preferred doing business with a woman or a man were more likely to find that person helpful than those who had no such preferences. Approximately seventy-seven percent of those with a preference for working with women found them actively helpful, compared to sixty-three percent with no preference; about eighty-nine percent of those expressing a preference for men felt this way, compared to seventy-four percent with no preference.

What we also noted was that the reasons given for preferences reflected some traditional stereotypes about the way women behave as well as about the styles of unethical behavior talked about earlier. Those expressing a preference for working with women, largely other women, did so because of emotional factors: they had a personal bias toward women or thought they needed support from other women. But those women and men

who expressed a preference for working with men often stated
that they believed men were less petty, less likely to play games,
or less likely to have personality problems. They tended to
convey opinions that many women act unethically—by being
deceptive, vindictive, and covert in what they do.

These findings seem to support the observation that opportunity and power are at the basis of whom behaves unethically to
whom. When people work together, when people have power
over another, they are in a position to either help or harm the
other. Women and men share a common thread here: the difference is that women simply have more opportunity to help or
harm other women as they work together more often. Men are
more likely to help or harm everyone; they have more power.
However, as women move up the occupational ladder, they gain
more power. But their opportunities for upward mobility are
more limited than men's; women often end up in a kind of
squeeze-play situation that can contribute to using unethical
tactics.

Because of their different styles of coping in the business
world, women act differently than men do when they act ueth-
ically. Women, according to the results of the survey, more
often act out of jealousy, envy, or fear; whereas men tend to act
more from ego motivations. The root of the difference lies in the
different balance of power and women's role as traditional
outsiders. To be sure, women are moving into positions of power
in increasing numbers, but they still feel that power differential—and that's reflected in the ways in which they act unethically.

The bottom line: it's a power game in a culture as success-
oriented as ours, and unethical behavior is part of it. If we want
to start changing such behavior, we have to come to terms with
the power issue. Its dynamics need to be investigated and
explored. And finally, a means of dealing with power more
constructively needs to be established—in ways that will help
both women and men.

Both sexes, then, may behave unethically. But when they do

they use different tactics, focus on different victims, and have different reasons for their unethical behavior. More often than not, women choose other women as victims. The reason? A partial answer lies in the climate of today's society and work-force.

Chapter 2

Ms.Perception

ALL WOMEN ARE NOT CREATED EQUAL

"She is a woman, remember, and open to attack/ as a woman."

Elizabeth to Burghley
Act One, Scene II

Unethical behavior between women occurs more often than unethical behavior between women and men. Why are women more likely to sabotage each other? And why are women likely to use covert, deceptive methods?

There seem to be eight major reasons, based on findings from sociology, psychology, demography, and history, among other fields.

First, women face more competition, due to current demographic and social trends: women struggle harder to maintain their position or to get ahead.

Second, modern society is experiencing a real ethical crisis.[1] Traditional values and morals are crumbling, and this has a greater impact on women.

Third, the workplace is still a jungle with everyone struggling to take advantage of opportunities and form beneficial alliances.

In the survival of the fittest, fought however subtly or overtly, some people are rendered obsolete and others get badly hurt or worse.

Fourth, women have demonstrated a more personal management style that can at times work very successfully but at times backfires.

Fifth, there are extra pressures women face in balancing their personal lives and the demands of the workplace, and many times these pressures create stress.

Sixth, some women are still held back from management positions because of the old stereotypes of how women should behave. To break out of that mold, women have to do more, accomplish more.

Seventh, women have been raised differently than men, and their attitudes toward morality develop differently: they have a more flexible, situational way of relating to the world, which sometimes can turn into unethical behavior.

Finally, women and men share very separate psychological realities: they relate to the world differently so they have disparate ideas about dishonesty and deception, attitudes towards competition, perceptions of self-esteem, and feelings about relationships. They also deal with feelings of anger and hostility differently.

Many people would like to deny these differences. They suggest that women in the workplace should be viewed equally with men. They believe that any discussion of differences only hurts women's chances.

But the point is these differences exist. To deny them is to be an ostrich sticking its head in the sand. There is no question that women should have equal opportunity and that women have the ability to do virtually any job on the same level as men. But that's a separate issue from recognizing that there are differences in men's and women's performances in the workplace and examining how these differences may sometimes interfere with women working more effectively together.

Conditions can be changed. Women can become more aware of what is happening and exercise more control over destructive behaviors in the workplace. Through knowledge, awareness, and confrontation, women can learn to support each other more and behave more ethically toward one another.

HOW CURRENT SOCIAL TRENDS CONTRIBUTE TO WOMEN SABOTAGING WOMEN

A key factor in what has happened between women is the rapid transformation of the workplace. Women have moved in growing numbers into the workplace and into higher-level positions. A *Business Week* article reports: "Women have seized two-thirds of the jobs created in the past decade. And they have been the linchpin in the shift towards services and away from manufacturing."[2]

Significantly, too, women, although still not earning as much as men, are making more money than they ever have. In 1980 women earned only sixty percent of what men earned, but as of 1984 it was reported at sixty-four percent. The trend should continue; it is estimated that by 2000 women will be earning at least seventy-four percent of what men do.[3] Why? The obvious reason is that women are getting more education, experience, and recognition and are moving into higher level jobs than have been traditionally open to them. And as women perform well in their new jobs, more doors are opening.

Statistics show this clearly. Since 1970 the number of women in management and professional jobs has zoomed; they have moved into professions formerly dominated by men. During the 1970s women held only eighteen percent of all executive, administrative, and management positions; by 1980 they held thirty percent.[4]

Yet the very social changes that have propelled women into these new positions also have created other pressures, including the increased divorced rate, the increased number of women remaining single, and the growing number of female-headed households. At the same time that women are gaining more responsibilities within the workplace, they also are gaining more responsibilities outside. On one hand, this means women have more freedom and control over their lives than ever before. But this personal power and freedom bring with them risks, for instance, women's increased financial responsibility for themselves and their families: it is a well-known fact that many single mothers are strapped by finances due to nonpayment of child support.[5] And, with or without children, some women may find themselves emotionally alone; in choosing to make a major commitment to work they don't have the time or the energy to nurture relationships. Women may make these choices because of necessity or freely, but they often feel under enormous pressure at work and at home.

One of the sources of these pressures is the wage gap. In spite of recent legislation, women still make less than men do, primarily because men and women don't have equal opportunities to perform the same jobs and because compared to men, women are more easily trapped into lower-paying, routine work. So women still are more likely to face blocks to advancements than men. Some women, of course, get through. But the narrower path to advancement means that women have to struggle harder with each other to get to those few available spots.

Statistics show this picture starkly. Although there are a growing number of successful women executives, the vast majority of all working women are still stuck in lower-paying jobs, sometimes called the "pink-collar ghetto": jobs in the service occupations, the helping professions, and secretarial-clerical work. In 1982, ninety-nine percent of all secretaries were women,[6] and while the secretarial route is often the way up into higher ranks in the company, to get there a woman still must break from the pack, which can be a source of resentment and hurt for those left behind, and which often involves keeping someone else down. So women may feel they have to resort to various forms of sabotage to get ahead.

The same sort of pressures can operate on women who are outside the corporation. According to the statistics, women represent the most active source of new business formation today. As of 1982 they owned 631,000 firms grossing \$40.5 billion, and they have been forming their companies at a much faster rate than men. In the five-year period between 1977 and 1982 the number of businesses they owned increased by thirty percent compared to a ten percent increase for men.[7] For the remainder of the 1980s, women are projected to continue to start their own businesses at a rate of three to one over men.

For many women, forming a business is a response to corporate discrimination. They feel blocked from top jobs in the corporation, so they form their own businesses as a way out. But once in business for themselves women can face even more pressures, since they are up against the traditional "old boy" network of businesses already created by men. Making the business a success can be tougher, although this pattern is gradually changing as more and more women are doing it, and— a vital ingredient—women are creating more support networks for themselves.

Men are in a more solid position; they have more power and more connections already established. Since competition is tougher, women find that they must be tougher, which may translate into women taking advantage of each other. As women compete to get jobs for their new businesses, just as they compete to move ahead in the corporation, whom do they confront who are more vulnerable and more likely to be blocking their way? Other women, of course. Therefore, they are more likely to direct their competitive actions against other women than against men.

Another contributing factor is that women have been shackled with certain expectations about what they should do and how they should behave. These old stereotypes suggest that women should do certain types of work, which emphasize their nurturant social skills, physical attractiveness, or domestic responsibility. Men are taught as boys to emphasize their technical skills, authoritativeness, and physical prowess. The reality was that women traditionally were counseled, programmed, and drawn to jobs such as nursing, teaching, or receptionists and office "go-fers."[8]

With the advent of the Women's Movement, extraordinary as well as average women sought to get out of this box. In order to do so, they often had to be extra tough—or at least perceived to be—to get the work done. Our studies show that women who don't break out of the old employment stereotypes can feel frustrated and trapped, which can lead them to lash out at those who do get ahead.

Thus, there's a kind of vicious cycle making it harder for all women—those who make it on the success ladder and those who don't. In turn, such difficulties are reflected in the statistics about who likes to work with whom. When Louis Harris and Associates did a survey of six hundred executives in 1982, they found that forty-one percent of them said men don't like to take orders from women, and thirty-nine percent of them said women also don't like taking orders from other women.[9]

According to a *Los Angeles Times* article by Kathleen Hendrix, the underlying reason for the resistance which women sometimes experience is what is called "the comfort factor." Even though other workers may recognize a woman executive's competence, they still feel some discomfort at fully accepting her in a position of power.[10] Why? Because old attitudes and patterns of behavior die hard. Women are playing a new role in the workplace, and many people, especially other women, feel uncomfortable with that fact.

A continuing problem for women achievers is that some of the strategies women pursue to break down the barriers are the same which lead others to criticize them for being too tough or critical. For instance, in a *Wall Street Journal*/Gallup survey, twenty-nine percent of the women said they would *rather* work for men, because they believed female executives were "too petty and overly critical." They felt that their female bosses were overcompensating for being female by being overbearing. The feeling was that since the female bosses had to work so hard to succeed themselves, they demanded much more of their subordinates. The participants in the survey also felt that some of their female bosses were too easily threatened: since there were relatively fewer opportunities for women, the ones who succeeded were more competitive.[11]

The transformation of the workplace through the Women's Movement and its advocacy of new roles for women has not only created new positions for women, it has also helped create the very situation which contributes to women behaving unethically toward other women. There are more possibilities—and also more barriers—as women work to gain these new opportunities which the changed economy has opened up, and this combination of forces has placed women under increased pressure. There are more options, and there are greater numbers of women who would like to take advantage of them; they have more desire to succeed, and yet as they seek to move ahead they confront the fact that there is a far greater number of women competing and struggling in business—and there is a lesser chance for them to move up than there is for men. Our survey revealed that women under stress do attack each other when one competes with another. And at the same time, they are more vulnerable.

It's this explosive combination that contributes to the phenomenon of women sabotaging each other. But there are solutions.

HOW THE DECLINE IN ETHICAL VALUES AFFECTS WOMEN

Ethical values have declined throughout society. Examples of this are everywhere: religious dissension, drugs in the schools, ethical debates over new developments in science and medicine, even apathy—many just don't care. In a thoughtful *Fortune* magazine article, "Battered Pillars of the American System," Peter Berger traces how religious, educational, and scientific institutions have been especially hard hit by these ethical declines.[12] One of his main points is that both secular and religious culture in America have become weakened and have undermined values; people have lost faith in their traditions and in their institutions.

Why does this change affect women? Because historically women have been most constrained by these traditional values, and as the values have changed so have the constraints on women. When beliefs about what is proper behavior and conduct break down, people become confused about what to do, about what is morally right and wrong. This is especially true for women who have found this past decade one of such radical change in opportunities and goals. Because of this flux, as the theories of R. H. Maslow[13] confirmed, people are more likely to engage in self-interested behavior with pragmatic ends: they become less concerned about the social consequences of their acts than they are in what's best for ''me.''

A related problem is the development of competing codes of ethical behavior which have resulted as society has become more complex. Individuals may have one standard of ethics, the companies they work for may have another, and the employees of those companies may have their own. It's a problem which Thomas J. Hayes describes starkly when he writes, ''The employee's dilemma is compounded when he or she seeks out a single moral standard to follow and one does not exist.''[14]

When moral values are unclear, in flux, or beset by competing interpretations of what is right or wrong, and when a situation arises where acting unethically can produce a meaningful personal gain, even though others or the organization as a whole might be hurt, some people become more opportunistic and the lures of unethical conduct become more powerful.

Some companies actually create the environment that contributes to unethical action. Different departments in the same company may have conflicting goals, or there may be a disparity between short-term and long-term profit goals. Or, when production problems arise various units in the organization may seek to shift blame to other units.

Certainly all of these value changes in society—the decline in social values generally, the development of competing codes of ethical behavior, a company environment that contributes to unethical action—also affect men. But our findings, as well as other important research, suggest that women are affected more seriously; they are under more pressure to perform due to their lower power position in the workplace, and, as the results of our survey substantiate, when ethical conflicts or opportunities for gain through unethical means arise in the workplace, some women take the unethical way out. The confusion of moral values tends to be a tempting excuse for those seeking personal gain.

The problem of ethical breakdown in our society is a serious one, because ethical values are a kind of social glue that keeps the institutions of our society functioning smoothly. When these common moral principles break down, so can the social fabric. As Harold Johnson wrote in *Business Horizons,* "Unethical choices may build through a chain reaction a new society of government intervention and control—or society may evolve into violent anarchy where it truly is 'every person for himself.' "[15]

This frightening new world Johnson describes may not have evolved yet, but our society definitely shows breakdown. Societal value systems have become unclear, and today, as David Linowes writes, "Our environment suffers from confusion as to what is morally right and wrong. The danger is serious, because immorality and dishonesty are contagious. They spread and grow when left in their own condoning environment."[16]

Certainly, this breakdown in values it pervasive in all levels of society—in religion, education, science, and business—and it has occurred in part because of the recent vast technological and social changes which have disrupted traditional roles, relationships, and values.

With this moral loosening, each person has become freer to act to his or her personal advantage, whether these actions are moral or not. And while neither men nor women are immune to this growing social virus, women are more at risk because their own roles and relationships have changed the most, leaving them with more disrupted social moorings.

HOW THE CULTURAL
AND SOCIAL DYNAMICS
OF THE WORKPLACE
AFFECT WOMEN

Just what are the pressures of the competitive workplace which are especially stressful to women? Is it office politics, or are there special circumstances which make women even more likely to behave unethically toward other women?

The first reality is that the large, complex corporation is highly politicized, and the struggle for power encourages a variety of coalitions and factions to form. On the one hand, such groups can provide a source of strength and nurturing; on the other, they can offer a power base for people working their way to the top. And as individuals move from one group to another on their way up, they can easily step on others remaining in the group, who may feel resentful, even hostile.

Many corporations have become more altruistic. They have, in the words of Mary Cunningham, become "more humane, more like a family."[17] One result of this is that channels to the top have become more open; there is more room for individual creativity. It also means there is more opportunity for people to develop different power groups, factions, and coalitions to achieve personal goals. One upshot of all this is that women are more apt to be victimized—or victimize other women—in the ensuing power struggles that result. They are more apt to take advantage of another, less powerful woman.

In *Corporate Cultures,* Terence E. Deal and Allan A. Kennedy describe these barriers that make it more difficult for women, like members of minority groups, to become integrated into corporate culture. As they found, most of the corporate women they interviewed felt perpetually excluded from important events at all stages in their careers, since the men already in power tended not to feel comfortable with them.[18] Women commonly react to such barriers by feeling frustrated and powerless. It would be difficult to take out their hostile feelings on more powerful men, which leaves the less powerful as the recipient. At the same time, knowing such barriers are there, some women struggle even harder to get into the power circle. If that means they have to push other women down to get there, their attitude is "that's the breaks of the game."

The development of subcultures in the corporation also can contribute to more unethical behavior. As Deal and Kennedy describe it, subcultures spring up for a number of reasons. They develop around functional differences—for example, groups centered in sales, research and development, or manufacturing, to name a few. They develop around economic, educational, and gender characteristics. Once developed, they each create their own cultural environment and world view. Unfortunately, individuals with low power in these groups can feel especially frustrated when their own values and world views are not recognized, and they can take out these feelings on others in their subgroup or on others with even less power.[19]

Secretaries are an example of this. As Rosabeth Moss Kanter found in studying men and women in a corporation, secretaries sometimes were caught up in struggles of power because each secretary's status in the company was linked to the status of her own boss. The secretaries of the higher-level bosses would dump on the secretaries of the lower-level bosses when they saw their bosses at loggerheads. Sometimes they even acted to undermine their own bosses when they had designs on their bosses' jobs— a situation that was more likely to occur when the boss was a woman, which made access to that position seem more possible for another woman.[20]

The move up the corporate hierarchy creates fertile conditions for unethical behavior to flourish, especially for a woman. Kanter noticed that some individuals would gain the advantage of being "fast-tracked" as prime officer candidates. They had more career reviews, and they were moved into positions where they were more likely to become the target of resentment by those not so favored. Meanwhile, many of their peers suddenly warmed up to them in order to be part of the winner's team.[21]

Getting ahead requires skill in maneuvering through the resentments of those left behind and the presentments of the fickle opportunity seekers. The game is stressful for both women and men, but women have acquired fewer resources and less skill for playing the game effectively, and therefore may be more likely to engage in questionable conduct against each other along the way.

There is another problem here. Since there are fewer women on the higher corporate reaches, women in these positions are more visible, and their behavior may be interpreted as being tricky or devious. It's often a no-win situation women face if they want to survive in the corporate world, and since the game is harder and has more constraints, and since many women don't know the rules, they have to be more calculating and tough to play—and then they're more likely to be accused of foul play.

Political game-playing can also result in women resorting to more covert tactics to succeed. Because it is still not as acceptable for women as it is for men to exercise power, women can't be as open and aggressive about wanting to get ahead as men, so they are more likely to engage in behind-the-scenes actions. But if these don't work and they find themselves stuck, they may experience the feelings of hostility that arise from frustrated expectations, such as Kanter noted in her study.[22] As she remarks, "Previous research has found that high-mobility situations tend to foster rivalry, instability in the composition of work groups, (and) comparison upward in the hierarchy."[23] And, since women are more likely to be in this situation than men when they try to get ahead, it's not surprising that they should be more likely to express this hostility/resentment pattern.

But what about those women who opt out of this upward struggle—the ones who settle for being secretaries, clerical workers, and lower-level managers? Does that mean they're more ethical? According to research, including Kanter's study, they also can be deceptive, sometimes vicious and vindictive to others. Those who are tend to pick on people outside their group. What happens is that these "lost-opportunity" people tend to develop close social ties with others in their group, which can lead to their striking out at those outside the group as a way of reinforcing their own low aspirations and group bonding. On the flip side, if anyone in the group has higher aspirations and tries to leave the group, she or he may be ostracized by the other members as a way of reaffirming the values and support of the group. Joking, ridicule and—at times—seeking to sabotage the accomplishments of the resented outsider are the usual means.

Again, this type of behavior is not exclusive of either sex. Both men and women in low-status positions are deceptive, but those who are are more typically women. As Kanter found, these were usually in the lower-status, blocked jobs, and their victims were most usually the women who moved up the hierarchy. Since they found fewer and fewer female peers on the way up, they were the most vulnerable to such attacks. The men, on the other hand, found a peer group at every level of the system.[24]

The reverse also happens. Those who move up sometimes act unethically to those they leave behind. It is a means of getting back at the resentment and hostility experienced or of cementing ties with the new group entered.[25] A classic example is the promoted woman who fires or gives negative references about the woman who helped her get ahead.

Even the mentoring system can lead to abuses. Some individuals use their connections with a sponsor higher up in the corporation to undercut his or her own boss whose position ranks lower down in the hierarchy. Or a person may act to ensure his or her own power base by making alliances with more than one mentor, so that if his or her own sponsor falls in power, he or she doesn't go down with the ship. Many men and women experience mentoring at some time in their careers, but our findings indicate the hedging strategy described here has become common among women. A woman mentor may be in a more tenuous position than a man; if another woman chooses to turn on her, she usually can be undercut.

The woman manager is in much the same situation. Overall, she has fewer power connections. Women managers tend to be in positions that are vulnerable to power squeezes, such as being a first-line supervisor of a staff performing a highly routinized function, where, for example, she has to carry out the demands of higher-level managers for results, and at the same time contend with the resistance of workers who feel stuck in their low-opportunity positions and resent her for getting ahead and who may engage in assorted actions, such as slacking off, to sabotage her, while she ends up acting like the stereotyped overcontrolling, critical, bossy boss in order to stay in charge. And the result is generally even more hostility and resentful behavior, leading to more efforts to criticize and control.[26]

The underlying problem is that women have much less power than men; when women assume power roles, they have more difficulty handling them. The bottom line is that the context of the workplace today is one which often creates an environment which encourages women to treat each other unethically.

So women trying to move ahead may strike out at other women to further their climbs. The way to the top is more restricted for women; the fact that upper management positions open to them are limited creates intense competition. At the same time, the women who are at the bottom, either because they feel stuck or have opted for lower status roles, are likely to strike out as well. They may feel resentful about other women getting ahead, or they may simply want to preserve the values of their status group. In either case, the result is that it is inordinately difficult for the woman who is trying to get ahead.

To a great extent the dynamics of the workplace are a major factor in leading women to sabotage other women. And while the same dynamics contribute to the unethical actions of men, women have a much smaller arena in which to play: not only do women have to contend with greater pressures, but when they do act unethically, the victim is more likely to be another woman because she is less powerful and less likely to fight back.

HOW THE DIFFERENT
MANAGEMENT STYLE
OF WOMEN MAKES
THINGS WORSE

When women do rise into management, they tend to use a more personal and sometimes overcontrolling management style that can be troublesome. Combined with the discrimination and resistances they may encounter in the workplace, it can contribute to unethical behavior.

The good news about women's management style is that they tend to be more concerned with the feelings of others and more alert to employer and customer needs. The bad news, according to a *D&B Reports* article by Kevin McDermott, is women are frequently thought to "lack the political skills of men."[27] When things go well, the advantage of this more personal management style is that it results in closer interactions with others and that people simply feel better about working together on a task. When things get rocky, this closeness may turn into hostility and personal conflict. And that's when people frequently act to strike back—in either direct or devious ways.

According to psychologists, one reason for the differences in management styles may be that men and women learn to operate according to different sets of rules as children. When Carol Gilligan reviewed studies of how children play, she found that the boys tended to play more competitive games with rules, while the girls tended to enjoy turn-taking games.[28] Through their games, girls learn to develop more empathy to others and to regard rules more flexibly—as something that can readily be changed if they don't work—but boys learn to become both more independent yet better able to work on a team and handle competition, so they can both "play with their enemies . . . and compete with their friends," based on the rules of the game.[29]

Such patterns of behavior, learned in childhood, can carry over in varying degrees of consciousness. If women are more willing to change the rules, that can mean a more flexible working environment in good times; but it also can mean that, because she is much less bound by the traditional rules, a woman manager can act unethically when it is expedient to do so. So, if women are less amenable to team play and the spirit of competition and compromise, they might be especially apt to attack and get back at a perceived "enemy" rather than regard any rivalry for position as part of the game, whereas men lean more to playing by the rules, holding back feelings of hostile rivalry for the sake of the team.

According to our research, the other major difference in many women's management style—the tendency to be overly critical and controlling—appears to come about because women are typically more threatened when they use power. Having power is newer to women. They are more likely to face challenges or resentments from those they manage, so they react by tending to overcontrol. Another major difference originates in childhood, where women have typically been taught to use persuasion and manipulation rather than direct orders to get someone to do something they want. When they move into management, they retain these techniques and styles.

In fact, more and more companies today are using this more personal style in management. It creates a more humanistic and supportive environment for workers, which encourages productivity and company loyalty. But it also can facilitate unethical behavior, because when there are difficulties people are more likely to vent their emotional feelings and hostilities toward one another. And they are more likely to bend the rules to act in whatever way seems most expedient and pragmatic at the time.

The combination of a personal, less-rule-bound style with a tendency to be tough and overcontrol can sometimes turn into a time-bomb which explodes into a no-holds-barred attack when a woman manager feels threatened and goes after the person who threatens or is perceived as threatening her.

In raising the question: "Must Women Executives Be Such Barracudas?" writer Judith Trotsky's answer was yes. She noticed numerous examples of this: one woman browbeat her verbally to get her to leave a project; another privately supported a plan, but then proceeded to sabotage it for her own ends. After talking to many executive women, Trotsky found they agreed that women were especially tough. Why? Because, they told her, if women want to get ahead, they have to be very aggressive. Some also suggested that women are trained to be more vicious and conniving since they're competing for men. As one woman said: "For a woman to get into a position of authority and power, she has to be something of a barracuda."[30]

Unfortunately, this kind of required toughness can place the woman manager in a pressure-cooker situation. The achieving woman often has to maintain a superior performance in whatever she does, and that creates tremendous pressure to do whatever is necessary to keep up. Garda Bowman and Associates conducted a survey of two thousand executives, half of them men and half of them women. They found that both men and women executives strongly agreed that "a woman has to be exceptional, indeed overqualified, to succeed in management today."[31] Or, as one woman manager said in an interview reported in *Savvy* magazine, "At each new level, a woman must gain credibility all over again, something a man seldom has to do." And as another observed, "It's a continuous process of gaining approval. Even though you've developed a positive reputation, you have to keep proving yourself."[32]

The woman manager, our respondents told us, easily can find herself in a high-pressure, double-bind situation: on one hand, it was felt, she has to be "hard-boiled" to get ahead; on the other, she is criticized if she seems too tough. It can lead others to view an aggressive, successful woman as behaving unethically, whereas if a man behaved the same way, his actions would not be suspect. To maintain their positions, some women may find they have to use their power in indirect, manipulative ways; they find it the only way to survive.

These problems and pressures occur for women managers because they face all sorts of stereotyped perceptions and expectations of how women should behave, and they are judged more critically than are men by others in the workplace. In a study of women in authority, Carol Ann Beauvais found that the members of a work group judged the women more harshly when they acted in a more instrumental, analytical way, which is more characteristic of the masculine style, but they were more positive when the women acted in a more expressive way, characteristic of the feminine style. The reason, according to Beauvais, is that when a woman tries to act in a more rational, non-expressive way, there is "greater sex role incongruity":[33] such a woman acts differently than people expect, and it results in confusion.

Women managers also have to put up with a variety of misperceptions noted in other studies—the belief that they aren't as competent as men, are too emotional, or are less motivated. There are some employees who are still not comfortable with women supervisors.[34] It's the familiar attitude of sex-role stereotyping, which still operates in many work situations to hold women back.

And while, as already noted, the more intuitive, expressive style of management is gaining more and more acceptance today, our research showed that many women still feel compelled to downplay their strengths in this mode of behavior and display a tough shell to shake off the old stereotype that they are too soft. What they're doing is buying into the traditional male business myth that a rational, analytical style of management is best—at the very time that it is rapidly going out of style.

What about women who use a considerate and human relations-oriented approach to management? Current research shows that women tend to do best with this style of management, yet women who adopt it, doing what works best, "run the risk of being seen stereotypically," because it has been identified as stereotypically feminine leadership. They often get caught in a double bind: others may believe they know how to work with people, but may think they lack other important leadership qualities, such as "emotional stability, aggressiveness, self-reliance, and objectivity"—qualities traditionally associated with men.[35]

The upshot is that women in management today are frequently

trapped in the conflict between the perceptions and expectations of women: their style of management, leaning toward more human relations and feminine style of leadership versus the persistence of the male management myth. Should women seek to manage in the more objective and aggressive way characteristic of how men have traditionally managed, they can get shot down for trying to be too tough. Should they adopt a more feminine, person-oriented style, they may be perceived as lacking important leadership qualities.

It's no wonder that women managers often feel under great pressure to perform and may either be perceived as behaving more unethically or actually act unethically to get out of the double bind in which they find themselves.

HOW THE PERSONAL AND WORK PRESSURES ON WOMEN CONTRIBUTE TO UNETHICAL ACTION

Attempting to reconcile personal and work demands puts a strain on many women. There are day-to-day problems at work that create ethical conflict situations that can undermine feelings of personal esteem.

There are four main areas of stress. First, women still have primary responsibility for the home, and they often are caught in a time squeeze. They have dual roles, and there are only so many hours in the day. Second, women still tend to receive less pay for equal or comparable work, and resentments build. Third, there are still instances of discrimination and differential treatment that also build resentment and anger. Finally, women can be their own worst enemies, as one woman seeks to get ahead and others resist her movement.

The pressures of trying to maintain a social or home life are especially acute for executive and professional women. As men move up the occupational ladder, they commonly find support from wives and girlfriends, who take over the running of the home or are willing to be patient when the professional male has to travel on business or put in extra time in the office. But the executive woman who is married usually doesn't get this kind of support. Much of the time she still has to do the work at home herself. If a woman is single, she is apt to find that potential mates resent her time commitments, and she may even have trouble finding relationships. In 1984 *The Wall Street Journal* and the Gallup Organization conducted a survey of 722 female executives (vice presidents, presidents, and CEOs) in major companies in which the participants consistently reported extra home and personal demands. The married women, even those earning more than their husbands, generally did most of the chores at home. The single women typically had to sacrifice outside interests, including personal relationships, to their jobs.[36]

As for receiving less pay for equal comparable work, studies show that this rankles many women. Women are well aware they still only receive about sixty percent of what men do, though the figure can go up to approximately seventy-four percent now for higher-level jobs.[37] Besides the economic strains this can create, self-esteem is a major factor—particularly for women who have to support themselves or take care of children. Since money is a measure of worth today, women who make less may have lowered feelings of self-esteem, and this becomes a breeding ground for feelings of resentment against those who are doing better, including women supervisors or women who move up the career ladder and out of a lower-status group. Women executives and professionals who feel held back and underpaid also may resent others they see moving ahead. If they act on those resentments, their victims are likely to be other women: they are more immediately accessible than the often distant company heads and board members who are making the overall decisions.

Also, the woman who *is* moving ahead and feels discriminated against sometimes expresses her feelings through resentment.

She finds she has to be tougher to survive, feels angry, and seeks out the most vulnerable victim—usually another woman.

Currently the major barrier to women in management occurs at the senior management level. Doors have opened up at the entry level, but as women reach the $75,000.00 to $100,000.00 level after several years in the corporate world, they suddenly find themselves stuck. Susan Fraker's survey on women's progress in management found that the key reason is that many of those in power positions still hold old stereotypes or misperceptions about women. Many employers fear that women don't take their careers as seriously as men, might leave to have children, or will find the pressures of work too great.[38] In reacting against these misperceptions, women typically feel they have to appear tough, which affects the women under them. One woman executive, writing anonymously in *Vogue,* said she had to develop a tough veneer and act more like a man to survive professionally:

> (As) a top executive in an important corporation . . . I am faced more and more . . . with the choice between compromising my human values as a woman, and accepting the dominant dog-eat-dog "bottom line" ethic, the choice between forcing myself to think more and more like a man or being classed as a "softie" . . . and served up as dogfood myself.[39]

A bank executive describing the perils of her own position in a *Wall Street Journal* article agreed: "You live in a fishbowl when you're the only woman. You have to be more credible than a man would—every day."[40]

It appears that wherever they are in the management hierarchy, women in power positions tend to have their power undermined. It's not surprising that women feel resentment toward others or engage in compensating behaviors, such as trying to be tougher and more controlling when they supervise. Women not only experience discrimination from those with more power, but they get undermined from below. As already noted, there is still a substantial percentage of employees who express a preference for a male boss—forty-seven percent of the women and forty percent of the men in a survey sponsored by *The Los Angeles Times*.[41] Other studies, including Marjorie Bayes and Peter Newton in "Women in Authority," found that subordinates often act in various ways to undermine a woman manager's power and that other women were often the worst offenders.[42] Typical actions are designed to challenge the woman's use of power: subordinates go over the woman's head to a male authority, purposely disobey instructions, pretend not to hear directions, or try to entice female executives to abandon the authority role. At times, these same subordinates might challenge the authority of a male manager, but when they did, they usually used the format of an open confrontation. When they challenged the women, however, their efforts were much more devious, or, as Bayes and Newton describe them, "unacknowledged, subtle and masked." Subordinates used "covert defiance, denial of subordinancy, or various attempts to seduce her out of that role." The perpetrators were usually women who didn't like the idea of working for another woman. Through scheming and plotting, they attempted to subvert the woman in an authority role.[43]

According to Bayes and Newton, the reason there was so much conflict between the women subordinates and their managers in their study is because women are normally socialized to take the Number Two position with a male in the first position. As a result, many women resist being subordinate to a woman because they have "been trained to compete with other women for favored positions with powerful men. It seems difficult for women to join in supporting or protecting another woman."[44] Bayes and Newton continue that subordinates may resist the more directive leadership from a woman which is needed to complete a task, since they are used to the woman playing a more expressive role. They think she should do things which are helpful and supportive and feel a sense of emptiness or abandonment when she plays a more forceful role.[45] They may react toward her with anger and resentment.

To some extent, both men and women may treat a woman in authority this way. But reputable recent research has shown this resistance is more likely to come from another woman. In a survey of executive women, Charlotte Sutton and Kris Moore found that men more than women were willing to accept women as colleagues and competent equals. They found a slight percentage increase in the number of male and female executives who believed that women are uncomfortable working for other women. At the same time the number of executives who believe that men would be uncomfortable working for women declined significantly from studies conducted twenty years ago.

Why should executives believe that there is a growing resistance to women executives from other women, while men seem to be accepting women managers more? According to Sutton and Moore, this apparently growing adversarial relationship between women superiors and their female subordinates could be developing for a number of reasons. First, the female boss may be demanding more now of her female subordinates in order to mold them into competent corporate women. Second, it may be that the subordinate not only resents the additional demands but also is disappointed she isn't getting the warmth, support, and encouragement commonly expected of the female boss. Third, the female subordinates may suspect that there are only a limited number of company positions open to women and so they feel competitive with their female bosses. And finally, there seems to be an even more difficult conflict when a younger woman is supervising an older woman.[46]

One male manufacturing vice president in Sutton and Moore's study summed up the central problem:

> It has been my experience that women in general are the greatest detriment to the success of other women. I have repeatedly witnessed the lack of cooperation by female employees with newly-promoted female supervisors and managers.[47]

As women have moved up the occupational ladder, they have encountered many stresses, have entered something of a hornet's nest of resistance, especially from other women. To a great extent, these difficulties are due to misperceptions of what women can do, discrimination against them, and resistance to their performing in their new management roles. Much of this resistance is perhaps due to the fact that there has been change and women in executive positions represent a new factor in doing business. Since women executives have a less secure power position, they have lower feelings of self-esteem in the occupational hierarchy.

This issue of cultural change is critical. Changes within an organization or business can produce hostility and aggressions; it can fill the organization with uncertainties and become threatening. Fear can be generated, leading to aggressive activity of various types, including griping, gossip, and behind-the-scenes sabotage. In many cases, women are both the victims and the perpetrators. They are experiencing the most change and the greatest feelings of uncertainty, and this can result in hostility, fear, and resistance to change.

Today women face a kind of "Catch-22" situation. To get ahead, they have to be tough. Yet that toughness provokes resistance, often in the form of hostility from other women who are unsettled by change. It's important to understand the dynamics of why women sabotage other women; we can then recognize the sources of anger, hostility, and resistance coming from each other and work on new solutions for strengthening our interpersonal and business relationships.

I believe that women's unethical behavior, as well as the fact that other women are principally its target, will change. The first step in this change is a clearer examination of the psychological, moral, and philosophical factors that have historically influenced women.

Chapter 3

Ms. Interpretation

WOMEN DISCRIMINATE

"If I were your daughter . . . would you think it fitting to lay such hard terms on me, . . . For I am . . . the daughter of a prince, softly nurtured."
Mary to The Old Man
Act One, Scene I

The way women have been brought up and their unique psychology affects how they act toward each other.

When I began to explore the issue of women's ethical relationships with other women, I knew it would be controversial. But I felt that if women were to find answers to working together effectively, it was imperative for the truth to be known about what destructive as well as supportive behaviors exist between women in the workplace—and why. Perhaps the most destructive of these negative behaviors are the ways in which women sabotage each other.

According to reputable theorists such as Jean Piaget and Lawrence Kohlberg, these are rooted in how female children have been trained in moral values, and in their way of looking at the world as a whole. My own research, and that of many recognized authorities, points out these differences as providing some meaningful explanations for women's work relationships with other women.[1]

HOW WOMEN DIFFER
IN THEIR MORAL
DEVELOPMENT

The notion of moral development suggests a scale of morality, which goes from being of low moral character to being highly moral. It also suggests that given certain criteria, one can judge what is more or less moral.

This is a sticky area. People have long argued over what is or what is not moral. Given these caveats, some researchers, largely psychologists and psychiatrists, have tried to look at moral values objectively to create a value-neutral means of assessing how far a person has developed morally.

Assessing what is moral is difficult. Basically, the evaluation of morality has been based on moving from a "what's in it for me" personal attitude to a more universal perspective, where personal gains give way to the notion of the greater social good.

Based on this approach, some researchers have argued that women, because of their different childhood experiences, have a less evolved moral sense than men.

The various arguments about moral stages put forth first by Piaget in 1932 and later by Kohlberg in 1969 appear to support this theory. In examining their theories, Ellen Dickstein found that moral behavior develops in a social context where one interacts with others. A person becomes moral by understanding the needs and desires of others and then acts so as to either benefit, or at least not hurt, others.[2]

How does this process of moral development occur? According to Piaget, Kohlberg, and others, each person has certain genetically programmed social tendencies. As the child begins to develop his or her thinking abilities, he or she learns how to engage in role-taking, and by doing this learns to see the world as others see it. Gradually, the child's selfish, me-first, amoral behavior becomes socialized into more acceptable channels. The result is a moral consciousness, and the person learns how to make choices about behaving morally or not in different situations.

The steps to moral development are typically divided into six or seven stages. People presumably can get stuck at any level.

At the first moral—or premoral—stage, everyone is completely egocentric. There is no thought about the wants or needs of others. Children behave because of practical considerations, such as a fear of punishment, not because they understand the moral rules or want to be good.[3]

As a child begins to interact with others, he or she comes to realize that there are other points of view and starts to consider the other's intention. Through this, the child begins to develop a sense of justice and fair play. He or she begins to realize that there should be equal treatment for all and recognizes that there are rules to obey and that it is "moral" to obey those rules.

This shift is Stage Two and occurs, according to Piaget and Kohlberg, because the individual is concerned with getting a favorable response from others: he or she wants to be liked or favored. So at this stage, morality becomes very centered.

Movement into the Stage Three level takes place as the individual interacts even more with others. It could be called the "golden rule" stage: do unto others as you would like them to do unto you. Conversely, if you wouldn't like it, don't do it to others. Essentially, the underlying dynamic at this stage is the notion of an idealized reciprocity. It's a kind of moral tit-for-tat which applies to everyone.

The maturing person soon realizes that there are different situations and different types of people, and that it is therefore necessary to make distinctions in how to behave. At Stage Four, the individual recognizes that moral behavior occurs in a social context and is related to a network of roles.[4]

Finally, in Stages Five and Six, the individual advances to an even higher level of moral development; at this point he or she can make moral choices based on considering all points of view. In effect, according to Piaget, autonomy has been reached; or as Kohlberg puts it, the person has arrived at the "level of individual principles."[5]

Presumably, all children remain in Stage One until at least two and a half years of age, and then may begin learning some of the role-taking skills necessary to move into Stage Two between the ages of two and a half and seven. In late childhood Stage Three is achieved; Stage Four in the teenage years, and then, if moral development continues, Stages Five and Six are experienced as adults.

These theories about different stages are significant because of what happens to women and men in the workplace. Individuals move into these stages at different times, some advancing further morally than others. At times, some individuals may exhibit different stages of moral behavior because of dissimilar circumstances.

We have already mentioned that leading theorists have determined that women and men may have developed differently in their moral outlook simply because they have had diverse experiences.[6] A crucial skill is the ability to understand the role of another, which is needed in order to develop a broader moral perspective. Most men learn how to work with others at an earlier age. They spend more time in team play, so they become more skilled in taking the role of the other and gaining a more autonomous moral point of view.

Why should these differences in growing up be so important? According to research by authorities such as Jean Baker Miller, since boys are more involved in competitive team games and sports, they learn early to see themselves as part of a team, and thus learn to adjust their behavior to the view of others. In contrast, girls, since they tend to participate more in individual play, become more egocentrically oriented. They also see themselves more competitively in relation to other girls because they lack that team-building experience. So they are more likely to engage in individualistic forms of moral behavior based on personal considerations.[7]

Another key difference between the moral behavior of men and women traceable to childhood is that many men seem to have broader networks of people whom they treat ethically. It has to do with in-group and out-group distinctions. If someone is part of the in-group, such as family or friends, one is more likely to behave ethically toward them, whereas one may feel freer to be cut-throat and devious with an outsider.

Much reliable research, such as that by Rosabeth Kanter,[8] has shown the importance of in-group and out-group connections. People are more likely to treat out-group people more exploitively, less altruistically, and less generously than the people they consider to be in their in-group. They are more likely to help and do favors for insiders.

These distinctions become relevant to what happens later on in the workplace. Many boys, because of their early team play experience, learn to create wider connections with others, so they engage more broadly in helping people later on. Most girls are more selective, so they may have fewer people in their inner circle later on.

Somehow, just stating this theory feels uncomfortable. As a woman making such charges about women, I find the theory especially upsetting. Yet, as I have argued before, it is crucial to look at these differences dispassionately even if we don't like them, for understanding them is the only way to change.

In a study on the relationship between moral judgment and ego development, Miriam Eiseman noted that higher masculinity scores on a Sentence Completion Test and Defining Issues Test were associated with the greater use of principled and moral reasoning; femininity scores with lesser use.[9] Dr. Lore Kantrowitz came to similar conclusions in her study of sex role development and its relationship to intellectual and ethical development in young adults. She found that high femininity scores were negatively associated with ethical development in women and concluded that the "traditional feminine role has had a more limiting effect on women than the traditional masculine role has had for men."[10]

These theories and research on moral development appear to support the view that, in general, women have a more individualistic mode of moral action. This individualistic approach to morality makes it more likely that women in combative situations will attack others in a weaker position—namely other women; whereas men are more likely to attack others on more indiscriminate grounds. The reason for the difference is that women, with little, if any, experience in team play, respond to such situations on a personal, self-survival basis.

This means that the individual guided by an individualistic morality is more likely to make a decision to act based on the values of a particular relationship, which in turn depends on the perceived value of the other involved.

Accordingly, if a person is less valued in a relationship, then a person with an individualistic sense of morality is more likely to act unethically toward that person. Translated into the work environment, this means it would be more likely for a person to act unethically toward a woman, since, in modern society, as in other societies, women are in general less valued than men, as unfair as that may seem. Furthermore, a woman would be more likely to treat another woman unfairly, since, according to some significant theories, women are more likely to use a more individualistic form of morality than men.

The relationship between moral development and moral action can be illustrated as:

	Women	Men
Childhood experience:	More individual play	More team play
Moral development:	A more personalized moral orientation	A more group-oriented orientation
Moral action:	More influenced by situational factors	More influenced by rules about right or wrong
Choice of Victim:	More influenced by value or status of victim (more likely to be a woman, since of "lower" status)	Less influenced by value or status of victim (likely to be anyone, regardless of sex)
Outcome:	Women likely to behave unethically toward other women	Men likely to behave unethically toward anyone

Certainly, these observations about moral development sound like a throwback to arguments on eugenics which suggest that some people are more genetically superior than others. The key here is that the differences arise out of cultural conditioning.

The premises of these theories may be somewhat upsetting. However, much research appears to support them. They suggest that women tend to be more unethical in dealing with other women than they are with men.

Though we may feel disturbed by these findings, the theories seem to have some validity and help to explain what we observed in our research. The answer is not to discredit them but to look back at the cultural experiences in childhood that lead to such differences and ask what we can do to change them.

HOW WOMEN DIFFER
IN THEIR PSYCHOLOGY

An important reason that women have a unique style of sabotage is because we think and feel differently. Women have a different way of perceiving or reacting to the world. Our early conditioning is one reason that leads us to develop a distinctive style of action. And while this sounds like stereotyping women by using traditional conceptions of whom women are or should be, research bears it out.

Much recent psychological research shows marked differences in numerous areas of development that may explain why women act in the ways that they do. There are male/female differences in rationality, superego strength, honesty, dishonesty and deception, competitive behavior, knowledge of the proper behavior, self-perceptions of status and power, attitudes toward success, and feelings of anger and aggression. Women tend to see themselves separately, see goals and relationships dissimilarly, have disparate notions about power, competition, and aggression, and, as a less powerful group in society, have a deep well of personal anger that may be expressed in various ways.

There are three books which highlight these differences: *Toward a New Psychology of Women* by Jean Baker Miller, *Women's Reality: An Emerging Female System in a White Male Society* by Anne Wilson Schaef, and *In a Different Voice* by Carol Gilligan.

Miller writes of women's subordinate status relative to men in explaining women's psychology. She observes that being in second place makes a big difference. Subordinates are continually trying to please the dominant group and develop the characteristics to do so: they are submissive, passive, docile, and show a lack of initiative. Subordinates also can develop childlike qualities, such as being weak and helpless, and often find difficulty in believing in their own abilities, often looking to dominants for cues on how to behave.

Presumably, according to Miller, this second-class status makes subordinates more intuitive: they learn to become highly attuned to what dominants want so they can act to please. And some subordinates may attempt to imitate or impress the dominants by treating members of their own group as destructively as the dominants do, which includes sabotaging them as a way of gaining acceptance from the group in power.[11] In this light, when women sabotage other women, they may be doing so because they perceive themselves to be in the dominant roles or they may see other women as an inferior group who don't deserve better treatment.

Miller suggests that the tendency women have to behave in covert ways may be derived from this subordinate status itself. Being devious is a functional way to deal with conflicts and difficulties when one has less power. Direct aggression or action won't work, so a subordinate learns to use a more indirect, devious approach. It's a little like guerrilla warfare. Those in power send out bombers and make direct confrontational hits. But those without power—the guerrillas—have to rely on being crafty and using their wits.

According to Miller, a young girl in growing up may use her wiles to get something from "Daddy"; a wife may cleverly manipulate her husband into doing something for her by making him think he wants it himself. By the same token, a woman may use deceptive behavior against other women, because she has learned that's how to get what she wants.

The competitive pressures of subordinates to be recognized by dominants may lead subordinates to use this competitive, manipulative, and deceptive behavior against each other. For women, this means competing with each other for men from an early age. When some women go to work, they transfer this pattern of competing against each other to the workplace.

Miller also suggests that a subordinate's attempts to sabotage others is a transformation of feelings of worthlessness, anger, and defensiveness into anger at others—as opposed to directing it inside oneself as a means of gaining a better self image. Women are frequently defensive about who they are and whether they are pleasing others enough. Women are continually wondering, "Am I giving enough?" or whether they are in the wrong. As the insecurity and hurt build up inside, it can easily turn into anger. That anger is released against other women, who, because they are less valued and more powerless when compared to males, are a safer, more legitimate object against which to express anger. They can also be effective victims for a woman who wants to ally herself with the male group in power.[12] Women may easily fall into the trap of victimizing other women out of anger or a desire to impress those in the higher-status male group.

In *Women's Reality,* internationally known psychotherapist and founder of the Women's Institute of Alternative Psychotherapy Anne Wilson Schaef takes a similar tack in contrasting the psychology of women as subordinates vis-à-vis males. She calls women's psychology the Female System and she views it as a kind of sounding board to the dominant White Male System. Supposedly, since women subscribe to the myth of the superior male system, they have trouble feeling good about themselves. They also feel a lack of power and an inner rage. So they glorify the male values that stress the ability to be totally logical, rational, and objective and put down their more innate and intuitive view of the world.

Like Miller, Schaef suggests a number of ways women compensate for this insecurity and low status they feel. The reasoning is slightly different, but the results are the same: women are more likely to sabotage women.

Schaef suggests that many women try to deal with this feeling of being less adequate by seeking to be overly fair and cooperative. As she describes it, it's a kind of strategy of "absolution" in which women bend over backward to be liked, to do good. But when women do this, they may become vulnerable and others may take advantage of their efforts to be just and fair. Those who are most likely to do so are other women who have adopted the male system of aggressiveness and competitiveness in order to win—and they will, since women who operate from the so-called female-fairness position usually expect other women to operate out of the same system. Fair-minded women can be badly hurt.[13] It's a classic ill-will, good-will situation. The problem is that many women do not realize which set of game rules—women's or men's—is operative.

As Schaef points out, women's expectations of fairness are often thwarted, because many women have learned to use devious tactics to survive. Or, as she observes quite poignantly, "Because our position in this culture is so shaky, we have learned to lie. We lie to men and to other women, but mostly we lie to ourselves. We lie about who we are and about what we want and need."[14] The reason for lying is survival, but, according to Schaef, this simply makes women feel more isolated and more angry—and can provide some of the impetus to strike out at other women, who are more vulnerable because they have less power and because they are trying to play fair.

The result is a disastrous no-win situation for some women. On one hand, some women feel especially isolated and angry. On the other, some feel openly vulnerable. Sometimes women feel both, which can result in their becoming extremely vindictive and devious with one another, especially when they are in a situation of intense competition for the limited number of positions on top.

As Schaef explains, such women can adopt what she calls the

"Queen Bee" syndrome. Such women already have bought the "White Male Superiority Myth" and dislike and distrust other women. They feel there is no room for another woman at the top with them, because they feel other women are inferior and they get their sense of validation and worth from not being like other women. Therefore, they actively set about to destroy their competition, and with such women in such situations, fairness plays no part.

Conversely, the woman who is expressing her inner anger and trying to compensate for an inferior position can be a dangerous opponent. Moreover, the woman who seeks to be super-competent can set herself above others and use her competence as a weapon to drive others, possibly to self-destruction. Gossip is another weapon sometimes used. Gossip may concentrate on maliciously attacking others—mostly other women—to express a hostile woman's rage. Even the "Good Christian Martyr" type can twist her anger into a process of manipulating and controlling others by inducing guilt.

Schaef's vision of such women does not present a pretty picture. These portraits show angry women who strike out at each other. Moreover, they convey the serious problems that may flow from women's traditional inferior status in which for so many years they have felt and had little or no power. Such dynamics can be changed. The first step is awareness.

While the subordinate status of women is a major factor in influencing ethical or unethical action, another key factor is the differences girls and boys encounter in growing up. These differences are highlighted in Carol Gilligan's book, *In a Different Voice*,[15] mentioned in Chapter Two.

The source of these differences, according to Gilligan, is the peer group and the differences in the way boys and girls play. At the elementary school age, the peer group is extremely influential: children soon learn what's expected of them. For girls, these expectations are quite different than for boys.

First, when it comes to rules, boys tend to play more competitively, so they learn more about the creation of rules and developing fair play procedures for resolving conflicts. But because girls are more apt to participate in turn-taking games, they are less likely to encounter disputes. They tend to be much more pragmatic in dealing with rules, more willing to bend them, make exceptions, or come up with innovations in order to keep the peace.

Second, boys' and girls' recreations are organized differently, and that also creates different lessons. Since boys tend to play in larger groups, they soon become adept at organizational skills and at dealing with competition in an open and controlled way. In contrast, since girls tend to play in smaller, more intimate groups, they tend to learn more about cooperation and primary human relations. It makes them more sensitive and empathetic to specific individuals. As a result, boys deal in a different way than girls with rules governing relationships in general.[16]

Gilligan argues that the sensitivity so characteristic of women can lead them into unethical behavior. It can also lead to a level of moral judgment beyond abstract justice. Why? Because, according to Gilligan, this sensitivity can lead women to listen to voices other than their own and to let points of view, appropriately or not, influence their judgment. The negative side of listening to others can readily lead women into a situational morality, where they change the rules, as they sometimes do in girls' games, because of pragmatic considerations resulting from their having listened to someone else whose rules or motivations might be ethically wrong.

The tendency to rely or depend on others can lead some women to give up their responsibility for the decisions they make. This unwillingness to make a choice can be characterized as the "poor little me syndrome": a woman thinks she has no choice, so she lets others make her choices for her. Then she can say she has no responsibility: "poor little me."[17]

The problem with this denial of responsibility is that because of it some women can act irrationally or unethically and feel the action is justified because other people are responsible. In addition, some women who fail to take responsibility for their actions also fail to believe themselves at fault for the consequences of their actions.

In growing up, women encounter all kinds of situations that

make the issue of independent choice problematic. Little girls learn to be more empathetic and compassionate. The result is that as adults they are more likely to make judgments based on feelings of empathy and compassion for a particular person rather than judging the situation in more general terms, as is more characteristic of men. Little girls learn to associate femininity with goodness and self-sacrifice, so as adults they may have more difficulty in taking independent stands in conflict with these early values.[18]

The result of all this is that from a very early age most women learn to make ethical choices based on their personal relationships with others, whereas men tend to learn standards based on general rules. Women's orientation is very particularistic and humanistic, and it can lead to some very compassionate actions. The downside is that, depending on the situation and the personal feelings of the individual, it can also lead to very destructive and vindictive actions.[19] There are broad possibilities for either evil or good—and frequently the deciding factor is the personal relationship one woman has with another.

Gilligan points out one problem with this open-choice situation: women can often be pulled in many different directions when it comes to making a choice.[20] They may want to fulfill their own needs, yet because of early conditioning feel they must be good and caring to others. As a result, they can feel frustrated.

This is one more reason why the anger which many women feel can continue to build and explode later. And when that happens in the workplace the target is likely to be another woman, since she is the most vulnerable and powerless target for such rage.

IS IT RATIONAL TO BE UNETHICAL?

Anger and emotional reasons are only part of the motivating factors that lead women to act unethically towards each other. Sometimes women act unethically simply because it's more rational to do so. Much psychological research illustrates how people act out of rational considerations, and women are no different. There may be a payoff from an unethical act that leads them to do it. By the same token, there can be more of a payoff in sabotaging another woman.

How do women feel when they do this? Do they feel any pangs of conscience? Eileen McDonagh suggests that women have what is called in technical jargon lower superego strength. Our findings indicate women are more likely to be in a situation which permits or encourages deceptive behavior.[21] What does research say about these patterns?

WHAT'S RATIONAL AND
WHAT ISN'T

Some current theories on rationality suggest there is a kind of economic underpinning for our actions. We act a certain way because there's a reasonable payoff. So when there is a payoff in terms of a situation, position, social contact or value for acting unethically, we sometimes choose such actions.

And while as yet there is no valid research systematically comparing males and females in terms of how they think and what they believe about different things, there are data which offer explanations as to why men and women have different views about situations and how their diverse views can lead to more or less ethical behavior.

Mary Zey-Ferrell, Mark Weaver, and O. C. Ferrell, among others, found this kind of relationship between associations with others, perceptions about the situation, and unethical behavior. They studied advertising people in a corporation and an ad agency. Their findings were important in determining why individuals engaged in unethical activities such as falsifying reports, padding expense accounts, and blaming errors on innocent co-workers. They found that opportunity often set the stage for doing something unethical. What was most important was the way the person perceived the situation and what he or she had learned from others about the appropriate way to act. The model showing their progression to making an unethical or ethical decision can be illustrated as:

Differential association with peers
(What I think my peers do)

to

Opportunity
(My perceived opportunity to engage in unethical behavior)

to

Unethical behavior
(My decision—what I do)[22]

They concluded that an individual can become "conditioned to unethical behavior" by learning, through association with them, that this kind of behavior is acceptable to peers.[23]

While the researchers didn't look specifically at how women and men compare in how they act unethically, their model provides an interesting way of thinking about women's situation in the workplace: perhaps if women associate with peers who are more likely to act unethically for various reasons, such as the emotional and low-status factors already discussed, they may be more likely to develop beliefs that it is okay to act unethically. If other people are doing it, an individual may reason, I must be okay.

Some research on the social exchange theory suggests that people may take advantage of opportunities to behave unethically because it's the rational, utilitarian thing to do. The basic claim of this theory is that people act out of instrumental considerations, which means they act to get more rewards and less punishment. It's an approach that sounds very much like common sense. We seek out the payoffs and when they don't occur we go the other way.

When this social exchange approach is combined with the differential association concept, it suggests that individuals will be more likely to think like their peers or take advantage of an opportunity to act unethically, because it is to their benefit to do so. It suggests that an individual will more than likely engage in unethical behavior if he or she believes or perceives that there is a payoff. Conversely, the less payoff the individual imagines there to be, the less likely he or she is to act in these ways.[24] These theories on utilitarian action and exchange can be applied to what happens to men and women in the workplace. They suggest that if women behave more unethically toward other women than toward men, they are doing it because that has more reward value; so, on a rational, utilitarian ground, it makes more sense.

DO WOMEN HAVE LESS OF A CONSCIENCE THAN MEN?

Assuming we act for utilitarian purposes, to get more rewards and avoid punishment, questions about the influence of conscience on the way women act become quite relevant. The conscience is a powerful force for convincing us to act one way or another because it is right or wrong. The conscience controls us because we get the reward or payoff for behaving as we should by feeling good. When we don't, punishment is in the form of guilt.

What if the conscience has less power or operates on different constraints? Or what if the person has less of a conscience? Then there's less guilt and more incentive to behave unethically if there's a personal gain by doing so. This dynamic is especially relevant for understanding why some women behave unethically toward other women.

Some of the basic research on this topic derives from the work of noted psychologist R. B. Cattell, who claims that superego strength is one of the most important factors related to ethical behavior. According to Cattell, a person with superego strength—also known as a strong conscience—is freely able to choose an ethical position out of a personal sense of responsibility or conscientiousness. Some people may seem to behave ethically because they are high in the other factor related to ethical behavior—Group Dependence; however, they only conform outwardly by doing what the group feels is ethical. According to his theories, a truly ethical person is one with superego strength—and that person will act out of a strong sense of what is right regardless of how the group feels. A person with a weak superego, on the other hand, will be less able to suppress the impulses of the id (such as feelings of anger, as in "I'll get back at her for that"). And so the person weak in superego is more likely to engage in unethical conduct, given the right circumstances.[25]

Cattell's work provides one possible explanation as to why women may be more unethical toward other women: they may have a lower superego strength as a result of their upbringing. Why? As pointed out earlier, males from an early age learn to submerge their own interests into the team goal—a kind of submerging themselves in the group consciousness; women are less likely to participate in this process. This theory suggests that, as a result, they are more apt to respond to their immediate impulses and act on their feelings, which are signs of low superego strength.

Cattell's ideas about women having less of a certain type of conscience are consistent with research findings which show that some women in higher level positions are more manipulative and Machiavellian than men. There is a connection: if women are less held back by the restraints of their superego, then they can feel freer to act manipulatively to exploit or take advantage of others.

The Machiavellianism (or Mach) Scale, which measures manipulative behavior, was originally developed by Richard Christie and Florence Geis and described in their book, *Studies in Machiavellianism*.[26] The name comes from their observations of the style of leadership advocated by Niccolò Machiavelli (1469–1527) in his books, *The Prince* and *The Discourses*. They noted that manipulative leaders behave in much the way Machiavelli describes: they don't seem much concerned with conventional morality, they don't seem to have any ideological commitment, and they seem to be motivated by a pragmatic, manipulative view of human nature.

Christie and Geis developed the Mach Scale to show the extent to which people show these Machiavellian-style behaviors. On the scale, the high Machs are the real manipulators. They persuade others more, they are persuaded less, and they win more. They attempt to manipulate more and are more successful at it. That might be considered the upside of this down pattern. The downside is that such people show little concern for conventional morality and are more likely to engage in unethical behavior when there is a benefit for their rational self-interest.[27] High-Mach manipulators are masters. They do what they do because there's a payoff. If someone else also benefits, that's fine. If not, they'll act for their own gain regardless.

For women who want to get ahead, such tactics can succeed. According to much research, women in general score lower on the Mach Scale than men, perhaps because they don't have as much opportunity to be in achievement-oriented, manipulative-type situations. Our research disclosed that often when women move ahead, they change. Or perhaps it's the more Machiavellian women that get ahead. At least that's what Shelby D. Hunt and Lawrence B. Chonko found when they studied professional men and women in marketing. The women had higher Mach scores. Hunt and Chonko propose that this suggests that there's some kind of self-selection going on in which women who expect to get ahead in a business setting must develop Machiavellian traits to be successful when they compete.

Yet when women do manipulate, they tend to do so in more subtle, indirect ways, according to this theory. Karen Van Wagner and Cheryl Swanson explored the differences in the way in which women and men use power in an office setting. They found that the women were more likely to use manipulative techniques to convince and persuade others. Men tended to use a much more immediate, "let's do it" type of approach.[28]

In turn, these differences may be influenced by the different ways women and men relate to power. According to Van Wagner and Swanson, both men and women have similar power needs. But women tend to be more concerned about using power to build up their internal strength; they're more internalized in their response, whereas men tend to express their power more directly by being assertive and other-directed; they are more interested in perceiving themselves as powerful actors in an external setting.[29]

When men have power, they tend to be much more analytical and task-oriented; women with power tend to be more concerned about creating a humanistic context and impressing management. Or, as Van Wagner and Swanson wrote, "Men are action-oriented. . . . This translates into a power style which concentrates on manipulating, analyzing, and restructuring the world around them. . . . Women, in contrast, have a contextural power style . . . they are concerned with the subtleties of interaction. . . . In comparison to the 'male' task-oriented power style, the female power style is more self- and people-oriented."[30]

Again, some researchers have found that these different styles date back to childhood. Dorothea Braginsky examined Machiavellianism and manipulative behavior in children and found that girls with high power needs tended to use subtle, evasive methods to create a good impression in order to get others to do what they want. Some typical techniques were bribery, denying they'd done something they had done, and blaming others. Boys with high power needs tended to be very direct and aggressive: they simply ordered others around to get their ways.

These power patterns continue in the workplace. Many women in power continue to use a subtle, manipulative style since it has worked for them in the past. And in fact, this indirect style may suit women well, since it tends to be more acceptable to both men and women who may be uncomfortable about women using direct power. Women attempting to use the more direct and aggressive male-management style often experience resistance, so they use what works.

There appears to be a kind of trade-off in which women use what is utilitarian for them. Manipulation can be part of that trade-off. If, as Cattell suggests, women have less ego strength, some may feel freer to be manipulative and exploitive, if that works. Likewise, if a more people-oriented, persuasive approach works better when women seek to exercise their power, they may use that.

In some cases, of course, manipulative actions can have good results. But they also can be directed to unethical ends. The goal is the maximum reward—and if achieving it involves unethical behavior, some may choose this path.

ARE WOMEN MORE DECEPTIVE?

Many theorists maintain that women are more deceptive: they are more likely to engage in behind-the-scenes gossip, backstabbing, even conniving actions to achieve their goals. Certain studies show that women are, in fact, more likely to be deceptive than men under certain circumstances, and there are some good reasons for it. Since women's paths to action are more blocked in many situations, they may feel that the only road open is the use of deception. In other words, deception can arise from very rational considerations, and much research has shown a relationship between deciding to deceive and the cost and benefits of doing it. The greater the benefits of being deceptive, the more likely a person is to be dishonest or do something deceitful. As David Farrington and Robert Kidd found when they dropped coins of different value on the street, people were more likely to make a false claim when the coin was worth more and when it cost them less to make the claim. And they found that the female subjects were more likely to falsely claim the money.

It's a far cry from being deceptive in a laboratory situation to being deceptive in the workplace, but researchers have found analogies. Such deceptions crop up in the course of everyday activities in the office, often as a way to smooth over relationships or save face: a person may claim a late project will be done on time to make someone else happy; a person will try to deny a mistake or cover it up. In fact, such activities are so common-place in some work settings that people often don't consider them unethical. They're just "bending the truth a little," or "being diplomatic." But whatever people choose to call it, those in a lower-status position are more likely to act in these ways because they have less power to get what they want, and women are more likely to be in the lower-status positions.

Our research as well as other reliable sources also suggest that women are more likely to dupe other women. Why? Because women tend to be more trusting and more easily fooled. A key reason for this is that women tend to be more field dependent in the way they perceive things, while men tend to be more field independent. This means that women are more likely to be influenced by the context where they experience something; men are more able to pull a statement out of context to analyze and assess it. For example, Paul John Lavrakas noticed this relationship between women and men and field dependence when he asked fifty male and fifty female subjects to judge the truth of a tape-recorded statement. The men were much more adept at doing this, as Lavrakas predicted, based on field dependence.[31]

Do women have more skill at justifying deception to themselves than men? William Pope did some research on how people react when they do something that violates moral standards. He found that people often try to justify or explain their own behavior to themselves: it's a way to adjust to the discrepancy one feels in doing something that goes against one's own standards or generally accepted standards of behavior.[32] Given that most women tend to be more verbally oriented than men, as research has consistently shown, and that many women tend to be more focused on their own internal processes than men, it stands to reason that they are more likely to think about what they do and try to explain their actions to themselves. And it is also reasonable to suggest that they would be more likely to try to justify—and therefore feel better about—engaging in deceptive behavior.

There is also some evidence that women lie more often and

are more deceptive as they move up the corporate ladder. Bella DePaulo and Robert Rosenthal found, when they did a study on lie-telling, that women's emotional styles cover deceptiveness more convincingly. They asked a group of men and women to tell them if they thought a man or woman on videotape was being honest when they said they liked someone. They discovered that the women tended to be more expressive whether they were honest or not. They also found that the deceivers who scored high in Machiavellianism tended to be even better as liars, in part because they tended to use a much more theatrical, hamming style of lying. It appears that putting a lot of emotion into saying something makes it seem convincing, even if the statement is untrue. DePaulo and Rosenthal commented, "People who tend to exaggerate sentiments of liking that they do not really feel, as well as people who exaggerate feigned feelings of dislike, are much less likely to get caught in their lies than are the less histrionic sorts."[33]

The implications of such research findings for women in the workplace are: since women tend to be more emotional in their style of relating to others, they may be also more adept at lying. Also, since women who rise up in the corporate hierarchy tend to score higher in Machiavellianism, it may follow that the higher and more powerful women might prove to be even more adept at lying.

Being Machiavellian, and more likely to use more expressive styles of deception that are more effective, women, it seems, are particularly well equipped to lie. And, if they find deceptiveness effective and, in fact, other more direct techniques of coping are closed to them, it follows that they would be more likely to act in this manner. As we have determined, people do things that have a cost-benefit payoff, and if a certain approach—such as being deceptive to get ahead—proves effective in obtaining a desired benefit, a person will likely use it.

Finally, there is some reliable research on the organizational context in which men and women work which provides still another reason why women may be more deceptive at work. According to Virginia Schein, deceptive behaviors occur in organizations because each setting is more or less a political arena where individual managers and others jockey for power and influence. Some settings are more fertile grounds for deception than others.

When an organizational setting is highly competitive and its members must make many rapid, non-routine decisions, people are less likely to engage in deceptive behaviors. They have to focus on taking care of the work. Schein terms this a "low-slack system"—one with little free time for off-the-job politicking. A basically stable environment where people participate in routine everyday activities Schein terms a "high-slack system"—where people have plenty of free time to pursue their own personal goals, since they can do so without disrupting the system. This kind of stable working environment encourages deceptive tactics because, according to Schein, people are likely to be bored performing jobs which are somewhat routine, even at the managerial level. They feel a need for excitement, and they express this through political warfare involving all sorts of little deceptions and intrigues to develop personal power.[34]

This research is particularly relevant for understanding why women might be more deceptive, because this is exactly the type of environment—routinized, low-power settings—in which women are more likely to work, even as managers, and thus more likely to engage in covert political intrigues to seek personal gain.

In short, the workplace for women is such that individuals are motivated to do something deceptive to achieve some personal goal. Other research seems to suggest that some women have certain personal traits that contribute to their acting more deceptively. At the same time they are more likely to work in a setting that encourages deceptive behavior. Is it any wonder that women have acquired the reputation they have for being underhanded and backstabbing to other women?

HOW ARE WOMEN
AFFECTED BY
COMPETITION IN THE
WORKPLACE?

What does competition have to do with the way women act? Could it be that the very competitiveness of the workplace and women's low power status in it contributes to this covert style?

According to the research on this subject, competition is very much a factor in women's behavior in the workplace, since unethical behavior increases in a more competitive environment—perhaps the urban equivalent of survival of the fittest in the wild. Intense competition increases the struggle between both men and women for success.

The research is especially relevant in considering the effect of competition on women, because it shows that the mangers who experience the most competitive pressure are not those at the top but those in middle management, which is exactly where many women in business are. Top managers set the goals; middle managers are required to meet them.

The problem is that a highly competitive business environment can stimulate unethical conduct among such managers. As W. Harvey Hegarty and Henry P. Sims, Jr. found when they looked at unethical decision-making behavior, in most competitive business environments the emphasis is on good performance and profit; ethics is a secondary and less-important objective. Productivity is what is rewarded, and business people only start to consider ethical behavior very important when it goes off course enough to draw legal action.[35]

When Hegarty and Sims examined the relationship between profits, productivity, and unethical behavior in a laboratory setting using business graduate students, they found that the more they rewarded the students with higher profits, the more the students were likely to look the other way when their "salespeople" were making unethical kickbacks. Moreover, they found that students with the highest Mach Scale scores were the most likely to choose the unethical path as conditions of competition increased.[36]   This research is very suggestive of what happens to women managers in the workplace. Earlier in this chapter, we saw that current research theories suggest that women become more Machiavellian as they move up the occupational ladder. If this theory is valid and people become more unethical as the pressure builds up, then the High-Machs are more likely to behave unethically. And as women move up to higher positions in the business world, there is more competition; they become more Machiavellian; and therefore they are more likely to sabotage others.

DO WOMEN KNOW THE RULES?

According to some theorists, another reason women may sometimes sabotage other women is that they simply don't know the appropriate business rules or because they have their own set of rules. Men have had a long history of developing support systems and "old-boy" networks. They know the ins and outs of mentoring. Sometimes women, as the new kids on the block, don't understand the expectations of help and support. So they may not always know the rules or play by them when others reach out to help them. Instead, they may take advantage of the person who helps. Or they may offer help themselves but then take it back when there's a better opportunity to do something else.

An article in *The Executive Female* makes this point. According to this article, women have been brought up forming alliances mainly because they like someone, whereas men, as little boys, learn how to get along with someone if they think them competent, whether they like the person or not. This early learning works well for men when they carry it over into a business setting. They network and support each other not so much out of personal liking but because the connection works. It's pragmatic. Things get done. And that's good for the men and the business. The problem for some women comes about because they try to bring their own rules into the business world. They may feel uncomfortable because they are working in an environment where liking is replaced by the ability to produce— a situation in which even some men may feel threatened and in which women tend to feel especially uncertain and distressed because they have even less idea as to what to do. They have to operate from a new rule book.[37]

One result of this, reported by Sheila Collins in a study of top and middle-level women administrators, is that women may not be very good mentors. For example, when Collins asked these administrators, with backgrounds in social work, nursing, and education, whether they had provided career assistance to other women, she found that the women generally scored low. Why? She didn't feel it was an unwillingness to help others, but rather that the women simply lacked the knowledge about ''the career development process for women and what is involved in serving in a mentor role.''[38]   Thus, some women don't follow rules in business simply because they don't know them. They may not support each other as much as they could or may end up sabotaging each other without intending to do so.

HOW LOW ESTEEM AND
LOW POWER
CONTRIBUTE TO
SABOTAGE

Another reason cited in recent studies on women's inclination to sabotage each other is that women, compared to men, tend to have feelings of low esteem and power. Again, research shows that feelings of low esteem and power may influence a person to act unethically. The upshot is a vicious circle: the sabotage contributes to women being held back in positions of low esteem and power, which contributes to the sabotage, which contributes to being held back in positions of low esteem and power. And so on.

Much of the research on the relationship between self-esteem and unethical behavior comes from psychologists doing experimental studies. E. Aronson and D. R. Mettes conducted a study in which they gave students a chance to cheat at blackjack. They found that the students who measured lower in self-esteem cheated more often.[39] In a second study, Richard Graf found that low-esteem students were more likely to dishonestly filch a dollar bill rather than return it to the experimenter.[40]

What is the association between dishonesty and low self-esteem? According to the researchers, cheating is a way to excel and correct a negative self image. There appears to be a relationship between lowered feelings of self-worth and doing something unethical.

Other researchers suggest that people with low self-esteem may be more apt to cheat because they feel more anxiety: if they can do something, by whatever means, to feel more power or control over someone else, then they feel better and less anxious. Carolyn Reed found this association between low status (which is associated with low self-esteem) and anxiety when she studied women at different career levels. She observed that as women moved up the career ladder their feelings of anxiety decreased, and the higher-status women were lower in anxiety than the group of average women.[41]

Women may also use manipulative behavior to get ahead because they are much like members of minority groups in low-status positions, who sometimes must resort to unethical and covert tactics to get ahead or even to survive. In her article, "Women and Power," Paula Johnson makes this point when she asserts that women often end up using more "indirect, personal, and helpless modes of influence," because in reality and in their own expectations, women have less access to other power resources.[42]

Arlie Hochschild, a sociologist at the University of California at Berkeley, has done extensive research on sex roles. She states that there is a relationship between low-power and minority status and manipulative behavior. In fact, she considers this a completely rational approach for a person in such a situation to achieve his or her goals. Since the person doesn't have the power to get something directly, it's only sensible to use manipulative strategies to get them.

So a woman may behave in a helpless fashion in order to get her own way. According to Hochschild, it's a rational thing to do in oppressive circumstances.[43] In using power in a quiet, covert way, women may help to continue their lower-power status because over the long term this strategy may backfire. If a woman covers up her power, others may be unaware of her potential and she therefore may be more likely to remain in a subordinate, low-status position. That leads back into a vicious-cycle mentality again, for in staying stuck, the person will continue to use an indirect and covert style of power. And in certain situations, women may use ingratiation or exact petty revenge. Men, on the other hand, can be more open and aggressive in using power. It's simply more expected and viewed as more legitimate for them to do so.

Some researchers also suggest that a person in a low-power position might behave unethically because he or she feels less responsibility to others or to the organization as a whole. According to Maury Silver and Daniel Geller, this may happen because a low-status person may feel dehumanized; he or she may feel less connected to others, and consequently may be more likely to respond to monetary incentives or other personal benefits without concern about the effect of these actions on others.[44] And, since women are more likely to be in low-status positions, they may be more likely to experience this kind of dehumanization, which could lead them to feel less responsible to the group as a whole.

This low-status association with unethical action also applies to organizations as a whole, as Arthur Selwyn Miller has found in studying the business morality of companies of different sizes. According to his study, the large companies with more prestige and status tend to adopt a more moral stance in regard to the general public, and their corporate officers are typically held to a higher standard of moral rectitude.[45] The smaller business or business person, in addition to having less visibility, is not held to such high standards and has more freedom to be less ethically responsible and so is better able to conceal unethical acts. This observation is especially relevant to women, who are starting small businesses now at a much more rapid rate than men. The research on which this book is based reinforced the findings of other recent studies that women in their own businesses had more experiences of unethical behavior than those in the corporate environment.

Some women may feel particularly jealous because of their lower power status, especially when they see other women doing well or on the verge of getting ahead. As a result, they may try to attack these achievers or sabotage them through criticism and gossip.

Psychologist Beth Milwid found this kind of dynamic operating when she did a study of thirty women in banking, law, and architecture. The women had had a difficult time breaking into office networks, and they had had to overcome the usual resistance to women in the higher levels of their profession. Yet, some of them, once they made it themselves, acted to block other women from making the climb. Why? Recent research findings suggest that they felt insecure about their own hard-won positions and threatened by other women joining them at their level. Also, they believed that other women from lower-power positions on their own hard-won levels would somehow diminish the value of their own accomplishments. As one woman lawyer from a prestigious law firm Milwid interviewed said, ''I think that now there's a 'princess bee' who doesn't mind working with another woman but doesn't want that other woman to be at her level . . . she wants it made clear that she's half a step ahead.''[46]

Our research suggested that as some women move up the ladder the specter of their former low status can influence and haunt them and can lead them to guard their positions and strike out at other women who seem threatening. Some feel threatened that someone else may outdo them; some feel vulnerable.

When they get some power, women are held to different standards of behavior. In most business environments they can't be as direct and aggressive as men in getting something done;

they have to be more indirect and offer rewards to get what they want. According to Mary Glenn Wiley and Arlene Eskilson, who surveyed ninety-six experienced managers, this indirect-reward type of power style is simply a more unstable base of power than that used by men. A woman is more likely to be judged harshly if she makes the slightest misstep or comes into conflict with someone else.[47]

Many recent studies show that an unstable base can lead a woman manager to feel her own power ignored or chipped away, so she feels resentful and hostile and acts hostilely or unethically in retaliation. Or she may find that when she tries to exercise power others are resentful and resistant: they may think she is behaving wrongly or unethically, when in fact she is doing just what a male manager might do without encountering such problems. The underlying problem is that the people with whom she works may feel she should be in a low-power position. They have trouble relating to her in this higher status.

Women traditionally have had little clout in the workplace. If they use the more subtle, manipulative forms of power based on reward—which is traditional for women—they have a less stable power base and they are more apt to find themselves in situations where others can deny or undermine their authority. Then they may come to feel hurt and resentful themselves. Conversely, if they try to be more aggressive in using power, others may resent them and accuse them of acting unethically. It's a no-win situation, and many women find themselves in it.

When women try to compensate for their lack of power they may find themselves in situations which produce even more pressure and conflict. For example, women are often more helpful and accessible to their staff people than men usually are. One would think this would help their staff people feel good about working for them and supporting them. Natasha Josefowitz studied the question of accessibility with a group of one hundred and seventy male and female managers. In the group, the women were twice as accessible as the males. They encouraged their staffers to seek them out, checked what they were doing more frequently, or kept their doors open. They often did so because they felt it difficult to say no. A key reason for this was because they felt more insecure in their management position. They were more anxious to please and avoid conflict. She found that in many cases, women managers were more accessible than they really want to be or should be, and this leads to problems.[48]

While this approach can work in creating a more open, communicative work context, it also can have negative effects in that a person who is overly accessible can feel under increased pressure. In turn, the result can be a kind of pressure-cooker environment: the increased closeness with staff members can combine with feelings of pressure which produce increased feelings of hostility and greater chances of conflict.

For a number of reasons, the dual problem of having low power and low esteem puts women at a higher risk of either behaving unethically or being perceived as behaving unethically in the workplace. They're in the classic "Catch 22" situation. Only if women become aware of what is happening and why it is happening can they work together to reduce these occurrences and get out of the box they are in.

HOW FEELINGS OF HOSTILITY AND AGGRESSION SOMETIMES AFFECT WOMEN

It may be difficult to get out of this box without working through some of the feelings of hostility and aggression which frequently arise in those who have lesser power and low self-esteem. Research studies repeatedly show the connection: individuals with lower self-esteem are more likely to feel hostile, show a lack of respect for others, and attempt to retaliate against others to save face in a difficult situation. Although these studies don't explicitly compare males and females, they do highlight a relationship that can be very relevant for women, who consistently have been found to have lower feelings of self-esteem when compared to men.

In a study she conducted at a Minnesota university, Penny Baron found that student volunteers who had lower self-esteem were more likely to rate another person's performance on a task less favorably. According to Baron, they did this because their lowered esteem made them feel more defensive, and they felt that by devaluing others they could build up their own self image.[49]

Dr. Milton Layden believes that a hostile response to others is a natural outcome of feelings of low esteem or inferiority. It occurs, he explains, because the emotional system, like other systems of the body, is controlled by a "balancing mechanism." When a person feels a lack of respect toward himself or herself, or feelings of inferiority, the mechanism is knocked off kilter and the person starts to feel hostile and anxious. These feelings then get translated into hostile actions.[50]

Women and men are likely to express such hostile feelings through quite different actions. One reason is because individuals who cannot express their hostility directly are likely to displace it. Women since childhood are more typically discouraged from the direct expression of hostility and aggression; so they are more likely to express their feelings in covert ways, such as quietly seeking revenge. And, being more usually in low-power positions and therefore feeling low esteem, they can be expected to feel more of this hostility—which then gets displaced.

Psychoanalyst Martin Symonds suggest that this displaced style of expressing aggression is characteristic of women not because of their sex but because they have more often been in a position of dependency. As Symonds explains it, men are more apt to use a "vertical" style to express their aggression through clear, direct, easily understood statements or acts designed to get the other person to obey out of fear. But women are more likely to use a "horizontal" style of aggression, in which they use indirect and guilt-provoking tactics to get the other person to comply. In Symonds' view, the "horizontal" style is more characteristic of women, because a person is drawn to this style out of feelings of dependency. The person feels powerless and helpless; when someone doesn't respond to these needs, the person wants to strike out but feels blocked from directly expressing aggressive feelings or has repressed them from awareness. So she (or he) uses the "horizontal," indirect approach.[51] An example might be a manager who uses ambiguously worded insults against someone she felt let her down.

Perhaps another way to look at this dynamic is the way psychotherapist Ray Greenburg does: in many situations, Greenburg states, a woman can't effectively use or threaten to use a directly aggressive approach. She isn't strong or powerful enough to back it up. She can't stand up and fight like a man, so she uses "horizontal aggression"—or drops out of the fight.[52]

HOW CONDITIONS AT WORK CONTRIBUTE TO FEELINGS OF HOSTILITY AND AGGRESSION

The settings where many women work are especially likely to contribute to feelings of hostility and aggression which lead to hostile and unethical acts. Our research and other recent significant studies suggest four major reasons which are especially likely to affect women: the frustration they feel, the provocations they receive, the negative feedback they sometimes get, and the crowding they experience.

Frustration is an important factor, because, as extensive research has shown, frustration typically produces an aggressive response. In fact, this association between frustration and aggression is believed to have biological roots, according to a theory of aggression proposed by Dollard, Doob, Biller, Mowrer and Sears back in 1939.[53]

However, there is a problem in giving vent to aggression in an organizational setting. One isn't supposed to express this aggression openly or directly, especially toward a boss or supervisor. Yet the aggression is still there, triggered by the frustration. What happens? More than likely it gets expressed indirectly, possibly in a variety of covert actions intended to hurt the employer or the organization, such as sabotage, wasting time and materials, or withholding output.[54] It may also be expressed through constant complaining or subtle acts to undermine co-workers.

When Paul E. Spector looked at the relationship between frustration and aggression in a mental health facility and in other organizations, he found a direct connection. Based on the responses of eighty-two employees to an "Organizational Frustration" questionnaire, he found that those with the highest scores were more likely to exhibit a number of aggressive behaviors, consisting primarily of hostility to others, complaining, and, sometimes, sabotage of property and equipment, as well as verbal attacks on coworkers and the instigation of arguments.[55]

Since women, particularly those who are trying to advance but encounter organizational blocks, are more likely than men to be frustrated in the workplace and are probably unable to express this through aggressive hostile behavior, it stands to reason that they use the kind of covert tactics described by Spector to express it.

Provocation also commonly leads to aggression, as researchers have found in comparing individuals in high and low provocation situations.[56] One reason is that a provocation can lead the provoked person to view that act as an attack and thus result in anger.

This research is particularly applicable to women in the workplace, because they are more likely to experience anger-provoking situations than men. Besides encountering the frustrations and blocks to advancement already mentioned, they are more likely to be attacked or provoked in other ways, due to their lower power status and their position as minority group members or outsiders in a male-dominated environment. Two of the major provocations are sexual harassment and sexism, which were reported as major complaints in our own study.

Besides the more blatant forms of provocation that might occur when a man inappropriately opportunes a woman, there are other more subtle ones which are designed to remind women that they play subservient roles, such as the classic situation where the male executives at a management meeting suggest that the woman executives get the coffee or take notes.

While some of these provocations may be minor in nature, even the feelings engendered by little injuries can build up over time and lead to anger expressed in various ways—sometimes directly and other times in unethical and covert aggressive behavior.

Negative feedback can be another anger producer. When people are given unfavorable evaluations, for example, they are more prone to express hostility to whomever gives them that feedback.[57]

Negative feedback produces this kind of response in the workplace as well as the laboratory, with an even greater effect on women. Women are more likely than men to receive negative feedback because of their lower-status positions. Women are often rated more critically than men whatever they do; they frequently have to do much more than men to gain favorable evaluations or promotions. Our research suggests that if women get more negative feedback they are more likely to react with feelings of hostility which translate into aggressive and sometimes unethical actions—often expressed in covert ways.

Another reason that women may experience more hostility, anxiety, and aggression under certain circumstances is that they are more crowded; they work more closely together. Lower-status individuals get less space. The top managers, mostly males, have spacious offices of their own. The middle managers have smaller spaces, though still private. Secretaries and clerical workers often get no more than a partition, or are situated in an open area near other peoples' desks.

This kind of close quarters by itself can contribute to tension. Psychologists studying crowding have noticed this negative effect. When Janice Zeedyk-Ryan and Gene Smith reviewed the literature in this field, they found that much of the research showed a negative effect associated with crowding, especially under high-density conditions requiring high levels of interaction.[58]

The results suggested that workers in high-density conditions with a high level of interaction are more likely to feel hostile and aggressive. Women are more likely to experience such circumstances because they tend to be in lower-status positions, which are allocated less personal space. Furthermore, women are more likely to be accessible and leave their doors open when they do move into management, so they are more apt to have a higher level of interaction with others on the job. Since women are more apt to express the types of behaviors which commonly result from crowding—hostility and aggression—that might lead them to behavior which can turn out to be unethical.

Low power and low self-esteem, aggravated by these workplace conditions, can fuel feelings of hostility and aggression, which women commonly express in covert and indirect ways due to their traditional style of doing things and the influence of the workplace. As Suzanne Gordon describes it in an article for *Ms.* magazine, many women seem to have this underlying reservoir of anger that bubbles up from time to time, because they feel so little power:

> . . . Any subordinate is in a position which constantly generates anger . . . anger is not there originally . . . the anger we know is developed by a cultural structure, which first incites an angry response.[59]

In short, much of the unethical, angry behavior which women engage in today is due to their social conditioning and the cultural context of the workplace. It creates situations in which women feel angry, hostile, and aggressive and can take out their aggression in covert and unethical ways. Any solutions must deal with this anger and aggression as signs that something hurts and must seek to change the situations that generate these behaviors.

HOW FEELINGS OF BEING AN OUTSIDER OR INSIDER CAN MAKE A DIFFERENCE

Finally, women may be influenced in whether they behave ethically or not by whether they are part of an in-group or feel like outsiders in the office. People tend to behave with more trust and cooperation to those in their own group; they communicate more. Conversely, there is less trust, cooperation, and communication, and more potential to behave aggressively or hostilely, to someone outside the group.

What makes this especially relevant for women on the way up is that other women may come to see them as part of an out-group, particularly since women who get ahead often adopt male practices and techniques to gain acceptance in the higher reaches of the organization. This is often affirmed by a woman's being praised to the extent that she "acts like a man." As other women of the group begin to consider the upward-bound woman an outsider, they may be more likely to direct any hostility or aggression they feel toward her.

Yet women within the group don't get off scot-free. They, also, can end up being subject to this anger when scapegoating is used to displace feelings of hostility which can't be released outside the group. In his studies on small groups, Robert Bales found that when people as a group feel angry they may select a scapegoat and direct their anger at this individual, so the group as a whole and the group leader is protected.[60] It relieves pressure on the group and the group leader and it helps those doing the scapegoating to feel better. The group can then continue to maintain itself and continue to function. Certain women are more probable candidates for scapegoats when hostility gets expressed within the group; typically a low-status member who has less power to protect herself than anyone else gets selected out, since this is the safest choice.

There is reliable evidence to show that women are especially likely to behave unethically toward other women at work or to be victimized by another woman. This may take all sorts of forms: the kind of double-dealing Mary Cunningham claimed she experienced by other women at Bendix,[61] behind-the-scenes gossip to cut a woman down to size or keep her in line, overly-critical office workers, and other barriers.

Women don't sabotage other women because of any genetic sex-linked characteristics. Rather, women are affected by certain social and psychological factors. These are:

- current social trends which create a more restrictive and competitive environment for women;
- the decline of ethical values throughout society which impact more on women than on men;
- the culture of the workplace where women are generally in a lower status or outsider role;
- the more personal management style of many women which can create more interpersonal conflict because people tend to get closer;
- the extra pressures on women due to the demands of their personal lives while fulfilling the demands of work;
- the stereotypes of expected male and female behavior, which can keep women in management positions from getting ahead;
- the more personal and pragmatic ways many women tend to deal with moral decisions, because they have experienced, in growing up, a different type of moral development than men;
- the different psychology of women, which leads them to feel more hostility and express it in covert ways.

Women have a different type of superego strength, which manifests itself in their attitudes about dishonesty and deception, in their perception of roles, in their feelings about competition, in their sense of self-esteem, and in their access to power.

They also tend to feel more anger and hostility and to encounter more frustration. And they are more likely to feel like outsiders in workplace groups.

If we want to start solving the problem of women sabotaging women and turn it into women supporting each other, we need to understand its roots. And this lies not only in the culture of the workplace but in the special early childhood experiences and psychology of women. Each of these factors contributes to an understanding of why some women behave unethically and why those that do principally choose other women as their targets. This is the place to begin—with awareness and understanding. With further knowledge, solutions can be developed to create the changes women need in order to find fulfillment—and success—in the workplace. But it is also necessary to understand the tactics unprincipled women use in their unethical behavior—and why.

Chapter 4

Ms. Conduct

WOMEN DO IT BETTER

"You shall not find me lacking in devices, in the/ word to drop here, the rumor started there. We must have . . . agents about her/ so that her acts and sayings may be mis/construed and a net of half-lies woven about her. . . ."

Elizabeth to Burghley
Act One, Scene II

Women are more likely than men to believe they have been treated unethically by another woman. The results of our study showed that only thirty-five percent of the men claimed a woman had treated them unethically, whereas fifty-three percent of the women reported that another woman had treated them unethically—fifty-one percent greater than reportings of unethical treatment to men. Interestingly, there was virtually no difference in the way both men and women reported being treated by men.

Many women in our survey reported that they had experienced indirect, vengeful, vindictive, and backstabbing actions at the hands of other women, and that these episodes occurred over relatively petty matters. They felt that many times women dwelled on minor slights and built them into causes of action. Some women reported that they believed other women were

87

often guided by jealousies, feelings of threatened personal secu-
rity, or low self-esteem in striking out at other women they
believe are moving ahead of them.

Some of the interviewees suggested reasons for this. According to their views, women depend much more than men on
personal power. They are more apt to psychologize, analyze,
and react emotionally to the situations they encounter. They are
likely to hold a grudge before retaliating, though there may be
long-term repercussions of such an attack. In contrast, the
interviewees felt that men tend to have official-position power
and relate to one another in terms of a well-developed system of
rules. Men act more pragmatically and are more receptive to
putting aside personal slights. They make the best they can of a
given situation, and consequently they are more apt to work
with past enemies.

Our reports showed that this behavior occurs in all social and
occupational contexts; it affects the type of jobs women hold
and wherever they are on the career ladder. Women outside the
organizational environment of large corporations are not immune to this situation. Nor are women who may be done in by a
former friend or colleague. Some cases have made national
headlines. Most do not.

When the women in our study reported unethical behavior by
men, it usually revolved around issues of sexual harassment,
discrimination in employment, and failure to be promoted. But
their reports of unethical behavior by other women concerned
issues of power and competition, reactions to personal slights
and envy.

The following cases illustrate the darker side of women, which
pervades many types of business relationships, organizational
settings, occupational categories, and status and ranking levels.
There appears to be a common link in the style of unethical
action. There is a certain type of vengefulness; a certain type of
retribution that characterizes these stories. Ironically, the level
of retribution often outstrips the original incident that triggered
the desire for vengeance. Then, too, there is that quality of
secretiveness, backstabbing, and behind-the-scenes manipula-

tion which infuses these plots of character assassination, power destruction, and monetary loss which causes one to ask if these women are reacting out of feelings of hurt at the actions of another person—often unintended and relatively trivial—or out of feelings of insecurity, jealousy, and fear.

LYING IN WAIT FOR
REVENGE

Nicole's case illustrates the kind of complaints of which many women in our study spoke. Nicole performed what she thought was a compassionate act for someone who was a former friend, supposedly in desperate need.

The incident began with a simple manicure. Nicole had gone to Diane's beauty shop and had given her a check for twelve dollars to pay the manicurist. Nicole went for occasional manicures at Diane's shop, and over the years the two had become friends. They shared a little of each other's private lives; their children had gone to school together.

A few days after the manicure, Nicole was robbed. Her purse and its contents were taken. Her bank opened a new checking account and closed the other. The twelve-dollar check was returned to Diane's bank marked "account closed." Diane immediately called Nicole. Nicole said she would send another check and include a note to the manicurist explaining the circumstances. Within a few days, Diane received the check. Nicole thought no more about it.

Nicole was completely unprepared for—and stunned by—the events that followed.

Diane's attack started with a seemingly innocent plea for Nicole's help. As Nicole recalls it, Diane contacted her after they hadn't spoken for months. She said she was desperate and didn't know where to turn. Things had been rough for her financially, cash flow had been erratic, and the insurance payment to keep her shop open was past due. Diane expected significant cash flow within a month. Nicole was very sympathetic. As a struggling young entrepreneur herself, one who had come over from another country with only a few dollars in her pocket, she had experienced dire poverty and felt the fear and desperation that goes with it.

Nicole offered to lend Diane two thousand dollars, personally taking it to Diane so she could take care of her obligation immediately. However, Nicole explained that she could lend the money only for a month, because she had commitments due then. She also asked Diane for a written promissory note. "Of course, no problem, no problem at all," Diane assured her about the note and the one-month obligation. "I only need it for a month."

A month later Nicole asked Diane for repayment. Diane made one excuse after another. "No problem, I'll send it." "Well, um, well, I'm getting to it." "It's in the mail." During later calls Diane was unavailable, at home or at the salon, at least to Nicole. Letters went unanswered.

Nicole couldn't understand Diane's lack of response. She finally found out from a mutual friend that Diane was angry over the twelve-dollar returned check, although she had never mentioned her anger to Nicole. Diane had told their mutual friend, "I really got her. Who does she (Nicole) think she is, a rich bitch, that she can let somebody wait five days to replace a bounced check?"

Diane felt that as soon as Nicole knew about the check, she should have jumped in her car and driven over with the cash, instead of using the mail. Twelve dollars to her was, she presumed, like two thousand dollars to Nicole. She never even spoke to Nicole about this concern; she just let her anger fester for months until she could "get even." She never intended to pay Nicole back. Whether Diane was telling the truth when she spoke to the mutual friend or just looking for an excuse is unknown.

Nicole was incredulous that anyone could act this way. As she told us:

It was a twelve-dollar manicure check! Would you believe that? And I lent her two thousand dollars. But for months, for somebody to hold (a grudge like that) . . . I never knew anything about it. I replaced the check. It took probably five days between the mail and her telling me and all that. And her thing was that I should have gotten in the car the moment I found out, driven up to her shop, handed this woman the cash, because for her twelve dollars is like two thousand dollars to me! If she would have called me and said: "Nicole, this woman really needs the twelve dollars today," I would have done it. Just like I had gotten up in the middle of the night to take her two thousand dollars. So, people are screwy. Truly, their heads are so twisted.

Nicole felt that Diane's covert attack was the result of a typically female position of low power, where a lack of self-esteem is reflected in a lack of assertiveness. As Nicole observed, the manicurist could have easily:

> . . . picked up the phone and said that she understood I had been robbed and my account was closed, but could I get this check to her other than in the mail which might take five days. She didn't do it. But then a person in that position or that lifestyle maybe isn't that assertive. Who knows. I have been very poor in my life, and when you are very poor, it is very hard to have the self-esteem to call up and say "Send me money because I am needy." You pretend you are not needy because you are so hurt or embarrassed or vulnerable. So when she didn't do it, I could understand.

Many currently held psychological theories substantiate the fact that when people are unassertive and don't stand up for what they really want, resentments, grudges, vengeance—even vindictiveness—become by-products. Our research showed that women may be more likely to hold grudges. Multiple studies illustrate that women psychologize situations more than men, who are more likely to be pragmatic and move on because it profits them to do so. As Nicole notes, "I think the difference between men and women is that men call you on it or they forget about it and move on."

Another reason that women may be more apt to act deceptively, as Diane did, is that they are less likely to voice their expectations. When they don't get what they want, they often feel resentful and hold grudges—as Diane did. In thinking about this incident, Nicole said that she had observed this pattern in a number of women: "In a way, women mix up social ethics with professional ethics. So they turn around in business and say 'she screwed me' . . . mostly what I am finding out is that women do not clearly put out their expectations. In the end, they feel screwed when in fact, they are partially responsible."

Finally, our study revealed that women tend to get more emotional and feel more strongly about situations than men do. They feel a need to "do something" when they feel they have been wronged. Nicole put this nicely when she summed up her own bad experience with Diane:

> I don't think men get so emotionally involved with a situation. They say, "That's just the way business is," and they move on. We personalize it and hurt. . . . We feel, we care, and then we overfeel and overcare and, because we are afraid to put out what we want, we make assumptions and then we feel screwed. So, I think that women do hold grudges more than men—and, we get stuck.

ENGAGING IN PUT-DOWNS OUT OF JEALOUSY

The results of our research led us to feel that for some women jealousy can be a motivating factor behind unethical behavior. When a woman, perhaps a colleague or fellow employee, gets ahead and is successful, other women may feel envious because they think they are stuck or not moving ahead as quickly. They may act to put the other woman down, embarrass her, insult her, damage her reputation, or upset her. Men do this too. But women do it more often to each other. Women tend to experience jealousy more intensely than men do. If they strike back, it is often in a devious, behind-the-scenes style.

A series of such incidents befell Susan, a successful seminar leader and consultant. When she was a teacher, she was eager to share what she did with other teachers and learn about their methods, thinking both could benefit from the exchange. She noticed that many women teachers hesitated to share any of their good lessons with other teachers. They seemed afraid that others would copy their lessons or gossip, even though there was minimal risk of this. Susan stated, "It didn't matter that the person was teaching sixth grade and you were teaching kindergarten and would be involved in just a concept exchange—there was a great deal of territoriality."

During this time, Susan had a car accident, which caused her to stay home from work for three months. She lost twenty pounds, looked thin as a rail and spent most of the day in bed or on a lounge outside. One day Jane came to visit her. Susan and Jane were close. They taught together, and Susan had organized three showers for Jane when Jane had gotten married. Two days after this visit, Susan received a five-page letter from Jane telling her she was "disgusting" for lying around and taking it easy when there was so much famine and disease in the world. Jane warned her that she would lose all her friends and the people who cared about her if she kept acting like this.

Susan was amazed and shocked. At a time when she most needed encouragement and support, the letter, ostensibly sent because the so-called friend was concerned about her, made her feel so terrible that she had a relapse. As she explained:

> Here I was recuperating from a car accident, so I was out of work. I weighed eighty-nine pounds and the only thing I could do was lay on my balcony. I was tan and I was thin, which might make anyone who wasn't thin annoyed. By that time, I had been out of work three months. I don't

know how I was acting that was supposed to be so disgusting. All I know is that I received this letter from someone who said she cared and wanted to help me. At the time of her visit, I was feeling better. When I got this letter, my emotional health and my back got worse. It actually caused me another three months out of work. I was so totally crazed by her letter. I couldn't believe someone who liked me would do that to me.

Afterward, when Jane tried to call, Susan hung up on her. Susan subsequently discovered through a mutual friend that Jane had been telling people there was something wrong with Susan, which was the reason she didn't have kids.

What did Jane have to gain by this? Initially, Susan didn't know her motive. Later, in reviewing her relationship with her supposed friend, she believed she found the reason. Susan observed, "She was jealous. She couldn't stand the fact that my principal and I communicated well while she seemed to upset him whenever she spoke to him."

Like Diane, who waited for revenge, Jane bided her time for a chance to act when Susan was most vulnerable rather than confronting and acknowledging her hostile feelings directly.

Some time later, when Susan was considering organizing a career-change workshop and leaving public teaching altogether, she and her mentor, another teacher, were laid off from their jobs due to a shortage of state funds. Although the school said the layoff was only temporary, Susan seriously though about other possibilities and believed there were other teachers who might want to do the same.

Driving to a luncheon together, she mentioned the idea of a career-change workshop to Becky, her mentor: "Why don't we train people and do workshops so that they can leave teaching?" Becky immediately put the proposal down, telling Susan that it was a bad idea. Susan pursued her idea anyway. After six months of research, she wrote up a proposal and submitted it to a major foundation for funding. She said nothing to Becky, who had been so adamantly opposed to it.

Ironically, the day after she submitted the proposal, Becky brought up the workshop concept. "You know that idea you told me about several months ago? I think it's a wonderful idea. I think we should write the proposal and submit it to someone." Susan explained that she already had submitted the proposal but that she hadn't thought Becky was interested because of her past remarks.

Becky became silent. Thereafter, she was extremely caustic and vindictive toward Susan, although she continually denied she had any resentment about the proposal. Subsequently, Becky made several insulting comments about Susan to an official from the State Department of Education. Susan tried to get Becky to be open about her feelings. Becky denied there was any connection between her remarks and the proposal. "Oh, no, darling," she said quite innocently. "I'm just fine with it."

Obviously, Becky was not. At a dinner attended by ten officials from the state of California, Becky made a number of innuendoes about Susan, implying that Susan was having an affair with one of the school superintendents: "Well, Susan and Peter are *very* close." When another superintendent wondered why Susan had been laid off, Susan managed to dilute the remark by making a humorous comment: "Well, I guess I wasn't very good," she laughed.

A year and a half later, Becky used Susan's casual remark to make further innuendoes about the supposed relationship. Over cocktails, Becky announced to several superintendents that Susan had dated this superintendent. When Susan commented that Becky was just kidding around, Becky became intensely angry. Her nostrils flared and she blurted out, "Don't tell me that! I know what I am talking about!" Susan was stunned by Becky's intensity.

In thinking it over later, Susan believed that Becky's remarks were due to a number of factors. Becky often drank, and during such episodes said things she shouldn't. The proposal Susan created helped establish a growing reputation for herself in a new field. Susan believed Becky's jealousy over being left out of the proposal was the motivating factor behind her verbal insults.

FORMER FRIENDS

Our research indicated that a woman may behave unethically toward another because she feels she is losing her influence and control over that person. She may strike back to show her anger. Certainly, the same kind of situation occurs for men, but again, the key difference seems to be in that a woman's reaction is often much more intense.

An excellent illustration of this is what happened to Laura, who became politically active in a high-income community. Laura was in her thirties and a former school teacher when she and her husband moved to the area in the early 1960s. Her husband travelled often, leaving her with some free time. She soon became active in community affairs. Initially, her involvement centered around the school her children attended. After a few years, she became a PTA president, a Girl Scout leader, and a member of the Welcome Wagon Newcomers group to help new people feel at home in the community. This is where she met Josephine, who was the publisher of the local newspaper.

Laura hadn't planned to enter politics. The availability of buses for the school children became an issue in the community. Laura wrote a letter to the mayor stating that she believed the community didn't have enough tax dollars and she preferred to have the money spent in the classroom rather than on getting children to school. If necessary, the children could walk. She also mentioned some of the other things she thought the township should do: the cross streets for children should be made safer and shoulders should be broadened on the roads for bicycles and horseback riders.

It all happened quietly, unexpectedly, and civilly. The community poured out the good neighbor spirit when individuals showed concern for good education, property values, and keeping the slightest whiff of crime or scandal away from their one-acre-plus homes. As a result of this letter, the mayor appointed Laura to the Walkway Committee, a group that dealt with the city's paths and trails system.

Laura still saw Josephine from time to time at Welcome Wagon meetings. Josephine once had been on the Walkway Committee and had offered helpful advice. At the time, Laura thought Josephine was simply being friendly and the two women became close. According to Laura, Josephine was the kind of person who liked to have control over the people she helped. She was also the kind of person who gets very angry when those people she has mentored try to establish their own identity. As she explained:

> Josephine never wanted to be a visible person. She just wanted to be the hoop roller and I was supposed to be the hoop. She saw I was going to be involved with the city; so she started watering me, nurturing me. . . . She always wanted to run things, and if it wasn't run the way she wanted, then she didn't want to be involved.

But initially, Laura saw Josephine as a good, helpful friend. The Walkway Committee led to other community projects; beautifying City Hall was one. The city had just built a new building and had no money to cover landscaping. Laura helped organize a project in which she persuaded all clubs and groups in the community to work together for one day to plant flowers and trees. As a result of this, she was encouraged to apply for an opening on the Planning Commission and was appointed. Josephine was also on the commission. Almost at once Josephine sought to get Laura's support for her own position. To some extent, acting in the role of a mentor, she helped Laura get familiar with the work of the commission:

> Josephine was very happy when I joined the commission because I was somebody she knew, and so right away she was going to tell me how to think and how to prepare myself and how I was supposed to vote. I just worked within her framework. But I was testing the waters, too,

and if I did have a job, I always prepared myself completely for that. If some of the information came from her, so be it. She was always willing to spend time with me to go over something or if I had a question. She had been around awhile and I used to ask her for help. She was one of my mentors, I guess you might say.

While Laura was on the Planning Commission, several men active in local politics approached her to run for City Council. After discussing the matter with her husband, she agreed to run. Then problems with Josephine began to surface.

A key issue was that Josephine didn't like Laura's low-key style of campaigning. Laura wanted to run on her record of being on the Walkway Commission and her desire to represent the people of the community. Josephine wanted Laura to sling dirt at all the "bad people" that were running against her. She was particularly eager to direct an attack against a specific woman she wanted off the council. Laura didn't know the woman or her record and wanted to avoid a campaign based on unfounded personal attacks. She refused to engage in any mud-slinging. This response angered Josephine and tension began to build:

> Things sort of went downhill from that moment on. I remember a couple of times I would come into the council chambers during the election and be very, very upset at Josephine because I would have this meeting or this coffee with her and she would say I wasn't cutting people down enough and we had verbal blows about it.

After Laura was elected matters rapidly worsened. Josephine made it clear that she wanted to give Laura direction on how Laura should vote at the council meetings. Laura stood up to Josephine, stating she would be her own person. When Laura was elected mayor, tensions increased further. Josephine believed that she had contributed to Laura's rise to power by mentoring her and endorsing her candidacy. Josephine had initially backed Laura because she thought she could manipulate her, but Laura had made it clear that she would make her own choices and rely on her own conscience. Laura described the growing tension between them:

> I wasn't looking to be mayor the day after I joined the council. I wanted to learn my job first (later I was elected). Then the first packet came for the first meeting. She told me before it had come to be sure to call her to go over everything together and she would tell me exactly how to deal with every subject and how to vote and so on, and this is when I said, "Hey, if you want to give me input, I appreciate it. And if you have any information, background, whatever, I want it. But don't tell me how I am going to cast my vote." And I said, "I'll make up my mind and I'll cast my vote from my own conscience and what I think is best for my community and from my point of view. You are not going to cut the corners and say this is how it should be done."

Josephine and Laura voted differently on issues at council meetings. Then Josephine began to make snide, negative remarks about Laura to friends they had in common. She began to engineer a way to discredit Laura who by now was gaining more and more power as mayor.

Laura and her husband were involved in a number of real estate properties. One of them was the building which was occupied by the local district attorney and the Board of Supervisors. Both had requested Laura and her husband to make certain improvements in the building. When Laura and her husband sought to collect for the completed improvements, the district attorney and board didn't want to pay. The funds had not been approved in their budget.

The situation dragged on for several months. Laura's husband wrote to the board saying the bill had to be paid or there would be a lawsuit. In delaying, the board asked the tax assessor to reassess the building. If the building was assessed at a higher rate, the township would get more in tax revenue. The extra revenues would cover a portion of the amount due Laura and her husband.

Meanwhile, Josephine, through innuendo and through derogatory articles in her paper, was able to get officials in other agencies interested in quietly investigating Laura and her husband. The investigation sought to imply that Laura had made political decisions in order to benefit real estate in which she and her husband may have had an interest.

The sting operation which developed was not entirely Josephine's responsibility: there were other members of the community who may have become concerned about Laura's growing political power and wanted to hold her back. But Josephine's activities behind the scenes acted as a stimulus for triggering the actions of others and mobilizing a concerted attack against Laura.

Laura didn't think that the township should contract with the county for police and fire services anymore because she felt the township could get better coverage for less money elsewhere. She understood that this position ruffled some feathers, but her arrest on fraud charges still came as a shock:

> I was arrested because an undercover operation had taken place to . . . destroy my credibility, and I think it is because they were concerned about my ability to get things done, and . . . wanted to destroy that. . . . The newspaper is the one we can point to, but whoever pulls the strings and discusses policy that gets into the paper is the "they" responsible.

In Laura's view, Josephine's articles in her local newspaper and her continual derogatory comments to key officials in the community, coupled with Laura's and her husband's demands for reimbursement for building improvements and Laura's position on the fire and police services, triggered the investigation.

Today, Laura is still trying to pull her shattered political career and business back together. She was successful in defeating all criminal charges against her. At the trial, Josephine was initially one of the star "mystery" witnesses. But the defense shredded her testimony as well as that of other witnesses for the prosecution. Those in the courtroom, including the prosecution, questioned how the case had ever got that far.

The prosecution withdrew all charges even before Laura's defense counsel presented her side. Still, Laura's legal fees amounted to hundreds of thousands of dollars. The state and county expenses were even larger.

Laura feels that the basic problem stemmed from Josephine's jealousy over her tremendous political success, first on the council, then as mayor, as well as various other positions, as well as her own refusal to kowtow to Josephine. Josephine, Laura said, bided her time from when Laura was first elected and rejected her interference:

> So this had been bothering her a long time. When I became mayor, she didn't like it. I was too successful. I guess I was too naive to realize what could happen. I guess I just felt so strongly that what I was doing was good, that everyone would accept it, and they could obviously see what she was doing was not good.

Ginny Foat's dramatic story is another example of the intense vindictiveness of which women who start out as friends are capable.

Ginny had become active in the National Organization for Women at around the same time Shelly Mandell did. Both soon rose to prominence in the organization, and after a few years became close personal friends. Shelly was president of the Los Angeles Chapter and was later elected to the National Board. She was instrumental in encouraging Ginny to run for the California presidency of NOW in 1981. Ginny ran and won. During this time they did virtually everything together; they were almost inseparable.

There was a spirit of openness and intimacy. Ginny shared her past life with Shelly: she had been married to an extremely exploitive man who had drifted into a life of crime. At one time he had accused Ginny of being an accomplice to murders in Louisiana and Nevada. She was innocent: the charge in Nevada was dropped and the charges in Louisiana were never prosecuted. She had revealed this information to others in the organization; now she wanted to be sure her legal situation wouldn't become a hot potato as her visibility spread.

In retrospect, Ginny thinks that Shelly considered herself Ginny's mentor, whereas Ginny considered their relationship that of "equals and allies." And, she thinks, that as her own star rose in the organization, Shelly came to see her as a competitor and resented her power.

Friction was generated when Ginny decided to back another woman for the national presidency instead of running herself. She chose to run for action vice president. As Ginny describes it, Shelly was furious. Her plans to be the power behind the scenes were scuttled because Ginny had taken the step without consulting her. The friendship ended.

Within weeks Ginny learned that rumors about the outstanding murder warrant against her in Louisiana were circulating. When she confronted Shelly with her suspicion that Shelly had started the rumor, Shelly denied it; she claimed she would never stoop to anything that low. But Ginny felt sure that Shelly was the source. Going into the election, Ginny had felt confident that she would win as action vice president; the flying rumors eroded that confidence. She lost and the rumors subsided. Ginny returned to California and concentrated on the California chapter as well as her involvement in the California Democratic Party politics.

A few months later she had another angry confrontation with Shelly—this time in the context of the Democratic Party. There was extensive infighting over the slate of candidates to run as delegates to the 1983 California Democratic Convention and this had weakened the coalition considerably. In an attempt to keep peace, Shelly's recommendations were included on the slate, and one of the politicans called Ginny to ask her approval of Shelly's friend. Ginny agreed, but the call provoked a hostile exchange with Shelly. As Ginny stated in her book, *Never Guilty, Never Free!*, "Who did I think I was, she wanted to know. She had more political power than I could ever hope to have. I'd find out who had the power."

That same night Shelly called Louisiana. She sent a letter on the stationery of the city councilman for whom she worked asking for information about any outstanding warrants against Ginny. Ginny was arrested a few weeks later. She spent seven months in jail in Los Angeles and New Orleans, where the case was tried, and hundreds of thousands of dollars in legal expenses which she incurred in fighting against a conviction for a charge that was based only on the testimony of a man who was the admitted killer and currently serving an indeterminate sentence in a Nevada prison. And, because of her political visibility, the case against her went forward in a glare of publicity.

The experience was devastating. Ginny saw her past life detailed in the pages of magazines and newspapers and on television. It was like being put under a microscope that explores and reveals every nuance, every crevice. She had to fight for her freedom and her life. But especially devastating was the realization that someone who was part of the Women's Movement, someone who had once been a close friend, would do this to her. Ginny writes in her book: "I don't think there's any way to describe the devastation I felt when I found out about Shelly, or that I still feel today. . . . The person who put me here (in jail) wasn't some impersonal outsider. Whatever our differences, Shelly was one of my own. She was once one of my best friends."

Ginny talked about the need for women to confront any anger they feel, rather than hide it, so it doesn't come out in destructive ways. She pointed out that women need to overcome much of the distrust, which dates from childhood, that they feel toward other women and that can lead them to see other women as rivals to be attacked. As she observed:

> Women do harbor that kind of resentment, pain, whatever the emotion is. They internalize it. When it is internalized, they don't know how to fight back. We have been taught to manipulate. We have been taught that it is not proper for us

to get angry. We are supposed to hide our anger. We are supposed to win things by manipulation, and so we don't learn the ground rules (for working together) the same way that men do.

Girl children are brought up to believe from everything, even starting with fairy tales written by men, that they are to hate other women, that other women are their rivals, that other women are their enemies. . . . You can look at every fairy tale there is and you will find the same thing, whether it is the evil witch, whatever. But it is the evil female figure that they, through the story, have to distrust and have to hate. That leaves the groundwork, as far as I'm concerned, for how we as women view other women.

Our findings indicate that if this distrust is combined with a feeling that other women are the less powerful, inferior sex, it can be an explosive combination. According to Ginny, as well as many other of our respondents, this can lead women to sabotage one another in getting to the top. Another woman is viewed as a contender for their own positions rather than someone who can assist them or someone they would like to help along. But this needn't be the case:

We have little girls who trust the other girls and other women, and then we have taught them that they are the inferior sex and when we continue that . . . (As a result) the rivalry for the football captain and all of that sort of thing is set up. If Joe, the football captain, asks you out and you have a date with your girlfriend to go to the movies, of course there is no question about it. You break the date with your girlfriend and you go out with Joe. On the other side of that, young men are learning to work together. They are learning to work together in the Cub Scouts, the Eagle Scouts, the football team. They are learning what teamwork is. They are learning to respect each other. So the star of the football team really understands that to be the star, he's got to have this team with him. There is this teamwork that builds up.

Many women don't learn this. Instead, their individualistic rivalry against each other destroys the feeling of being a team, so these women don't support each other as they should:

> We have the old tapes from the fairy tales and from the books, and all of a sudden, we are facing a job, maybe a promotion, but we don't know it is important for us to take other women with us, to help women up the ladder with us, because we are still viewing women as our rivals and competition, so we are not taking them along. We are not grooming them behind us. Only recently am I seeing that change a bit.

Mostly, this occurs at the lower echelons of the corporation where there are, in fact, more opportunities for women as a group. Still, many women in the executive suites fear that if other women rise to the same level, the other women will take their jobs away.

Certainly there is some truth to this fear as long as high-level jobs for women remain limited. And yet, in the long run, the more women that move into higher positions as a group, the more opportunities there will be for all women. Or, as Ginny put it:

> We are not holding our equal shares of board of director seats, corporate leaderships, CEOs. We are not there yet. So in a lot of ways, (we think that) a pie is a pie (and power is limited). . . . But until we have come to a place where we recognize that if you slice the pie and you give away a pie, you haven't given away part of your power, you've made your power increase. I don't think we have gotten to that point yet.

Ginny suggested that the number of opportunities for women in power can be increased if women will only take it upon themselves to create more opportunities. In turn, the more opportunities created, the more the market expands.

Ginny's experience also points to the need that women have to acquire more confidence in themselves so they can feel secure about their own power and about other women having power. If Ginny's former friend has felt more secure she would not have felt so threatened when Ginny also gained power in the organization. And perhaps then she would not have taken steps to sabotage Ginny. Ginny commented:

> I think it has to do with confidence levels. Women have to develop a confidence in themselves and who they are. That is what we are in the process of doing, because we can then develop a confidence in other women.

Ginny's has gone on to work with other women in supportive ways. She is running The Langtry, a bed and breakfast inn in San Francisco for women travellers, and is active in Legal Advocates for Women. Her attorneys are handling a lawsuit she filed against the woman who sought to destroy her by willfully and maliciously revealing information about Ginny's past to hurt her. Her goal is to use the system in order to achieve justice. In turn, it might be seen as a way of sending out a message to other women that they can't behave unethically to hurt one another— that unethical actions have repercussions that also can hurt the perpetrator. Ginny Foat's experience has come full circle. She was sabotaged by a woman. But the support, caring and belief of other women brought her through her ordeal.

When women help one another, a climate of sharing and support that can help all to get ahead is born.

PLACING THE BLAME
ON SOMEONE ELSE

Our research suggested that another way women sometimes do each other in is by setting up another woman to take the blame rather than facing the music. Women don't have a monopoly on sloughing responsibility for their own acts in order to protect themselves; men do it too. But there is that certain style that those in our survey seemed to feel is characteristic of women: deception, manipulation—almost as though a trap has been set.

Rita Lavelle's story begins on a high, in her key, visible position in the United States Environmental Protection Agency. Her division regulated business environmentally. She noticed early in her employment that her boss, the head of the agency, had a number of problems. The woman was highly visible in the Washington political scene, but when it came to doing the job she was hired to do as agency head, she just wasn't performing—at least not well.

The agency was set up with six assistant administrators directly under Anne, each in charge of a separate environmental program. From the beginning, Anne had difficulties with her staff. Within six months, she had fired four of the administrators she had hired when she was first appointed to head the program. Replacements were appointed, and Rita was one of them. Soon it seemed as though Anne was constantly at loggerheads with the administrators over something. Rita said:

> I realize now—I didn't at the time—that our motivations were in direct conflict from the beginning. While I was seeking to prove I could be a successful manager—harnessing and directing the technical talent of the agency, freeing it from the bureaucratic red tape so elaborately woven by the attorneys—Anne sought to become the hottest female political figure in the land.
>
> In an agency like the U.S. Environmental Protection Agency, whose actions or inactions so dramatically affect the quality of life for all citizens, this conflict spelled disaster. All of my actions were designed to provide the meat, all of hers to attract the sizzle.
>
> This may be an example of a typical male versus female view of careers. Men utilize a job to gain externals, women to gain *internals*. A woman looks at a job as an opportunity to prove she cares, that she is capable—in short, that she is worth something because others need and rely on her. A man looks at a job as a stepping stone to an even bigger stone. The ability to climb is too often related to his style, not his substance. I have heard some men say that perform-

ing too effectively makes them indispensable, precluding their opportunity to climb to more money, prestige, and power—all typical male goals.

According to Rita, not only did Anne have trouble with follow-through on the job, she was often not in the office when she should have been:

> She had no interest in follow-through on projects and was often unavailable to her managers for weeks on end. Failing to realize that she felt follow-through was completely unimportant, I mistakenly made excuses for her when she really sought none.
>
> We almost became the antithesis of each other. I was working sixteen hours a day to get results. She appeared at the office less and less, but when she did, it was always in a dramatic fashion. I was soft-spoken, conservative, and always promoting others as a means of achieving results. When necessary, I could come down hard and say no, demand accountability or better self-discipline, but I was never at ease in center stage.
>
> While I was announcing sites for government cleanup efforts, down-playing the risks and accentuating the positive, she was holding a press conference announcing a "new list of ticking time bombs." When I worked out an excellent agreement with an assailed Democrat governor that not only protected the environment and local jobs, but also his political career, she attacked me as disloyal to the White House:
>
> "How dare you let him announce that decision," she screamed. "He is a vulnerable incumbent. We could have used the firing of all those people to crucify him at the polls. You had better learn the game or get out."

According to Rita, Anne was used to hearing continual compliments from her personal staff members. She wanted her administrators to do the same. When they didn't, she became annoyed:

Rather than seeking management input on direction and policy, she sought constant feedback on how she personally was perceived. She forbade meetings between more than two of her administrators without her presence. Rather than convening meetings, herself, to resolve policy disputes or provide definitive direction, she relied on her staff to bring news on her administrators' performance, especially when she was out of the office so often.

The only thing that was constant about her was her need for constant change. We all knew in our guts that Anne would have dumped any of us if she could have—after all, she had fired four of her first six top assistants within six months. Since we had our own political constituencies, she couldn't fire us, but she certainly succeeded in making life miserable. Every one of her top administrators—there were six of us—came to me at least once, asking assistance in seeking a new position.

To some extent, Rita felt this behavior was due to Anne's being under a great deal of personal pressure, including an ugly divorce. Anne was physically ill, taking many weeks off work to recuperate. Out of loyalty and concern, Rita tried to help Anne both personally and professionally. During Anne's custody fight, Rita assisted her in getting the court records sealed. At the office, Rita and other employees often covered for her, doing what she was supposed to do since she was rarely there.

While I naively thought—despite our differences—that we were settling into our respective roles and strengths, the situation became a powder keg. In my eagerness to defend her management idiosyncracies, I missed the fact that her attempts to obtain good media coverage for herself were only too transparent to reporters. Rather than discussing agency results, her interviews constantly focused on her unique style, with emphasis upon how Reagan women were a unique breed. As her administrators worked overtime to try and reshape the focus of the coverage, the focus became more and more centered on her as a personality. Next to her flamboyant quips, jewels, designer dresses, and endangered species furs, my insistence on citing results paled miserably.

Rita believes that Anne became increasingly jealous and hostile toward her because she was performing so well at a time when Anne was not. Anne's haphazard management style helped to contribute to the problem. When she would literally abandon ship at times, others continued to act in her absence to do things which had to be done.

Because Anne would not allow staff members to hold meetings without her, there were very few staff meetings and, therefore, a lack of formal structure and organization. Each administrator ran his or her own program independently, communicating directly with her or her own employees. But, in terms of overall coordination of the agency, things were rapidly getting out of control.

> She was feeling very vulnerable. She was rather insecure in her position, because while she is a very gifted lady, very talented, very articulate, very physically beautiful, she got there totally on her politics and really didn't even know that much about the (work of the agency), didn't care to become involved and frankly wasn't even involved in the decisions that we were making day in and day out.

Under these circumstances, the agency was wrecked by Anne's "me-against-them" policy. When political pressures mounted against her, Rita feels, Anne found a scapegoat: Rita. In Rita's view, Anne settled on her out of jealousy. Rita was doing well in managing the most successful program in the whole agency. With her management, Anne's prestige and authority were eclipsed. Anne couldn't stand that.

Rita felt that there was no other reason for Anne to act as she did. Rita had shown her great loyalty, assisted Anne when she went through her divorce, and generally did everything Anne wanted her to do in carrying out policies.

I had my job to do. I had been given the guidelines and the policies. I had cleared all my policies with (the supervising government agency) and with her. . . . I knew exactly what I was doing and I can think of only six or seven things that she overturned that I did that weren't really that major, so I was in synch with her at all times. She reviewed my budget, she reviewed my performance standards, and so it was ludicrous that she should claim that I was performing in a manner that she had no knowledge of or that she could some way disagree with.

In retrospect, Anne's criticisms of me were always related to externals—my dress, my makeup, or my speech mannerisms. I never realized why it hurt so much, but now I can see that while she would attack me for that about which I was so sensitive, she would never acknowledge the strengths which I considered so important—program results. Thus her criticism and accompanying absence of praise was devastating.

I remember one exchange in particular. After a very heated four-hour session before an abusive Congressional chairman noted for his rudeness in conducting hearings, Anne refused to discuss what *I* wanted to discuss—how the agency attorneys were sabotaging our testimony with unauthorized, unsought memos which were then leaked to Capitol Hill. Instead, she insisted on criticizing my dress as too drab and my makeup as too scant. She urged me to "get my act together and start representing the administration with *some style.*"

"Rita," she cooed, "I never have a problem with him (the chairman); I just get dressed up and bat my eyelashes, asking for help and sanity from his committee. He especially likes purple and it photographs well."

The same contrast in motivations was evident in our management styles.

In order to obtain national attention and realize her goal of becoming a political force, however, Anne sowed the seeds of her own destruction. She made the mistake of

playing her political games against the masters of form, the
Department of Justice attorneys and White House syco-
phants. Unable to recognize a policy if it hit them between
the eyes, their only criterion was how the issue would 'play
in the polls.'

Rita believes that as soon as there was some bad publicity
about the agency in general, sparked by political infighting in
Washington, Anne used her to take the heat from herself. Rita's
success had made her feel more vulnerable and insecure of
herself.

> Anne was getting a great deal of anti-publicity from the
> press, though this was not necessarily because of the pro-
> gram. The program and I . . . and all the administrative
> assistants in our various programs were showing a lot of
> very good, long overdue results. So we were getting pretty
> good press, and she, in turn, because of her antagonistic
> style . . . was getting very poor press.
>
> Some of us administrators had talked about the fact that
> she would probably seek a scapegoat, and each of us
> thought it was going to be one of us at a given time.
> However, everybody was shocked that the scapegoat would
> be me, mostly because my program was so successful and
> she was claiming credit for this program all over the coun-
> try. So I assumed I was safe, and there was total shock
> when it came down on me.
>
> She told the Justice Department that "Rita held up the
> grant and embarrassed the Administration" and that she
> couldn't continue with Rita in her present position.
>
> Surprised at how easily the White House permitted her
> to dismiss their protégé, she went on to charge that the
> Justice Department attorneys had sent her out on a limb
> and then sawed it off. As the Department of Justice sought
> to correct the record, she declared that the White House
> staff was seeking a scapegoat. Obtaining immunity from
> prosecution in return for her agreement to resign, she then
> proceeded to stab the Administration publicly before recep-

tive Democrat Congressional Committees for policies she maintained were forced upon her against her better judgment.

Having worked overtime to deliver results, I was now devastated by the personal attacks delivered on the front pages daily by "anonymous" sources. Nevertheless, an ingrained team player, as Anne attacked, I continued to defend her and my now-silent teammates, right up to the time I was indicted for "lying to Congress" about the date of a meeting.

I asked why I should have lied about a completely innocuous date, still studiously avoiding criticism of Anne whose actions *had* been significant in the case in question. But by now, the Department of Justice, intent on displacing attention from its own mistakes in the "executive privilege" argument, had orchestrated a twenty-day discrepancy into a major crime. So intent was the Department upon convicting me that for eighteen months it succeeded in withholding documents that proved the entire case was a plot against me by Department of Justice and EPA attorneys.

Sinking further into shock and disbelief, I was unable to convince a jury that I didn't lie. The chief prosecutor claimed—with no evidence—that I had engineered the date discrepancy in return for a "big bucks job" after I left government. I was sentenced to six months in prison, five years' probation, and community service, a ten thousand dollar fine, attorneys' fees which I will never be able to pay, and a lifetime label of convicted felon.

Anne, financially secure, her attorney fees paid by tax dollars, remarried to a wealthy high government official, continues life in Washington as a "victim" of the Department of Justice and the White House.

Now, why did she do this to me? Because she felt threatened for her own job, and I think that she thought I might be the replacement.

I also think she chose me because while she was going

through this rather heavy time emotionally and politically and not performing on the job, I, in turn, was performing very, very well and delivering results and now, all of a sudden there was a political controversy about the agency.

In plain English, I had done everything politically that she was supposed to have done and we were in a very successful position. It was the outstanding program of the agency . . . so she was feeling vulnerable in her position— she really couldn't claim responsibility for our results.

What made the betrayal particularly galling to Rita is that she feels she was so loyal to Anne. She had done everything in her power to cover up for her at times when Anne was lax. In Rita's view she had done these things because Anne was a woman and Rita had strong feelings that "sisters" should support one another; moreover, Anne needed all the help she could get in Washington, D.C., a "very male" town. Rita continued, "I would say that I was like a sister to her, that's how I felt. That is why I was flabbergasted by the whole thing happening."

Indeed, once Anne began to attack Rita, she continued by embarrassing her with her peers and pillorying her in public. Before the political uproar, Rita had told Anne she wanted to go into private enterprise after her appointment was up, in particular as a vice-president of a particular company. In turn, Anne had shared her own dreams of a bright political future. When the problems with the Justice Department began, Anne used this private conversation against Rita. She called the president of the company Rita wanted to join, whom she had met through Rita, and told him she had been forced to fire Rita because she was a liar and incompetent. The only reason Rita could fathom for Anne's calling him was her anger and hostility towards herself.

In addition, Anne actively sought to discredit Rita by proclaiming her incompetence to the general public. Anne went to the press and claimed that the "only mistake I made was hiring Rita." She claimed she was forced to hire Rita by key officials in government. Anne suggested that Rita was not only incompetent, but a fraud:

I think that the tools that a woman uses appear to be character assassination and backstabbing, rather than direct confrontation, while with men it is direct confrontation, sexual harassment, and discrimination. Men are direct rather than indirect like Anne.

Rita attributed the intensity of Anne's attack to another quality she identified as peculiarly feminine—the difficulty some women have in separating personal and business issues. It is a theme that was recurrent in many of the women interviewed.

Rita, along with many of our interviewees, felt that women are less likely to separate personalities and issues and that when the chips are down women are more likely to personalize what happens, intensifying the retaliation on the individuals who opposed them. Anne was under a great deal of pressure, and she already felt insecure, vulnerable, and scared. Rita—a successful woman who threatened to overshadow her—was singled out for the brunt of her attack. Rita's previous loyalty and performance counted for nothing; Anne wanted to save herself and assuage her feelings of jealousy at the same time.

Rita ended up doing a term in jail for lying, while Anne managed to get out practically scot-free. She pled guilty to some charges at the same time she accused Rita of various crimes. But since she had immunity, the government never prosecuted her. To the public, she appeared the victim, not Rita.

ENGAGING IN
SABOTAGE OUT OF
JEALOUSY

It is common knowledge that women are frequently in the underdog position. Our research findings indicated that because of this position they sometimes resort to sabotaging other women.

Tina was a financial officer in a large leasing company. She had been hired at a time when the company had gone through a period of losses. Her primary function was to tighten up the financial controls in the finance department. There were eighteen people in the department, mostly single women.

The company's policy was to promote from within. Tina was brought in from the outside. The woman in line for the job was sloppy in her appearance, not meeting the image the company wanted to project. When Tina was brought in, this woman was transferred to another department.

For a time, everything seemed to be running smoothly as Tina supervised her department. Tina made a point of getting along with everyone, and especially Linda, who had been there for several years and had built up a tremendous amount of loyalty to herself, and also had some specialized knowledge about part of the accounting system. Linda had to train many of the people in Tina's department in what to do, which gave her power over others: if other employees didn't do what she wanted, she could always withhold her power to teach them.

At first, Linda seemed to cooperate with Tina. Tina thought everything as fine. However, under the surface, problems were building up. Reflecting on Linda's actions later, Tina felt that one major problem was that Linda was single and not completely happy with her own relationships, while Tina was not only a manager with more power and money, but was also enjoying an active social life. As Tina told us, "I was in a steady relationship. I did a lot of skiing, travelled around the world, and discovered that a lot of jealousy was generated within my organization and my staff."

One of the reasons Tina generated this jealousy is that she mixed business and pleasure. She opened up her social life to her staff members by inviting them to some of the parties she had at her house. As many as eighty or ninety people attended at one time. Separately, out of concern for the singles in her office who weren't dating, she would invite them to dinner at her home. At other times, she let some of them use her ski cabin when she wasn't there. And she partied hard herself. The upshot was that while enjoying these parties, many staff members, and Linda in particular, were jealous and resentful at how much Tina seemed to have. "The more she saw of what I had," Tina observed, "the worse it got."

There was lingering resentment over Tina having been brought in as an outsider. Finances were tight within the company. Both of these factors contributed to an increasingly tense, low-morale atmosphere on a day-to-day basis.

During her first three months, Tina observed that Linda took much more time than necessary to complete a particular job: she required eight hours to do a two-hour task. Initially Tina believed that there were some inefficiencies in the way Linda was doing the job. Since Tina's management style included a rotation of positions and tasks, she decided to rotate Linda into another position. At first Linda fought her bitterly, insisting she should stay where she was. Tina persisted, and instituted the rotation. Tina then discovered that other employees completed Linda's job in a fraction of the time. As she related:

> Well, when I rotated it out, I found out this game she was playing where two hours of work was all she was doing all day long. It made her mad that I figured it out. She was really angry that I was on to her. I knew what she was doing.

Shortly after this, Tina conducted an individual review with everyone in her department. Following company procedure, she noted the discrepancies in Linda's job performance in her personnel file. This had been the second such write-up in Linda's file. A third report would lead to termination. It pushed Linda to the point of retaliation.

In looking back, Tina identified two incidents that she believed caused Linda to act. During Christmas week, Tina's boss hired a temporary secretary. When he went out of town for a few days, he sent her red roses. The women in Tina's department felt somewhat resentful: after all, they felt, they had worked with this man before—why didn't he send red roses to them, too?

At the same time, the manager of a smaller division of the company took his three staff members to lunch. Tina's own staff of eighteen had a Christmas lunch the following day, but the company didn't pay for it. Tina's employees thought everyone should be treated the same—budget considerations were not their problem.

Linda chose this moment to get even with Tina. Her ingenious act of sabotage entirely disrupted the activities of Tina's department.

In the final week of the year, Linda organized a lunch with others in Tina's department. They didn't come back from lunch. The timing couldn't have been worse. The last cash for the year was coming in. The financial department needed to finish balancing the books. The following week, the entire office would be closed. Tina was thrown into a panic when they didn't return. The work had to be done, but there was no support to do it. Frantic phone calls were made to other departments to recruit extra help. She cancelled her plans for the following week and spent countless hours getting the work done.

Tina called around to try to find the employees. She located a junior staff member who broke down and cried on the phone. She said everyone was afraid of Linda. "Why?" asked Tina. "And why didn't you all return?" The story unfolded.

The members of Tina's department were feeling some resentment. The flower incident, no Christmas bonuses, not even a holiday lunch or party sponsored by the company, were all used by Linda to ignite them. Most important, Linda had leveraged her power in the office. At the lunch, she threatened not to assist anyone who didn't join her in the walkout, which would mean they wouldn't be able to do their jobs. Linda played on her coworkers' feelings of hostility and browbeat those who hesitated into joining.

The result? Linda was fired and is now employed at a major bank. The others returned to work.

TAKING ADVANTAGE OF WOMEN'S TRUST IN WOMEN

Finally, our research indicated that another way women differ from men in their unethical behavior is the way some women take advantage of women's propensity to trust other women. This occurs because many women believe that women are more trustworthy than men; they feel that somehow a woman in business will be more forthright and open; they believe that the bond of sistership will create the foundation of a stronger, more ethical, honest relationship. And, of course, for many women this happens.

Yet, as the previous discussion has shown, some women can be extremely devious, deceptive, and unethical. And this problem can be compounded when a woman acts in good faith, believing that another woman is behaving with integrity because she is a woman. When a woman takes advantage of that special trust and behaves unethically, the results can be disastrous, as happened to Carolyn.

Two years ago, Carolyn was working as an entrepreneur with her own consulting business. She had spent several years as an engineer in the corporate environment, and had felt burned out by her struggles to gain acceptance from the male engineers and managers she encountered in what she described as a "white male engineering structure." While she had become a manager, she felt some bitterness at having been passed over several times while incompetent men had been promoted ahead of her. When she became involved with one of the male managers, Carolyn suddenly felt a loss of support for her work as a manager. She was cut out of the information pipeline—a manager's life blood.

As a specialist in marketing and strategy, Carolyn successfully entered the world of consulting. Eager to work with women, she and four others set up a consulting group based on a spirit of trust.

At that point, Carolyn met Katherine through a women's

organization. Katherine proposed organizing a series of seminars for women. Ostensibly, it seemed like a highly profitable
idea, because at the time, as Carolyn explained, "Women were
very hungry for information. So being able to go to a seminar
and meet the top women in a particular field and get information
was perfect at the time."

Katherine was excellent at expressing other people's desires
and wishes. She understood the psychology of people; she could
immediately sense what they needed, but she claimed she was
disorganized and not very good about detail. It was far worse
than that. Katherine led people to believe she had certain
connections and commitments from others, when in fact she did
not. She concentrated on working and dealing with women only.
And she was so good at getting other people to believe the
fantasies she spun out that she got networks of people involved
in the project. As Katherine's foundation for her claims began
to shake, when the time came to produce results, the whole
scheme she had set up quickly began to fall apart.

In one incident, Katherine claimed that she had a certain
woman committed to be a keynote speaker or seminar leader at
a scheduled event; it came out that this woman had not made
any commitment—had not even been contacted about making a
commitment in the first place. In other telling incidents, Katherine claimed that funds were needed for a certain purpose; but
after she received the money, it wasn't used for that purpose.
She simply pocketed the funds by putting them in a second
account that was in another company name, but not accessible
to Carolyn.

According to Carolyn, Katherine had an incredible ability to
get people to believe her and cooperate, and then to create a
screen of ambiguity and confusion so that they couldn't initially
see through her lies. Carolyn felt Katherine was so convincing
because she had excellent communication skills, and she gave
the appearance of being so sincere that everyone simply believed
her. Also, she used her keen insight into the psychology of other
women to manipulate them. As Carolyn explained:

Katherine is one of the most effective liars that I have ever been able to meet. . . . She understands the psychology of people and what they want and need. So Katherine also deals in wish lists. Because of her ability to lie and weave webs of intrigue, she was able to pull together lots of resources, and because the people came from so many different areas, they weren't able to check up on each other. The left hand didn't know what the right hand was doing.

Katherine also has a very strong set of communications. I mean, she is good in her communication style. She is also very good, as I think any kind of sociopathic person is, at being able to create ambiguity, but nobody can put his finger on exactly what the problem is.

Carolyn also believed Katherine was dangerous because she felt free to manipulate and use people to her own ends without compunction. She simply involved everyone in her scheme without concern as to whether the scheme itself would work or whether people would benefit from their involvement. When things fell apart, she felt completely free to walk away from the situation. She didn't care what happened to anyone else, only herself.

As Carolyn described Katherine's role in the mess that finally occurred:

The problem, to me, is that Katherine is a true sociopath in that she is absolutely incapable of feeling anything about anything. An opportunist can be a person who observes a way to take advantage, but they can do that without bending ethics. However, what makes Katherine so deadly is that there are no ethics. There are no rules. She is totally amoral and she has no feelings, so she can do anything to anyone.

What she does is she sets up systems and she builds systems on top of systems, and she gets people to buy into these particular things, because . . . most people like to take advantage of opportunities, even if it takes hard work.

But the underlying problem is that she really is not invested in the scheme at all herself. What she is invested in is the process of scheming.

Carolyn's downfall was her total spirit of trust for other women. She didn't pay attention to the kind of warning signals she would normally have noticed, which would have suggested a shaky business deal. Instead she trusted, and Katherine took advantage of that trust, as she had in the past with other women. As Carolyn explained, Katherine effectively played on the trust women commonly have among themselves to ensnare them in her scheme. According to Carolyn, Katherine easily gained access to the women's market because she is a woman, whereas a man might have met resistance. Carolyn said, for example, if a man had described the same business plan that Katherine did, Carolyn would have asked more questions rather than accepted everything as readily as she did—which is exactly what happened for the other women who also were taken in by the seminar scam. As Carolyn put it:

> I think that a man can behave the same way, because a scam artist is a scam artist. I think though, from a woman's point of view, if this had been a man, I would have questioned a lot more. I would have questioned a lot of things.
>
> But because it was coming from a woman, I wanted to trust that. You know, it is like a marriage with a person. If you feel that the person is committed, you trust a lot of things, even if they are bizarre and your common sense comes back and says, "This isn't right," and you say, "Oh, there must be a reasonable explanation for it." So it's a trust level thing, and I think that fundamentally, women trust women more, or more easily, than they trust men.

According to Carolyn, it's a kind of subconscious reaction, because women feel a sense of connection with each other, or as she said:

> I think a lot of times women trust women more easily than they trust men, and they do that without even thinking.

They do that on a subconscious level. It is like if you look at a woman, you can draw some kind of connection with her. It is like a species sort of thing, and therefore, a lot of times, women establish a very quick trust level with each other.

Having this kind of trust in other women when it is unwarranted can be disastrous, as Carolyn discovered. She assumed that "all women had the same set of ethics, the same integrity, the same sense of business."

Carolyn's "investment" with Katherine has cost her about $150,000.00 so far—not only because of the funds she lost in the scam, but because of attorney and court costs. It has been five years since the original incident occurred, but the financial fallout from it is still going on. It's uncertain whether Carolyn will ever get any of her money back, since Katherine left the state and uses another identity.

Then, too, there is the emotional stress and pain of what happened, which Carolyn is still dealing with and may continue to deal with for years to come. Carolyn explained her continuing pain:

Katherine created a very frenetic situation . . . you are just constantly driven to try to make things work, and consequently there was all of that loss of energy.

I think the other part, though, was that hostility you feel. Not just over the loss of funds, but over the ridiculousness of the situation. Over something that could have potentially been very good but was set up as a scam from the very beginning, and of course, every time you sit and have your deposition taken or are sitting in court, you know the anger just sits and steeps, and I don't think that it ever gets that dissipated. I guess it also hurts because of the realization that a person like Katherine can wreak havoc, cost a lot of money, tear up people's lives, leave the state, change names, go on to a different kind of scam, and there is really not a lot you can do.

Today, Carolyn is a much less trusting person. She asks more questions and scrutinizes every situation and person she meets more carefully. No longer does she trust people automatically as she once did and she no longer extends a special trust to women.

Her response is understandable, yet unfortunate. As was the case with many women to whom we spoke, Carolyn has discovered that women in business can be very unethical at times. They can use the trust of other women to do serious harm to them. She said, "Women feel a sense of sisterhood and connection with other women." When women use that special trust like a poison, they may destroy other women as a result.

Examples like these—of revenge, jealousy, betrayal, and misplaced blame—appear on the surface to typify unethical women's business tactics, while men are seldom characterized in such ways. But, as I point out in Chapter Five, it is possible that such traits are typical *not* of all women, but of anyone who is in a position of minimal power and whose early psychological conditioning made them feel inferior and taught them different game playing techniques than males.

Chapter 5

Ms. Play

HOW WOMEN AND MEN PLAY GAMES

". . . I set myself to cull you out and down, / And down you are."

Elizabeth to Mary
Act Three

When women act unethically towards other women in the workplace, there is often an undercurrent of anger, hostility, and vindictiveness that is not characteristic of men's unethical behavior. Vindictiveness is the operative motive, particularly when the other person is another woman.

The responses to our interviews and questionnaires indicated that women's unethical behavior is often undercover or deceptive. Covert anger can fester quietly for a long time without the victim even being aware of the perpetrator's hostile feelings. In contrast, when men act unethically, they frequently do so overtly, more dispassionately, and they're more direct.

According to some research studies, men seem to be more democratic about acting unethically. They're less personal when they decide to step on someone who gets in the way: anyone, man or woman, is fair game. Women's actions seem to be especially vicious and vengeant; for example, as we have seen in Chapter Four, a woman will often take personal information shared in more amicable times and use it to hurt her victim, who then feels not only injured but also betrayed.

Why the difference? The results of our research seem to suggest that women are much more likely to respond out of emotions and feelings and hide behind the "poor little nice girl" image. Men are more likely to act out of carefully crafted self-interest and be more frontal in their attacks; they have the power.

While one would think that the traditional images of the emotional woman and aggressive, nonfeeling male might not be as relevant today, our interviews have shown that they are. The old trappings of the traditional ways of acting and responding are still with us, coloring the differences in how men and women behave. The way we are brought up and socialized is a very powerful force.

According to reliable researchers such as Carol Gilligan and Jean Baker Miller,[1] many of these differences in the expression of aggression go back to infantile feelings and how women and men are taught to express them. Men learn early in life to express any aggression openly, to get it out and then go on with their relationships. And, once the aggression has been expressed, it has been released. Most women learn as girls to be nice and well-behaved, to keep aggressive feelings in. So the anger builds; the resentment simmers. When it is finally released it is often through covert and deceptive means. It takes on the form of getting even for whatever initiated the anger which could not be expressed right away. Men learn early in life to compete, fight, and let the best man win with no hard feelings. Women tend to get caught in their emotions: they may worry about hurting someone else's feelings, getting their own feelings hurt, and thinking they shouldn't act aggressively in response to their feelings, because "it isn't nice." But the pent-up emotions have to be expressed somehow, some way; the result may be revenge that is distorted in relation to the actual wrongdoing.

These old patterns continue to carry over and result in characteristic styles of unethical behavior. We need to look closer. If we really want a more equalitarian society today, changes are needed. Awareness is the first step to creating change.

IT'S ALL IN THE GAME

These differences between men and women's unethical behavior are pervasive—not just in the workplace, but in the way men and women play. They can be traced back to the ways boys and girls play childhood games, which reflect a basic difference in their orientations to life and relationships that are later reflected in the business game of battling for success.

A classic example of these differences was observed by Lesley, who played soccer on a company co-ed team. What stood out most in her particular experience was the ways the men and women in her company played the game and what happened when a conflict arose.

She commented:

> I noticed that when men and women play on a competitive team, men want to win. They go out to win and that's all there is to it. They don't go out to socialize or all this other stuff. They may socialize, but mainly they want to win. Women are not necessarily out there to win. They have other motivations.

Lesley also noticed that the men in her company tended to be more philosophical and accepting about whatever happened in the course of play. The rules were laid out and they abided by them. So what if someone bumped them; so what if the referee missed seeing a foul; so what if a teammate blocked a kick or got in the way. They would yell and holler, but there would usually be time to make another shot. They just tried to play better. The women were different. When something adverse happened, they frequently got upset, reacted emotionally, often carried a grudge quietly and later tried to get revenge. Lesley explained:

> I notice that the women will usually make an issue out of it
> (a rule violation), or they will act like one's mother and
> say, "You better not do that." The most common practice
> I found was that nothing would be said if I got in the way
> of a female teammate. Later in the game, I would get
> kicked from behind.

Another difference Lesley noticed was that men were more
openly competitive and aggressive. If anything incited them
during the game, they expressed it then and there and it was
over. In contrast, while many of the women didn't seem to put
their hearts into the competition, anything that happened to
upset them stayed with them. Anger wasn't expressed on the
spot. Their resentment showed in hostile and often covertly
vengeful actions—later.

> The men on the team were always coming up to the women
> and saying, "We can do it, we can do it," and getting us all
> excited to play harder . . . However, I noticed that some of
> the women didn't really put their hearts into the competi-
> tion. I often got the feeling that it was unfeminine to be
> really competitive.

Lesley believed that many of the women tended to be a little
more timid and less assertive. It was usually the men who
pushed through the defense to score. The women tended to hang
back, although a few were very good players and just as competitive as the men.

The women, while not as openly aggressive in playing the
game itself, often expressed aggression covertly, either during
the game or long after it was presumably over. The men expressed their competitiveness and aggressiveness according to
the rules of the game.

Lesley recalled instances when the men got into some pretty
heavy skirmishes on the field and tempers ran high. At times the
referee had to separate people. But once the game was over, the
men would go off together and have a beer, as if the anger had
never happened. They were finished playing, they were part of a

group of friends, and any incident was in the past, but if a female teammate was mad about an action, she carried it off the field. The men often included the women in the after-game beer, but Betty observed that this wasn't reciprocated.

Once a man knocked a woman down on the field and then went over to her to apologize. She wouldn't accept it. "She wouldn't have anything to do with him. She wouldn't talk to him," Lesley said. Later in the game, she sneaked up on him and hit him. In fact, she had a penalty called against her for doing this. Lesley believes this is a classic male-female behavioral difference that has its roots in childhood.

She remembered that as a child she used to sneak up from behind to get even with her brother; she wouldn't retaliate face to face. And she noticed that the other little girls were also indirect, whereas the boys were straightforward. Little girls, she observed, "will sneak the toys away and hide them. A boy will just go up and grab it." The key difference is the way it's expressed. Males—as little boys and as men—are more openly aggressive; females from the very early years express their aggression in more deceptive, roundabout ways.

Finally, Lesley noticed a kind of team spirit and support which the men tended to have for one another. If there was a fight, they would rally around each other, and if the referee ruled against them they would accede to his ruling, grumble, then forget the issue and keep playing. The women tended to split up and take sides, depending on what they thought was fair or not fair. They would make an issue of the situation and then become angry if they didn't like the referee's ruling. As Lesley commented:

> I did notice that when fights broke out, the men wouldn't say who was right or wrong. If it got pretty nasty, they would go break it up, but they would usually stand behind their teammate, even if the teammate was wrong. If a foul or action was really bad and the teammate was blatantly wrong, that person was taken out of the game. I didn't notice women doing that. If there was a fight going on,

women would jump right in and say "That's not right, that's not right," and get into the moral issue instead of just standing aside and letting those people work it out themselves and letting the referee decide who is going to do what. Then I noticed that the issue was talked about during halftime—"that wasn't fair; he shouldn't be allowed to do that," and that kind of stuff. Their idea was that the next time they got a chance, they would knock him down. That was their way of getting even.

Occurrences similar to those in a play situation show up in the business world, and in a sense, a game can be looked at as a microcosm of the way people live their lives. The interviews we conducted reinforced that the patterns of play which Lesley observed are characteristic of how men and women act in the business world. And that might be expected. When we learn to play games as children, the interaction patterns we learn in the games help to prepare us for how we are going to behave later. As we get older, advancing to other games, these interaction patterns carry on.

Lesley described a racketball game she played with a woman friend and her husband which reaffirms the differences in game styles between men and women. When she played with the husband, she was close to beating him; he did everything he could to keep from losing. In the end, she won; caught up in the challenge, they both had fun. There were no hard feelings; both simply wanted to win.

When she played his wife, it was quite different. The other woman wasn't very athletic and soon began apologizing for not providing enough competition. Lesley felt horrible. Even though the other woman clearly wasn't good at the game, Lesley felt that she might hurt her feelings if she won. She was even concerned about any hostile feelings that might surface long after the game. Her soccer experience lingered on.

Feelings. Resentments. Deceptive, covert behavior. Being outwardly nice. We feel that these may be keys to understanding how women play the game differently from men—in the business world as well as in the sports arena.

THINGS ARE NOT WHAT
THEY SEEM

Sometimes, to keep up the illusion of being nice, women hide things. The results can be much worse than if the problems were confronted in the first place. Miriam's situation illustrates this.

Miriam was hired by Lori when she went into the executive recruiting business. Miriam, 23, was working in a personnel agency. Initially, Lori encouraged her and worked closely with her to give her support.

Things seemed to be going well, although there were a few signs of problems. Lori had a sink-or-swim philosophy about training. She urged Miriam to do what she could on her own. She told Miriam that she had "the smarts" to manage and that she, herself, didn't want to be a manager. The agency felt that Lori should act in this role, to be there if Miriam needed her, but that Miriam should "always think things through first."

Occasionally, Miriam went to Lori when she really got stuck on something or was attempting a brand new area she didn't understand. According to Miriam, "Lori was always there for me." During the four years they worked together, there was nothing to lead Miriam to think Lori might harbor any negative feelings. Lori even helped Miriam get her next job. Lori had assured her, "Well, you know I am a good reference for you." After Lori left the agency, someone called to say there was a position available at a research firm; Lori referred Miriam.

Three years later, Miriam applied for a corporate recruiting position. She again used Lori as a reference. She told the company that Lori knew her very well, so the company gave a lot of weight to her opinion.

When the company called, Lori voiced all her negative reservations about Miriam's lack of initiative and inability to think for herself. Miriam didn't get the job.

The issue is not Lori's revelation. There was some truth to what she said about Miriam's difficulties on the job. But most of these occurences happened when Miriam was first hired. As Miriam had worked with Lori over the four-year period, she had improved in many ways. Miriam thought Lori had acted unethically in leading her to think she would be a good reference and then bringing up her negative rather than positive qualities.

Why hadn't Lori been forthright in telling Miriam how she felt? Why had she led Miriam to believe she would be a positive reference? It seemed to Miriam that Lori's motivation was a desire to smooth things over; to appear nice and receptive when Miriam asked for a reference, rather than bringing an issue out in the open which was critical.

NOW I'VE GOT YOU

Our research substantiated the fact that women sometimes act unethically toward others because as they move up in the business world they are particularly prone to feelings of insecurity about how much power they really have and how well they are performing. With fewer openings for women in upper management, more pressure is felt. If anyone threatens to disturb their power—or if they perceive anyone who threatens to disturb their power—they may lash out, and when they do they are apt to use more deceptive and manipulative techniques.

While it's also true that men act unethically to protect their own status and power, the control issue seems to be particularly powerful for women, and it could be because women perceive their status as somewhat more tenuous. In many instances when women act unethically they appear to do so to stay in control over someone else as a way to affirm their power. Often they play a kind of "Now I've got you" game, where the victim ends up feeling trapped in a web.

A classic example of this type of game happened to Bernice when she worked in a bank for an assistant vice-president, Marta. Bernice replaced a man who had worked for Marta and had been promoted. Everything seemed fine at first. Marta seemed to like her, and they hit it off very well. After a few days, Bernice began to see signs that Marta was insecure and wanted to control other people.

The first sign of the problem came when Bernice sought out the man who had worked for Marta and was supposed to train her. She couldn't find him. "He just made himself very unavailable," she told us. She eventually learned that before his promotion he had pleaded with Marta to let him transfer to another area, and she had resisted him for six months until he finally went to her manager. As a result, Marta had to let him go. Management told her they would find a replacement. Over the months, she had interviewed and rejected numerous people. Subconsciously, she hadn't wanted him to leave and had rationalized not finding an adequate replacement. She was finally pressured into hiring someone for the position. In a sense, Marta may have been feeling a loss of control that threatened her feeling of power when Bernice was hired.

Bernice was skilled in working with people and developed a good rapport with many of the lower-echelon employees who worked for Marta. Bernice was outgoing, less demanding; Marta was the opposite, and had trouble relating to her own team of people. The rapport that Bernice had with her coworkers ultimately led to conflict with Marta. "Nobody could get near her," Bernice recalled. " 'You have a problem, you solve the problem. If you solve it wrong, I'll tell you.' That was her philosophy."

The people who worked with Marta were very frustrated and began to come to Bernice for advice and support. Marta noticed and called Bernice in one day. She complimented Bernice on her effective way of handling people, something Marta said she was never able to develop. "What would be nice," Marta said, "is if you could act as my liaison, and when they come to you and tell you their problems, then you could come to me. It would work well for me."

Bernice thought there could be some ethical problems and wasn't sure she would feel comfortable with such a procedure:

in some instances she could go to Marta; in others she felt she couldn't because she would betray a confidence.

Bernice resisted. Marta turned against her. But Marta's actions were not direct; she did not confront Bernice about why she was angry. Instead, she created a strange double-bind situation: she began to criticize Bernice's work, but would not let her transfer to another department.

This went on for about three months. Marta put Bernice on probation, and Bernice had to satisfy certain demands which she had earlier been told she was satisfying. When Bernice befriended another woman her age in a very high-ranking data processing position, Marta advised the woman, "You know, it doesn't help your image to be known as a friend of Bernice's." When the friend asked what Marta meant, she said, "Well, she is only a secretary."

A man who worked for Marta had run into problems and confided in Bernice about his difficulties working with Marta; when Marta heard this, she got angry. Bernice was again on probation for going over her head and talking to another employee. As the situation deteriorated, Marta had Bernice write reports that she was inefficient and file them in her personnel file.

Eventually Bernice threw in the towel. She told Marta she would go as long as Marta fired her, which would allow her to collect unemployment. Bernice left the bank. It was a totally shattering experience. She had been caught up in a no-win situation.

Reassessing the situation, Bernice felt she had threatened Marta's feeling of control. Marta's confusing actions toward her had started soon after Marta had suggested that Bernice act as her liaison and Bernice refused. According to Bernice, "She started to harass me and insist that my work was not satisfactory." Bernice wasn't sure how to deal with the continuous criticism and expressed her concerns to Marta's manager, Linda, a vice-president in the same area of the bank. Bernice confided, "I don't know why she is picking on me, and I don't know how to please her and I don't know how to handle it."

Linda advised her to hang in. A few months from now, Linda said, her own assistant would be leaving to have a baby and she would love to have Bernice work for her.

Bernice felt encouraged, particularly since a position with Linda would be a step up. After Linda's assistant resigned, the position was offered to Bernice but Marta wouldn't release her. Linda backed off, saying she couldn't fight it. "Bernice, you must be doing something right because Marta wants to keep you," she said.

Bernice began to understand what was happening. She realized that Marta was getting back at her for resisting her power and at the same time holding on to her to show that she was in control. On the surface Marta showed support, but beneath the surface she was trying to do her in. Bernice confided to Linda, "You don't understand her psychology. She is out to 'get me' and she is not going to let you interfere with that process."

There was no way Bernice could get out of the destructive situation short of leaving the bank. Bernice believed Marta was isolated from others and insecure and therefore took out her frustrations on her employees. When Bernice confronted her, Marta still refused to let Bernice go; instead she used her power to turn Bernice's working situation into a veritable nightmare. "Look who's in charge. And see what happens if you dare to taunt me."

UNDERMINING

When they are insecure, some people seek to undermine others. The experiences related in some of the interviews we conducted highlighted various differences such feelings produce in men and women. For one, women are likely to maneuver behind the scenes when they seek to undermine other individuals. Our findings revealed that if a woman is the victim, the hurt she feels may be used as a basis for setting up the person who hurt her for a similar embarrassment. A man, on the other hand, is more

likely to simply blow up at the time he discovers that someone
has undermined him, rather than plot out a scheme to get even.

Josie, a nurse, found these patterns as a result of three such
experiences—two with women, the other with a man.

The incident with the man occurred when she was working
with a male doctor in a clinic. A woman scheduled for an
appointment called to cancel because she couldn't get a babysitter for her two-year-old. Josie erased her name from the calendar
and rescheduled her for a later date. Later, the doctor noticed
the cancellation and asked why. When Josie told him, he called
the woman and said: "No problem, my nurse will babysit for
you."

Josie was annoyed at her boss's behavior. She had been hired
as his assistant, not as a babysitter, and she would not be inside
the examination room when the doctor examined a patient, as
she normally was. However, she held back her feelings and
acceded to his wishes. When the patient arrived and Josie
directed her into the examination room, the woman commented
to Josie, "I don't think I am going to like this," referring to the
examination without a nurse present. Josie responded, "I don't
think I am going to, either," referring to her babysitting duties.
The child panicked when the mother disappeared, creating
havoc in the outer office.

As it happened, the patient mentioned Josie's comment to the
doctor. When he finished the examination, he marched into the
back room where Josie was cleaning up. Josie's back felt an
electric charge as he entered the room. His face was beet red;
he was furious. He stuck his finger in the middle of Josie's chest
and screamed at her, "You are fired!" And that was that. Josie
got her things and left.

The doctor charged Josie had undermined him to a patient.
He wasn't going to let an employee get away with it. His
response and retaliation were open and immediate.

Josie's negative encounters when she was employed by a
female nurse supervisor were very different.

In another clinic Josie worked for a year under Rhonda, the
supervising nurse. Working for Rhonda was like being on a

rollercoaster. She was a homosexual and seemed to have trouble dealing with the stigma that is sometimes attached to being a lesbian. She also had trouble keeping her weight down and was very sensitive about it. She had twice attempted suicide. The work environment was infused with feelings of insecurity. Rules were changed from day to day. Initially the nurses gritted their teeth; eventually they turned hostile to her as well as to each other. "In the year that I worked there, there were nine nurses and six quit or were threatened with termination. The atmosphere was so charged and so hostile that nurses would walk out of meetings," Josie said.

However, Josie enjoyed working with the patients, and they responded favorably to her tender, caring attitude. She discovered that Rhonda felt threatened by Josie's good clinical and social service work. Josie observed:

> A lot of my concern centered around the social needs of these patients in addition to the health care needs. . . . So I built up tremendous rapport with the various agencies in the county and with the social worker on staff (of the clinic) in dealing with my patients. . . . Well, she didn't like that. She said I spent too much time on the phone.

Rhonda dealt with her insecurity by harassing Josie. She criticized her continually for the support she provided to the patients and their families even though Josie had letters from them thanking her and telling her how much she had helped. Rhonda told her her communication skills were poor, when, in fact, this was one skill for which families routinely thanked her. She issued negative reports about Josie and threatened to withhold her pay. Josie felt that Rhonda kept reloading ammunition against her. She finally quit under the pressure.

A few years later, Josie took a staff nurse position in a hospital with the promise of taking over a supervisory position within a few weeks. For months Josie waited, believing that she was being strung along. A supervisor was fired and Sarah, the nursing director, needed someone to fill the slot. Josie was promoted with promises of training, but none was given. When Josie made mistakes, Sarah quickly condemned her.

Things went from bad to worse. Sarah was friendly with another nursing supervisor. The two of them frequently "ganged up" against various nurses, including Josie, for what appeared to be no reason:

> They made my life miserable. They made the life of every nurse in that office miserable, some more than others. The uneven personnel policy and underhandedness was unbearable at times.

Josie said that the two women, acting in concert, spread negative rumors about other nurses, passed around confidential information, and reprimanded others, often for no reason, in front of other people. They criticized Josie for fraternizing with the other nurses. Josie felt they did this because they perceived friendships as a threat to their power. They also set up conflicting requirements for her to meet. Rarely was she invited to attend the federal or state meetings which govern Medicare or medical policies dealing with home care, one of Josie's responsibilities. Yet they expected her to know all of the rules and regulations.

Josie took a vacation day to attend one of these meetings. At a subsequent staff meeting, Sarah humiliated her when Josie asked a question:

> Every person on the staff was there. I asked this question and in front of sixty people, she turned to me, her eyes cold as ice, and said: "You were at that meeting, why are you asking this question now?"

Josie was mortified. The question had concerned a new Medicare form and the nursing director certainly could have answered the question, since, as Josie said, "she knew the regulations inside and out." When she later asked Sarah why she had responded as she did, Sarah's reply was "You were undermining me." Sarah was suspicious of Josie's motivations and believed that Josie was trying to put her down. So she struck out first.

In assessing these three incidents, Josie commented on the differences she had experienced with men and women. Like other people interviewed, she found the women more deceptive and the men more direct and open. As she put it:

> I think that men in many ways play a little bit more with an open deck. Their cards are on the table. "This is the way it is. Let's get down to business and work, and we can have a beer and have some fun while we are doing it." But getting the work done is the essence. Women are more subtle and devious. I think society has taught women to be that way. . . . Women can be very, very petty and bitchy. I don't think men stoop to that level . . . In my experience, I would say that women are far more deceitful than men.

UNFAIR GAME

Another critical question to ask in examining the whys of unethical behavior is: exactly who is being unethical to whom? In our survey, we found that men reportedly behaved unethically to both men and women alike while women seemed to be more likely to behave unethically towards their own sex. The same patterns were observed in the interviews. Interviewed participants reported incidents in which a man who wanted to get ahead simply stepped on everyone in his path—and it didn't matter whether the person was a man or a woman. But the women tended to be perceived as somewhat more tricky in their dealings; as more likely to use deception against another woman.

An excellent example of the man who democratically shafts everyone was the man who worked with Tessa. She worked in the sales office of an insurance company. The policy of the firm was that the salesperson at the counter would write up any new business under his or her own code number. However, if the new client had previously spoken with another salesperson and asked for that person, then whoever was at the counter was required to use the code number of the salesperson making the first contact.

Ronald didn't do this; he simply used his own code number whenever he was at the counter. This continued for months with no one realizing what was happening. Tessa was one of the first to catch on:

> A person had come in and asked for me. Ronald said that I wasn't there and went ahead and wrote the application, putting his code number on it so that he would get the commission. About a week later, I discovered what had happened when, by chance, my contact's name was sitting on the underwriter's desk waiting for approval. The following week, another salesman caught him doing the same thing. Several other men suspected him of doing that to them also.

Ronald was democratic: he took advantage of men and women alike. What is interesting is the difference in the way men and women reacted. The men who caught him or suspected him of cheating confronted him angrily and directly; a few even threatened him with physical violence. Tessa confided that if she had been alone when she encountered him after discovering his cheating, she would have merely talked to him about what happened. "I certainly wouldn't have threatened him with physical violence."

Also, Ronald's actions in getting the extra business had been purely pragmatic: it was for monetary gain. When that strategy no longer paid off and he was threatened with losing his job and with physical confrontations, he stopped.

Edith's experience illustrates a more personal, behind-the-scenes method that, according to our research results, is more characteristic of the way women take advantage of other women. Edith was working in an administrative position under Darlene. When Darlene was away on vacation, Edith made a business decision on her own. Edith admitted that it was questionable whether she should have waited and checked out the decision with Darlene. When Darlene returned, she disagreed with the decision and was extremely negative and critical of Edith. She spent some time chastising her and telling her why her decision was wrong.

However, it turned out to be a good business decision, one that was focused on at a meeting at which both Darlene and Edith were present. Darlene immediately took the credit, as well as adulation and praise. Edith said nothing and carried her resentment for a long time. "That really ticked me off," she said. "It's one thing to take credit for it, but chastising me for it and never apologizing for it is another."

Edith never confronted Darlene about her behavior, but the hurt festered inside her for several weeks. Edith observed that if she had been a man, she might have been more direct at the time and said something like: "I don't appreciate you doing that" or "I expect an apology." Instead, she held the feelings and pain in. Summarizing her thoughts, she said: "Women, I think, internalize things more or think about it more before acting; men's reaction time is quicker."

THE EFFECTS

Our survey and interviews indicate that when women act unethically they do so in a different manner and they are more likely to do so to other women. In such cases, the effects are more harmful for several reasons. First, women tend to act in more devious and deceptive ways when they act unethically, so that the victim, caught off-guard, is more shaken by the action. Also, since women are more likely to share personal information with others than are men, those who go after others often use this information against their victims, who consequently feel even more betrayed and pained. Finally, women who have been hurt are more likely than men to keep it in—to avoid the immediate outburst of anger that men display and the immediate venting of emotion that such outlets provide. Instead, women's anger characteristically turns inward and becomes depression or intensifies hostile feelings.

So, men and women have different senses of self. Their

business behavior differs in part because of role modeling and different game playing experiences in childhood. And women victimizing other women can be in part explained by the fact that women occupy the low rungs of the power ladder and there are few men there to victimize. Chapter Six takes a deeper look at this lack of power and its impact on women's attitudes and behavior.

Chapter 6

Ms. Representative

WHAT YOU SEE IS NOT WHAT YOU GET

"Your life was a threat to mine, your throne to/ my throne,/ your policy a threat. . . ."
Elizabeth to Mary
Act Three

Why don't women support each other more? And why do women sometimes treat each other so badly? Our research indicated that one very basic reason is that many women feel insecure, inadequate, and uncertain.

The theme of insecurity came up repeatedly throughout the interviews we conducted. One woman, Priscilla, experienced a series of backstabbings from other women in non-profit groups. She expressed the rationale as:

> The whole thing lies in terms of strength. The stronger you are, the more ethical you can afford to be, the more fairly you can deal with other people. It's the old "you can walk softly because you are carrying a big stick." When you are weak, and all too often women are in the weaker situation, you don't have the courage to walk straight out. The weak people sneak up and try to shoot from behind a tree.

So my theory isn't so much that there's a genetic difference, although there may well be one. But women in our
society in most cases are in the weaker position. Therefore,
they take these sneaky trips around somebody else,
whether it is male or female, and they are more likely to do
it to someone who is female because of her perceived
weakness.

This same complaint was echoed repeatedly throughout the
interviews: women have fewer advantages; they are in a weaker
position; they can't be as open as men in getting what they want;
they feel uncertain and unsure—and as a result they adopt
deceptive strategies.

History shows many examples of people who, because they
were weak, were forced to use devious methods to get what they
wanted. Priscilla referred to the situation in Northern Ireland.
Like women in the workplace, the native Irish Catholics are in a
weaker position than the Protestants. So, as she put it, "They
bomb cars. They sabotage rather than just plain coming out and
putting their cards on the table and negotiating a kind of straightforward approach."

While women haven't gone to such tactical extremes, the
principle seems to apply. When one is weak, one feels insecure
and is more apt to use guerrilla tactics, such as sabotage, to
achieve one's goals.

THE INSECURE WOMAN
BOSS

During Priscilla's career in sales and sales management, she had
worked in a company that promoted women into positions of
power. She recalled that many ran into problems. Outwardly
they had the trappings of executive prerogative, yet didn't feel
that sense of strength within. Many at times engaged in unethical
actions in order to achieve their aims. She observed:

For some reason in their childhood or wherever, they didn't develop a sense of strength. So they may have had a title, but they abused the power that they had and didn't use it in a straightforward manner.

She recounted the times when the female bosses had problems with the employees. Strong bosses simply brought the employees into their offices and told them they weren't performing up to par. A strong boss, she felt, might say:

"Here are ten tasks you are supposed to be doing. It has come to my attention that in five of these areas you are not doing a good job. What resources do you need to do this job well? How can I work with you so that you can be a better person?"

However, a weak boss might find such a confrontation too threatening. Instead, she might use a more indirect method to let the person know she's dissatisfied with her work. Priscilla continues:

If I feel weak personally, I start spreading rumors. I give the person bad looks. I somehow or other sabotage her work. I destroy her credibility with others in the organization, but I never bring that person in and straightforwardly say: "Look, Jane, there are some inadequacies here."

According to Priscilla, even if the woman owns the company herself and is completely in charge she still can feel weak inside. Priscilla had a number of devastating experiences with women in their own businesses or in corporations whom she felt sabotaged her for exactly this reason. In Priscilla's view, they felt insecure about themselves, resented her for her success, and engaged in behind-the-scenes efforts to sabotage her.

In one instance a woman who had disagreed with Priscilla on numerous occasions regarding her leadership tried to undermine the growing non-profit organization which Priscilla had founded by spreading rumors that the organization owed Priscilla a lot of money. The essence of the rumor was true: Priscilla had put much of her own money into the group to get it off the ground; however, the rumors suggested that the organization was about to go bankrupt, and when it did each member then would be assessed several hundred dollars in order to pay Priscilla back. This was untrue, yet the woman spread the rumor as widely as she could. Priscilla believed that in harboring a grudge about their earlier disagreements, she did this to discourage other people from joining the association.

Unfortunately, some of the women who heard the false story never bothered to check it out. They accepted it as true. Priscilla is of the opinion this acceptance came about because they didn't have the courage to ask her directly what was going on. She explained,

> We deal with volunteers, and we have those who are very new to the business world who have come to us to seek the support they need to break into something where they can grow, and then we have others who have a lot of experience. The ones who believe these rumors are the inexperienced ones. But I have to feel that the stronger person, the one who doesn't have doubts in herself or himself, who hears something like this would pick up the phone and say, "What the hell are you doing there?" And if you say, "Wait a minute. Let me tell you the truth in this," they respond, "OK, fine."
>
> But people who are weak themselves don't have the courage to call up and ask the questions. So that weakness again gets them into a double bind for having believed somebody; then they get embarrassed about it, and then they don't even have the strength to apologize. The stronger you are, the more able you are to say, "Gee, I'm sorry. I made a mistake." But you can't do that if you are weak.
>
> Weak people sneak around, spread rumors. Strong people ask questions in an attempt to seek the truth. In our society, by and large, there are more weak women than there are weak men, and if you don't think you can win the

race, you are more likely to want to tie your competitor's shoelaces together. If you think you could beat your competitor, you hope they are running and having their best day so you can really beat them in a fair race. If you know going into it that you are probably going to lose, tying shoelaces together can be effective.

WOMEN UNWILLING TO
ASK FOR HELP

In our interviews, women repeatedly shared stories of women who felt afraid, threatened, and insecure, and who struck out by attempting revenge against other women. Sometimes they made incredible errors that cost employers and associates huge sums of money because they weren't able to be open or ask for help.

Another of our interviewees, Kathryn, had an experience with a woman who was unwilling to respond to criticisms, accept help, or acknowledge that she needed it. Kathryn had entered a development partnership with Andrea, a personal friend who was active in real estate and the community. When Andrea told her about the real estate arrangement she was putting together in order to buy, improve, and manage a building, Kathryn was impressed and became one of her partners.

The problem was that Andrea was good only at putting the initial deal together. As Kathryn explained, "She was great for going out and negotiating. But when it came to business, she just didn't know her stuff." After Andrea put a deal together, she didn't know how to follow up and make sure it was managed properly. As Kathryn put it, "The key to all real estate is management, and if it is mismanaged, the greatest investment in the world can go down the tubes."

As Kathryn related, Andrea didn't want anyone to know that she wasn't knowledgeable about all the detail areas. She wanted everyone to see her as the powerful real estate wheeler and dealer. So she wouldn't accept advice or help. The result was that after the package was put together, things began to fall apart. All kinds of problems surfaced: tenants who didn't pay rent; people who broke their rental agreements and moved out; and accidents leading to strict liability suits. Even as the deal was coming unglued, Andrea stonewalled. When Kathryn confronted her and told her, "You wouldn't admit you were having problems; you wouldn't let anyone help you," Andrea replied, "That's completely untrue."

"She was afraid to let down her guard and ask for help," Kathryn said, "because she felt so insecure and vulnerable. Others would find out she wasn't as successful as everyone thought." Kathryn's attorney succeeded in getting her out of the litigation. Others weren't so lucky. Going in, the deal was financially sound and should have been profitable for everyone who invested in it. Unfortunately, the daily details were mismanaged. Andrea was removed from all management, but it was too late.

THE INSECURE OR
JEALOUS EMPLOYEE

Instances of insecure and jealous employees doing something underhanded to undermine their bosses came up frequently in our interviews. Sally experienced this when she managed a small office in the personnel field. She did an excellent job in turning the office around. Within sixteen months it was transformed from a money-losing area into one that was profitable and able to pay back preceding bills. Joyce, one of her key recruiters, after commuting for nine months, decided it was too difficult and resigned to work for another agency closer to home.

Sally proposed to open another office of the company in an untapped market, which happened to be closer to Joyce's home. The head office agreed. Sally offered to rehire Joyce, and Joyce accepted immediately.

Once Joyce had her old job back, she began working behind the scenes to remove Sally. Unknowingly, Sally created a situation where Joyce had an excellent opportunity to do this: she split her time between the two offices, and when she was not in the new one, Joyce worked to take it over. One of the ways she did this was in fabricating stories to the company owners that made Sally look incompetent. Sally said, "She started by telling the owners the things that she felt I was doing wrong and the things I wasn't doing that should be done . . . She made it sound like my office was a mess."

Sally found herself caught up in the same problem with the women owners of the business that Priscilla had experienced with the women who heard negative gossip about her organization. The owners didn't bother to check out the stories with her. They were jittery about their new business and the expansion. Sally said they simply accepted the damaging stories Joyce told. Soon, they accused Sally of doing all sorts of things, including working on deals outside when she wasn't in the office. They chose not to listen to Sally's explanation that she was helping out at the first office to make things go more smoothly.

Sally was infuriated. She related:

> By the time I got this from the owners I was fed up with them, because it seemed like all I was doing was defending myself to these women. They had absolutely not the slightest concept of what was going on down here, and so in my estimation they were listening to the wrong people. Because of it, I left. I just didn't feel at that time that I needed to sit there and defend myself again and again when I had come in and made a profit for them and opened up another office that was almost instantly profitable. For them to listen to someone who was working for me and not say to me: "Well, gee, we understand this is happening, and we are just a little concerned," but come in with accusations instead is unconscionable.

In Sally's view, the owners and Joyce acted in this deceptive way because of their own insecurities. She had noticed similar things happening with other women with whom she worked in the past. Generally, she found these dealings characterized by behind-the-scenes backbiting and a lack of candor.

"Any time I have ever worked for a woman," she told me, "I have never known where I stood. I want people to know where they stand with me and I want to know where I stand with them. I don't like playing footsie with people."

Sally said she found the environment in working for women quite different than in working for men, because of the "catty-mouse, talk-behind-the-back, backbiting kinds of things that you don't normally find working with a man."

As had Priscilla, Sally attributed such behavior to the under-lying insecurities many women feel:

> Men are brought up in the team environment. Boys are into the more aggressive, this-is-how-the-game-is-played type of thing, while girls sit in corners being very docile, domestic types.
>
> I think that women, because they are not sure of who they are and where they are in the business world and aren't satisfied with themselves, don't know how to act in the workplace. So they feel insecure.

THE "BLAME IT ON THE BOSS" SYNDROME

A related problem to the insecure employee who tries to make her boss look bad by making up stories is the one whose own jealousy makes her distort reality. In this case, she really believes the worst about her boss and then spreads stories about him or her. Often, the employee sees herself as truly innocent when in fact she is behaving unethically—at least according to Maureen, who related the following experience.

She was working at a senior-level marketing position in a large drug company. She agreed to hire Robin, who was working at the time for Brian, the head of the department, as her secretary. Brian also was Maureen's boss. Robin had been with the company for several years and was miserable working for Brian. She told Maureen that she felt ignored, overworked, and had a personality conflict with Brian. Maureen thought she could solve two problems: she needed a secretary and Robin wanted a change. She hired her.

If Maureen had checked with Robin's previous bosses, she would have found that Robin had a history of trouble in getting along with people. And soon after she began working for Maureen, Robin began telling others that Maureen was treating her unfairly. As Maureen describes her behavior:

> She did everything she could to undermine me. She made jabs at me to all the women in the department. She was trying to set me up to make me angry, and at the time I thought, "God, what a witch!"

According to Maureen, Robin went around telling people that:

> I did this wrong and that wrong, and I didn't dress right, and I didn't do anything right.

Robin complained that Maureen never invited her out to lunch and wasn't as friendly with her as she was with other secretaries in the office. To complicate matters, Robin began having problems fending off Brian, who was pursuing her romantically now that she no longer worked for him. She blamed Maureen for not warning her about Brian so she could better handle him. Yet, when Robin had begun working with Maureen, Maureen had, in fact, warned her about Brian's conquests.

The rumors and the buildup of tensions between them got so bad that Maureen decided to confront Robin. She felt that Robin was openly blaming her for all sorts of things that weren't true, and it was time to put an end to the stories:

> I went into her office and said, "Robin, you are telling people that I have never invited you to lunch and I'm not friendly with you. That is just not true. Many times I have offered and you have turned me down every time. You must have forgotten."

Robin was furious and blamed Maureen for all the problems she was having with Brian. Maureen retorted:

"How can that be my fault? Look, I was the one who warned you. I warned you that this guy was very unstable. You didn't listen to me. Instead, you took the information and went to my immediate supervisor and made me look bad. Here I was trying to be a good person and you go to my immediate supervisor and tattle on me and make me look unprofessional. Now you are undermining me with everyone in the office. It doesn't make a lot of sense."

Maureen said that Robin suddenly grimaced. It was as though she realized how absurd her actions had been. "She was projecting onto me, trying to make her problems my problems." After several months of embarrassment and conflict, Maureen finally felt she was able to contain the problem. But until then, Robin's hostility had created a difficult situation and Maureen's character was undermined. For a long time afterward, the incident made her untrusting of other women.

THE UPPITY EMPLOYEE

Women sometimes encounter employees who treat them with a lack of respect simply because they are women. It's the kind of sexual discrimination women commonly have associated with males who don't feel women belong in the old Establishment or Club, but it hurts even more when it comes from another woman, and especially from an employee who innocently acts as though no sexual discrimination is meant.

This happened to Martha, a supervisor of thirty different departments specializing in environmental concerns for a state government. And it happened at a time when her department had received an award from the governor for doing an excellent job and saving the taxpayers more than two hundred thousand dollars a year.

Martha had been assigned a new secretary, Wilma, by her project manager. For a few weeks, Wilma did a good job with Martha's work; then, apparently decided she had better things to do. Martha said:

She came to me and said, ''I'm not going to do your work anymore. I don't have time. I have to work on these other interests that I have. I'm interested in upward mobility and I am going to work with this other government office taking on extra projects.''

It would have been acceptable for Wilma to seek a transfer if she had gone to Martha's project manager who had made the original assignment. He could have then assigned another secretary to Martha, and the transfer could have been done quite smoothly. But when Martha asked her whether she had spoken to the project manager, Wilma answered in a condescending way, ''Oh, no. I haven't even talked to him about it. I haven't had time.''

When she asked if Wilma had spoken to the office administrator, who would assign Martha another secretary, her answer was much the same. ''No. You'll just have to do that yourself. I don't have time.''

Martha was amazed by Wilma's lack of concern about what she was doing and by her attitude of disdain. ''I thought, when does a secretary go in and tell anybody that she is not doing her work for her when she is assigned?'' she said. ''Have you ever heard of such a thing?'' In Martha's view, Wilma wouldn't have done this if she had been working for a man. Martha felt that because she was a woman, Wilma didn't give her as much respect.

Another of Martha's secretaries, Tina, simply delayed doing Martha's work because she didn't think it was as important as work she was doing for someone else. But she would lead Martha into thinking she was getting the project done. Martha described the situation,

I would give her assignments three and four weeks in advance that she could easily do in, let's say, three or four hours. And I would say, ''Now, I don't need this for two or three weeks, but in the meantime, you can fit it into your work.'' Then, two weeks before I needed it, I would say, ''Well, I need that in about two weeks. Are you working on it?'' And she would say, "Well, yes, I'm going to get to it." Finally, after I had reminded her a week and then three days and then two days before it was due, the last day she would say to me, "I can't get that done now. I have this rush for somebody else to do."

In Martha's experience, the person with "this rush assignment" was always a man. She found that the secretaries in her office consistently gave this priority to male executives when they were working for a number of bosses.

Many of the women in secretarial positions in her company, she noticed, had an attitude of less respect for women in authority positions, which was expressed in the kinds of minor day-to-day sabotage which she experienced. "I don't think they would do that to a man," Martha concluded, "they would treat him with more respect."

PUTTING OTHER
WOMEN DOWN

Other women to whom we spoke in conjunction with our research reported that women in positions of power felt threatened by other women and responded by working behind the scenes to put them down. Our female respondents observed that when they had unethical run-ins with men, the men retaliated in a more direct fashion, at times even using the political team-working process to form coalitions against them, whereas the women were more likely to engage in their unethical schemes on their own or involve others as unwitting participants.

Donna observed this mode of operating after several difficult situations with both men and women. Her encounter with the men occurred when she was working in real estate and several men, to push her out of the field, filed a ten million-dollar lawsuit against her. The court subsequently tossed the suit out. In commenting on the style the men used in treating her unethically, Donna observed:

I feel the men sabotage someone by working together and making no bones about it. They like to line up powerful allies, legal and political or whatever it takes. When these men filed a ten million-dollar lawsuit against me, you could see it in their manner and their behavior, that they were so sure of what they were doing, and that there was no way I could stand up to that. They tend to go for blood. They like to intimidate, take a hard-line position. In my case, it was almost as if the men wanted to encourage a battle. I saw big egos and a lot of what I thought was inflated self-worth.

Donna found the women in her field who treated her badly tended to have feelings of low self-esteem. They were jealous or felt threatened by her, and they tried to put her down in quiet, indirect ways. She referred to the "Queen Bee" syndrome, where a woman thinks "I got where I am, and I am going to keep everybody else down." Primarily, she felt this occurred because the woman was scared by competition from other women.

Donna experienced this syndrome several times. When she was working in sales for a gas company, she was asked to do some modelling and TV commercials. The woman for whom she worked, Joanne, became very jealous. While she had been very cordial to Donna, she suddenly became distant and cool. Donna said Joanne actually planted mistakes that were attributed to her and spread false rumors to top management. Nothing Donna did to stop the problem worked. She tried to be very nice to Joanne, offering her assistance with projects, but she said, "The nicer I was to her, the worse she became. There was an obvious jealousy factor there that was impossible to try to cope with— the Queen Bee syndrome. Somebody that has been there for a long time is very threatened when someone new comes on board."

Donna had a similar experience when she was working part-time in a library. She had a master's degree in library science and a teaching credential and had worked in a multi-media center. Elsie, the district librarian, had none of these credentials. Elsie had been established in the district for years; Donna only worked there part-time a few days a week. When the school district began to make job cut-backs, Elsie, showed signs of intimidation. She began a surreptitious campaign to put Donna in a bad light. She made comments to other librarians about the poor job Donna was doing in the district. She gave Donna assignments of projects that couldn't be done, such as hunting for books that had been lost for years. Yet she never expressed any of her concerns openly to Donna.

In commenting on what had happened, Donna said she felt the key reasons why Elsie acted in such unethical ways were fear, jealousy, and envy. She believed Elsie saw her as a threat to her job.

Both Donna's negative experiences involved women with low self-esteem who were frightened by her as a powerful, accomplished woman. As Donna described it:

> This is a very subtle thing which occurs when women have other women underneath them or have other women they have to work with—women who are in titled positions of power are intimidated by seeing somebody who has a good education, sometimes younger, has more pizazz in dressing, or is more worldly than they are.

Another experience of the kind she had with Joanne and Elsie occurred when she worked on a national sales promotion campaign for a company manufacturing a specific item carried by several department stores in the country. Donna had done well for the company and herself; on some days, she exceeded one hundred thousand dollars in sales. Then, with little explanation, the company owner, a woman, told her she had decided to bring in a new person to replace her. The person the owner had selected had minimal sales and promotional experience and was a part-time aerobics instructor. The owner said this was a great advantage to the company because they could mold her right from the start.

If Donna was doing so well, why did they do this? Donna was convinced it was because the woman owner was afraid of her and wanted to bring in someone with limited experience so she could keep control. Otherwise, the decision economically made no sense. Donna believed the owner reacted this way because,

> As I got more confident, I knew what I was doing and was doing a good job. I did not have to ask the company owner questions as much or depend on her for help. It was a very small company and I think she felt that she was losing control. So she wanted someone to train who would be very, very dependent.

At the time she was fired, Donna had been with the company several years and knew all the inside workings. Not only did Donna make a lot of money for herself and the company, but she knew operations. She also thought that scared the owner. With a newcomer on a lower commission schedule, greater profits would remain for the owner, at least if the sales remained constant. If sales declined because Donna was not there, then the commission savings would backfire. They did.

DEVIOUSNESS AND DISCRIMINATION

Another woman who encountered the threatened female boss syndrome was Joan, and in her case, also, the boss avoided a direct confrontation.

Joan had worked as an administrative aide to a woman in a land title office. After a few months she noticed an unusual pattern. Her supervisor, Lois, who supervised a staff of fourteen, had been newly promoted to her position. "The women who worked for her were treated terribly and the men were not. She was threatened by capable females."

The women who were willing to keep their mouths shut and let Lois rewrite their letters under her name and take credit for the work did fine. But women such as Joan, who were confident and could handle things on their own, had problems. Joan's surfaced in the form of an extremely negative performance review.

Prior to the review, Lois had never commented on any faults she found with Joan's work. According to Joan, she never tried to meet with her and let her know that she would like Joan to make any changes, a reasonable request if an employer or supervisor is dissatisfied. "She never said 'Let's do this instead of that, or let's reevaluate, or I think this is a better approach, or whatever,' " said Joan. So her complaints on the performance review came like a bombshell. "She waited the entire year and said nothing. Then the performance review she gave me was outrageous."

In fact, it was so outrageous Joan spoke to one of the vice-presidents in the company, who agreed that Joan had been doing a terrific job for the company and her review was totally off the wall—the kind of hatchet job that would make it tough for her in getting ahead in the company. He recommended that she should seek a transfer to another department—as soon as she could.

But Joan discovered that she couldn't get out. Lois didn't want to release her and made a transfer impossible:

> Company policy was that you could not inquire into pro-motional or lateral moves without advising your supervisor that you were doing so. So I had to indicate to her that I was interested in moving to additional learning areas, which is how I tried to phrase it, in the company.

It was as if Lois took Joan's request as a personal insult. Joan related:

> Every time I would go back and talk to a new department, they would call her up and ask whether I was a good employee. I got bad reviews continually. And yet other people moved easily back and forth throughout the company. She was able to do that to all fourteen of us. So all fourteen of us left.

Joan believed the woman felt threatened by her. Lois was insecure. Why? Joan continued:

This lady had come up the ranks from a secretary in fifteen years, and I was brand new with the company. I had a lot of skills, I wrote the whole tech guide and went out to all the field officers with a training team who were all much higher in level than I, and did a bang-up job. And she had her part that she was doing and each department had its part. But I was in charge of the problem-solving as the system was then installed, so I got the phone calls.

Getting the phone calls! That meant that Joan was up front and visible, while Lois was more in the shadows. Rather than dealing with the ego problem directly, Lois expressed her hurt by stifling Joan and the other women in the office who posed threats. She held onto paperwork that came through her office, couldn't delegate, held Joan and the others back. "She was really threatened, not only by men, but by other capable people. The guys in her department were given promotions, but the women couldn't seem to get out."

WOMEN HOLDING OTHER WOMEN DOWN

While Lois's response to her insecurity was to try to keep the women in her department and hold them back, our research showed that many women do not give lower-level women employees even that chance. They seek to keep them down because they view other women moving up as a threat—not only because these women might take their positions, but because having other women up there with them might weaken their standing. If the division they manage consists primarily of women, it may be viewed as less important, since women have traditionally been viewed as low-status employees.

Virginia is the director of a large business association. She noticed this phenomena occurring in numerous companies based on her own work experiences and those of several friends. Women managers simply wanted to keep other women out of their divisions to keep up the status of their work group. As Virginia explained:

> There is really no such thing anymore as female networking or women really supporting one another within a corporate environment. There is a jealousy and fear that if too many women come into your division, it will become a so-called golden ghetto, and that position will lose its credibility. So I think keeping other women down is not only a protection of one's own position, but also a protection of the integrity and credibility and viability of one's own department or division.

Virginia found that some of the women managers for whom she worked were more likely to "go by the book." They were too insecure in their positions to be more flexible. In some cases, that led to holding other women back.

Virginia recalled an experience that occurred when she worked for a government department. The female employees believed they had been discriminated against because they hadn't been advancing as quickly as the men in the department. The consensus was that there were unnecessary restrictions in the language of the job descriptions and requirements which made it more difficult for them to move ahead and that if the descriptions were to be interpreted more broadly the restrictions would be nonexistent. The head of the department was a woman. She followed the guidelines to a "T," never veering from the old restrictions. Eventually, the other women filed suit and won restitution for the difference in their salaries and those of their former supervisors, all of them male, for a twelve-month period. The court also ordered the department to look at the career advance process and designate specific milestones that people in different positions could follow.

In Virginia's view, a key reason the woman didn't respond to the predicament of the other women was that she felt insecure. She had recently been promoted from manager to director and didn't want to rock the boat by trying to equalize the pay scales for a group of female employees. Virginia suggested:

I think that if the director had been male, we probably would have had our problem looked at more carefully, because it would have been someone who was secure in his position. I think sometimes corporate females adhere more to the book because they feel less secure.

Virginia restated her idea that this woman had recently been catapulted up the hierarchial ladder due to affirmative action. She had been at the lower levels of the organization for nine years and knew her work from a technical point of view. Yet when she was thrust into leadership and rose from a lower-level manager to a vice-president of the department within six months, she wasn't ready to take on a leadership position. She expressed her fears by holding other women back, rather than working on overcoming her fears and moving on.

Our research findings showed that a double-edged sword exists. Many women were thrust, unprepared, into upper management when the affirmative action doctrines were put in place. The "Patty Principle" emerged side-by-side with the "Peter Principle." Placing individuals in upper-management positions without training them to take into consideration new employment and personnel considerations can lead to unfair conditions within organizations.

SETTING OTHER WOMEN UP

Our studies disclosed that still other women react to their feelings of insecurity or jealousy by maneuvering the women they resent into embarrassing or difficult situations. In brief, they set them up so they will fail.

Cheryl experienced this scenario when she worked in a sales position in a medium-sized company. Her relationship with the other saleswomen had been fine so long as she was on the same level. Once she was promoted, the other women resented her. Alice found a way to retaliate by setting her up.

At her sales meetings held in the showroom, Cheryl would play a song on the tape—it woke everyone up in the morning and gave them a success message as well. Cheryl's manager planned to have a special meeting. Alice suggested that Cheryl play the song, "The Gambler," for the meeting. "It has a nice hook," she said, "and it gets a good point across: 'know when to fold them, know when to hold them, know when to walk away,' and people don't forget that. Is there some way you could play that song?" Although Cheryl hadn't planned on including "The Gambler" in her presentation, she welcomed Alice's suggestion and played it.

What Cheryl didn't know is that Alice, who had dated the manager before coming to work for the company, knew he hated the song. She had even heard him to say to another salesperson, "I hate that song. I think it's awful."

The day after the meeting the general manager called Cheryl into his office and told her the song was "the worst thing he'd ever heard." She was stunned. He went on to say that he had previously told several of the salespeople, including Alice, that he didn't like it. Cheryl responded that Alice recommended that she use that particular song. Immediately, she realized that she had been set up.

The general manager stuck up for Alice. "He told me I was crazy to think she would do such a thing." Cheryl backed down, and eventually the incident was forgotten.

She believed that there was hostility and jealousy reflected in Alice's actions. Alice had no particular reason to resent Cheryl, except that Cheryl had previously been her peer and was now her manager. Alice never outwardly expressed anger; she held it in, and, when she had a chance, set Cheryl up to embarrass her. It was a way to put her down.

THE CUT-'EM-DEAD
APPROACH

In the workplace, individuals who feel insecure and threatened by others still have to work with them. But under other circumstances, it's possible to use avoidance, or cut-'em-dead, techniques to keep someone out.

In a different experience, Cheryl went to a meeting of an advertising club. An associate had invited her as a guest. The president was pleasant and appeared very interested when Cheryl mentioned that she had been in advertising and had taught seminars. Roxanne was enthusiastic and suggested that Cheryl make a speech at one of the group's meetings.

Cheryl was delighted at Roxanne's interest and gave her a copy of her promotional package. They talked about the possibility of Cheryl joining the group. Roxanne seemed encouraging and supportive. As she glanced through Cheryl's packet, one of the men passed by and gave Cheryl a rave review. "He said something like, 'Oh, you need to get Cheryl. She's the vice president of this and she's done that, has been on all these television shows and spoken to many broadcasters.' "

> All of a sudden, Roxanne's attitude changed. She suddenly became very cold. The men around her were saying all these favorable things about me and she took on the qualities of ice. Then she said I didn't need to apply for membership because I obviously didn't need the group.

At first, Cheryl couldn't understand Roxanne's sudden shift of attitude. A few days later, she called a friend on the board of directors and the club and told him she had a funny feeling there was a lack of rapport between her and the club's president. Did he think there was any problem? He said, "No, not at all. I'll send you a membership form with my name on it as sponsor."

Cheryl completed the forms and sent in her check. Roxanne returned them with a letter saying that she was sorry, but the board had turned her down. Cheryl called the man who offered to sponsor her. He said her membership had not even been submitted to the board and what Roxanne had done wasn't allowed. Under his advice, Cheryl sent her forms and check in again.

Why should Roxanne act this way? Cheryl speculates that she felt threatened:

After she saw my packet, she perceived me as having more power than she did. She probably saw that at some point in the future, we would both be going for the same thing and I had better credentials and would get it.

Cheryl concluded that Roxanne wanted to be sure that didn't happen and went to great lengths, including lying to her about membership, to keep her out. At the same time, she refused to talk to Cheryl about it. It was as if she didn't exist. Cheryl said that after Roxanne received her application, she would not communicate with her:

> She wouldn't even talk to me that day after she saw my packet. She'd been friendly until she saw what I'd done. And then I felt completely cut off.

Cheryl experienced similar feelings when, at another time, a woman acquaintance took her off a speaking program. Again, Cheryl believes, it was because she felt threatened. Susan was the head of a non-profit organization to which Cheryl belonged. The program director had asked Cheryl to participate on a panel of speakers at a major conference. Cheryl began to work out the final arrangements, including reservations and the outline of her speech, several months in advance. A month before the program, Susan called her to say there were two new people on the program and that there just wasn't time to hear everyone—and that there was no longer room for Cheryl.

Cheryl was furious, but there was nothing she could do. Why did Susan really take her off the program? Cheryl thought it involved jealousy. "She was basically threatened. I got paid more money than she did. I guess she resented me."

Cheryl also speculated that Susan might have feared that as Cheryl gained more visibility within the group, her own position at its head might be threatened.

WOMEN, MEN, AND
JEALOUSY

These stories have a common thread. They show that women frequently strike out at and seek to undermine other women because they feel insecure, jealous, or resentful. Sometimes the other women can be employees seen as threats to their own positions or to the image of their work division as a whole. Sometimes the other woman can be a boss who is resented because of her senior position, so the employee does all she can to bring her down. At times the employee may do this consciously through fabricated stories; at other times, the employee may really misperceive the real situation because she operates out of jealousy.

This is not to say that men don't feel insecure and jealous at times or that they don't express those feelings in hostile acts toward women or men at work. But our research indicated that their style is very different. When men are unethical, they tend to be motivated by money, short-cuts to professional advancement, and in some cases rejected romantic feelings. Or they may use the tactics of sex discrimination to reaffirm the traditional male position and keep women in "their place."

This happened to Dawn. She got a job in the products development area in a high-tech company, and the man she replaced, Mark, was promoted to product manager. Part of her job was to research existing products and part included providing information to the product manager so he could use it in positioning and marketing the product.

Soon after she took the job she discovered a major flaw in one of the products Mark had researched. If it had been uncovered earlier the product would not have been accepted and Mark would probably not have received his promotion. When she went to her own boss about it he was impressed with her findings and told her, "This is a very important breakthrough. We may decide to drop the product and not pursue it further."

As her boss was deciding how to handle her revelations, Dawn learned that Mark had romantic feelings for her. Both were in the process of divorces; they were drawn together primarily for mutual support. They had a brief romantic encounter when they were on the road for a product presentation.

Then Mark learned that Dawn had discovered the mistake in his earlier work. He became angry and upset. He told Dawn that it was too hard to work with her anymore. "He said I was a distraction because every time he saw me, he had sexual feelings and couldn't work," she said. He went to Dawn's boss and told him he could no longer work with her. "He told the boss I was difficult to get along with," Dawn said.

When her boss confronted her, she was at a loss as to what to say. "I couldn't defend myself; I couldn't tell him why."

Dawn was able to get out of the situation. Her boss asked if she was having problems getting along with men in general. She suggested he speak with all the other product managers. "Find out if they agree," she said. "If they agree they can't work with me, it's clear I shouldn't be here." The other managers informed him that she did excellent work and was quite supportive. She survived.

But it took a long time to smooth over her relationship with Mark and get it back on an ordinary professional basis. In looking back, she felt that their brief romance had intensified Mark's feelings of insecurity and jealousy which had begun when Dawn discovered the flaw in his work. He saw her as a threat to his status and power in the company because she had exposed him, and he resented her ability to discover what she had.

The remedy was easy enough: get rid of her by putting her down. And he lied in the process. But note the differences in his method. Contrast his behavior with that of the insecure women described earlier in this chapter, who reacted through behind-the-scenes backstabbing and gossip. Mark confronted Dawn directly with his anger and then went directly to her boss. Certainly, he presented his complaints about Dawn in a misleading way; he blamed her for doing a bad job, when in fact he was angry at her and torn by his romantic feelings. But he acted openly and aggressively.

Our research revealed that this reflects a pattern which men generally seem more likely to use than women: lying openly to get what they want, whatever that is. Being insecure and jealous can be one reason for using the lie, but other factors can motivate this type of behavior too, such as wanting to buy time or take advantage of a competitor.

When Katrin worked for a newly organized high-tech firm, things began getting tight after the first year. The company was running out of money and having trouble raising funds. One of the backers saw a way of using this to get rid of the other investors and he told Katrin what he planned to do. "We have other investors that we don't like. They are pains in the ass. So what we are going to do is put the company through bankruptcy, reorganize it, and squeeze and flush them out." Katrin reminded him that the other investors had been there long before him. That didn't matter. Richard saw a way to use the situation to his unethical advantage.

In another case, Joan had a job where the head of her department promised her she would keep her job after another company took over the firm and put a freeze on hiring and job remodifications. Had she known there was any question about her job, she could have gone out and found another one. With Greg's assurances, she didn't bother to look.

There were layoffs throughout the company, but he assured her, "I already told the company head that I have already done my laying off and that is it. Stop worrying. You won't go. You would be the last one to go. If you leave, this whole department falls apart. You are guaranteed your job."

Four months before the rest of the department was laid off, Joan lost her job. And because this meant a loss of four months of salary before she was able to find anything else, she had to sell her house and experienced tremendous emotional stress.

Why hadn't Greg told her the situation right away? And why had he kept her hanging by letting her think her job was secure? In Joan's view, he lied because this was a way to keep her in the company while he needed her; when circumstances changed, he let her go. It had been an empty promise, and he knew it at the time. However, it served his immediate purpose of keeping the department together until Joan was no longer needed.

Women's "characteristic" lack of power, then, can lead some women to a "characteristic" style of unethical behavior that includes lying, sabotage, and covert activities. But there is another factor that also affects and differentiates many women's business behavior—the lack of experience with contracts, agreements, and bonds that generally help teach codes of business behavior to men.

Chapter 7

Ms. Lead

RULES ARE MADE TO BE BROKEN

"I learned to play it young, / . . . It's thus if you would rule; Give up good faith, . . . and/ love/ Where your interest lies, and should your interest change/ Let your love follow it quickly. This is queen's porridge. / And however little stomach she has for it/ A queen must eat it."

> Elizabeth to Mary
> Act Three

Many women are new to the business game. They don't always know the rules to follow; and even if they do, they may be uncomfortable following a code of behavior laid down by men.

We discovered this theme in interview after interview. Many of the women described growing up in a world where they were never expected to encounter the ins and outs of competition in the business world; their bastion was to be the home, where the image was of the good, moral woman who was a beacon of truth, honesty, and justice. In the envisioned protected family environment, this encapsuled world of integrity could be kept pure and unstained. It would not be subject to the day-to-day pressures and games faced in the business jungle.

Certainly this is an overly-idealized image of what life as a homemaker and helpmate should be like. Thirty, forty, even fifty years ago, many women tried to create it. This created a sense that women would be, and should be, more loyal, honest, and more imbued with integrity than men. But the women in our survey continually related unethical incidents involving women in the world of office politics. And often, it was revealed, the beliefs of these women, brought up by mothers with high ideals about the basic trustworthiness of other women, contributed to their own hurt.

Their own idealism had led them to have expectations of or enter into agreements with other women without taking sufficient precautions, whereas they would have been more cautious in dealing with a man.

What the women we interviewed also found was that not only were many women unfamiliar with the traditional rules but those who had managed to learn them were unethical in using them, and many broke them. Or, in vindictiveness, used the rules against someone else when they sought revenge.

BLACKBALLED, BADGERED, AND BEWILDERED

One woman discovered the fury of another woman when she stepped into her territory. And while men long have had their own territorial battles, this situation illustrates that when some women fight about territorial rules it can become especially bitter. Many of our subjects felt that women, as the "new kids on the block," were particularly threatened when someone else stepped into their arenas and the reaction was to fight back— with attacks that were long and intense.

Linda, recalling her career as a paralegal, said that over the years she had found it more difficult to work with women than men. Her experiences revealed to her that women in business have a heightened sense of territorial possessiveness and fear of invasion by other ambitious women, and often put up blocks in their paths. As Linda told us, "I have been blocked numerous times in getting ahead as far as getting more responsibility, more pay, a better job title, or even utilizing my ability on the job— because of women feeling threatened."

With Marjorie, for whom she worked in a large San Francisco law firm, the reaction to threat was even more extreme. Like many women working for or with other women, Linda and Marjorie had shared many personal things together off the job. Linda had been to Marjorie's house several times to visit and had done some house-sitting for her. They had also revealed certain confidences to one another. The incident started innocently enough when Marjorie went on vacation for three weeks and left Linda in charge of the office. Linda was to take care of the clients and see that the office ran smoothly, which she did. When Marjorie returned she was livid because, according to Linda, "she was upset that the office had succeeded without her."

On the premises that Linda had made decisions she'd had no right making, that she'd taken on responsibilities she should not have taken on, and that she had not been in the office consistently from 9:00 to 5:00, Marjorie told Linda she was going to put her on probation. Linda bristled at this suggestion. "I had already worked for her for a year, and I told her that I wouldn't be put on probation. There were no grounds for it. She told me that I was either going to be put on probation or be fired."

The upshot of this confrontation was that Linda announced her resignation, but Marjorie responded with a display of her power. She warned Linda that she would never work again in the legal community as a paralegal if she quit. Linda felt that Marjorie had no valid reason for anything she was doing, and she considered her threats of blackball idle ones. She decided to leave immediately.

She then discovered that Marjorie did in fact exert her power to see that she didn't work again. Although she had interviews every day, she couldn't find a job for three months. Finally she got a job with another attorney. She had been working for a week; her employer told her he was pleased with her work and that she was "doing fine." That Friday, when her employer's assistant took her out to lunch, Linda happened to mention that she had previously worked for Marjorie.

The following week, her employer called her into his office and announced he had to let her go. He gave no details. "He just said that it was nothing personal," Linda explained, "but he had to let me go."

In Linda's view, the main reason Marjorie had blackballed her was because Linda had posed a threat to her area of authority. By showing her skills in managing the office, Linda had made Marjorie feel less valuable herself; she felt she had to get rid of Linda to preserve her own esteem and used the rules—the firm's probation mechanisms. When Linda challenged Marjorie's reason for doing this, Marjorie reached out vindictively to do everything she could to destroy Linda rather than confronting the underlying reason.

In retrospect, Linda said she ran into difficulty because she simply didn't know the rules, nor could she really understand them because Marjorie had created her own. Marjorie's campaign of hatred and her original rationale for firing Linda left Linda feeling bewildered and in the dark. Since this skirmish, Linda has become wiser in recognizing the potential pitfalls and land mines. As she said, "I have been very naive and unsuspecting in a lot of situations. I now see how the game is played. Now that I have observed it being played, I feel like I am more capable of existing in this world, even though I am no expert at playing—yet."

Linda's story also brings up the issue, mentioned in previous Chapters, of mixing personal and business relationships, which creates a whole new series of rules for what is appropriate business behavior. Certainly, many men develop off-the-job friendships. They go to clubs together, play golf, visit one another, bring their family members along and the like, but there is a more external, hail-fellow-well-met kind of camaraderie that develops. Most men share their outer, but not their inner, selves—at least not in the beginning. In fact, men are more likely to keep up that outer front that permits them to appear strong, successful, and independent to others, no matter how they feel inside.

What is different about women, as our research revealed, is the in-depth nature of the sharing that goes on. It's like being back in high school and sharing girlish confidences. It's like having that special friend to whom you tell everything.

When women share, they tend to share from the heart—their feelings, their fears. It appears that they develop a greater sense of intimacy and trust. The other side of this closeness is the deep feelings of hurt and betrayal that occur when one believes this intimacy has been breached.

Was Marjorie's reaction to Linda's competence one of vindictiveness that led to revenge—or was it a protective screen? When one is very open, there is often a feeling of vulnerability and exposure. This feeling may threaten a person, who can in turn respond quickly—and this response can include lies and vendettas—to create a screen of protection against someone who is perceived as a threat.

During an interview conducted for this book, psychotherapist, stress expert, and author Barbara Mackoff stated that women often can be their own worst enemies. "When we deal from the heart and show our feelings, we are more vulnerable," Dr. Mackoff says. "And because we share personal history of some sort, we assume that a special bond has been formed. What happens, instead, is the woman opens herself up much more than she needs to. The end result, if the deal doesn't work out and the business situation goes sour, is a feeling of betrayal."

Men in our survey reported that they rarely shared personal data. They would feel out any new situation: size it up, measure it, then possibly—at a much later date—share.

Diane, like many of our female respondents, reported confusion about the rules, and the consequent variations on this central problem—sometimes in the context of political infighting, sometimes in hidden agendas, sometimes in personal lives creeping into the business arena. She, like many, found that most of her problems with unethical behavior were due to rule breakdowns which came from women, not men.

Her first encounter occurred when she was working as a job developer for a company specializing in career counseling for displaced homemakers. Her responsibility was to interview corporate clients and learn what kind of jobs might be available for these women in their organizations. She also took over an additional responsibility as a workshop coordinator in charge of putting on seminars and workshops designed to help women learn to prepare for jobs. After about a year and a half, the board of directors, which was predominantly women, decided it needed a new director. They hired Alice.

Alice was not really qualified. According to Diane, if Alice had not been chosen, Diane probably would have been offered the position. Diane believed the stage was set for a confrontation when the new director began to feel threatened by Diane's professional abilities.

Initially, Diane didn't perceive a problem. The office seemed to be running smoothly, and Alice was seemingly pleasant to her. Diane proceeded to follow what she thought were the guidelines for professionalism. As she told us, "I was dressing for success, I was reading every single one of those books, following them religiously, and boy, I thought I was on top of it all. I was going to be this crackerjack corporate type, and I was putting across the correct image."

But, as she later realized, she didn't know enough to understand the inner game of office politics that goes on behind the scenes. "No one had ever taught me the undercurrents of human emotionalism and power," she observed. She had never had any experience with individuals who were apparently sincere, yet two-faced. She became too good at her work.

One of Diane's jobs was to contact the media for publicity. As a result, she had numerous calls from television and radio stations and from the newspapers. Since no one had taken the time to tell her the appropriate "house" rules, she didn't realize she should have referred the calls to her superiors instead of handling them successfully herself. She simply thought she was doing her job. Later on, a coworker told her that this was one of the main reasons that behind-the-scenes moves were put into place to ensure her leaving and that Alice had taken an active role in engineering Diane's ouster by persuading the board that Diane didn't know how to follow the rules. But could Diane have known what rules to follow if Alice had a different agenda? Alice perceived Diane as a threat. Perhaps because Diane performed her job correctly, she further alienated Alice.

Our research indicated that such feelings of being threatened by another powerful woman can result from the deep insecurities women may feel at suddenly being thrust into a new business context. They are not sure of the rules themselves and do not know how to comfortably support or guide others. Diane believed this is what happened on this job. She later had experiences that only confirmed her initial observations. As she said:

> And that was the first time I learned that one of the biggest problems of a female manager is the threat to her personally. I am generalizing, I know, but I think women tend to take personally the work of other people as a possible threat to their positions and power rather than supporting or accepting an individual's talents—encouraging and mentoring. When I first started working, women managers didn't know how to mentor. They thought of those under them as adversaries.

And, as we have already shown, women in lower-level positions may be jealous of those who move into managerial positions. They seem to feel that somehow a woman doesn't belong in such a position and sabotage that woman's performance of the managerial role. Again, the problem arises out of the assumption of new roles and rules, which can lead to conflicts. Some people in the workplace don't accept those new roles and rules, or even feel comfortable with those who do.

A study completed by Charlotte Decker Sutton and Kris Moore and published in the September/October 1985 issue of the *Harvard Business Review* illustrates this. The study was a "revisit" of executive women, twenty years later.

Twenty years ago, less than ten percent of the men in this survey reported that they would be comfortable working for a woman. In 1985, almost fifty percent reported that they would be comfortable in that situation. Twenty years ago, slightly more than half the women in the study reported they would be comfortable working for other women—and that percentage remained the same.

Indeed, after the career counseling company experience Diane echoed the discomfort many people feel working with women managers and she decided to find a job working for a man. She became an assistant to a male executive promoting and marketing a business degree program for a school catering to the adult-in-transition market. Eventually, due to declining enrollment and conflicts between her boss and his own boss in charge of overall operations, her boss was fired and she was moved into his position.

Diane had all the qualifications to take over the job of management. She had finished her MBA; she had taken extensive course work on human behavior and organizations; she used all the techniques that modern managers use, such as sitting down with all employees to determine what they wanted to do, where they felt their skills could be best utilized, and what they wanted to work on. In fact, these were human resources-oriented approaches that her own boss had never used.

As soon as she took over, her relationships with the other women in the office deteriorated. While she had been an assistant manager, as she said, "I was a peer. I was seen as part of them." With her promotion, everything changed. "The second I became their manager, the sabotage started," she said. As Diane described it, some of the women began calling people around the campus to tell them what she was doing or what was happening in their office. A friend in another office reported that he had been getting calls from the secretaries. They reported that Diane's former boss had been set up. Feelings of resentment surfaced against Diane for taking his job. According to Diane, "Almost anything I did was viewed as negative. I think deep down they felt jealous they hadn't been appointed."

Nothing Diane did seemed to work. On the surface, all seemed serene. But the sabotage level was running high, with the women in the office communicating with others behind Diane's back or promising to do something, then intentionally not doing it. Diane felt:

> I don't think men would have acted in the way these women did. I think women are used to getting even in subversive ways. Men are confrontative, overt. If they don't like something, they let you know. There are some men who are manipulative, like women, but women bring a tone of vindictiveness to it. Men's manipulation is sort of a jockeying, one up. Women are often expressing anger or seeking revenge.

The beliefs of both Linda and Diane were confirmed by Burt, a sales trainer and consultant, who was one of the men interviewed.

He concurred with the hypothesis that our moral upbringing has a strong effect on our business actions. As a result of that upbringing, many women act in covert ways, while men act in overt manners. "Women will operate by the rules as long as they serve their purpose, then change the rules to suit," Burt said. When we asked him how men and women would react to a situation involving unethical behavior, his immediate response was that, depending on the gravity of the situation, in his experience most men would be likely either to ignore or report it while most women would save it for ammunition—invoking their own rules.

Louise, another of our respondents, described an incident that originated from her not knowing or following the rules. She had accepted a position as assistant to Georgia, the president of a company in the information-processing field. After she had been there several weeks, she was directed to put together a management team to run the company. Georgia didn't want to deal with the day-to-day operations of the company, but wanted to focus on long-run strategic planning, deal making, and negotiations. Georgia hadn't taken into consideration the potential hostility that any change within the company would cause. Several of the existing managers thought they should have received this position.

The hostility surfaced almost immediately in the form of resentment directed against Louise by the other employees. Louise tried to confront the problem: she sat down individually with each of the managers in order to convey that each was a contributor to the organization. "I tried to make them feel they had real value, that they were being reshuffled or put into positions where they could do what it is they thought they really wanted to do—what they did best." When she thought she had the problem resolved and had gained the support of the managers, she discovered that a few were suggesting to Georgia that she declare a different policy. Typically, when this kind of situation occurs in companies, the senior management backs up its executives to preserve the organization's chain of command. In this instance, it didn't happen. Instead, Georgia changed her policy again, but didn't inform Louise of the revision. Soon Louise's management authority was undermined.

As Louise emphasized, Georgia's approach was completely wrong, completely against the usual rules for doing things:

> The problem wouldn't have happened if she had stood by her guns and supported me. It was wrong of her not to. In a male organization, in a corporation, when push comes to shove, unless it is blatant, you support your management people.

After Louise got through that early crisis, she found that her boss consistently misled her by telling her she supported a certain vision of the future organization when, in truth, she did not—and in fact regularly put obstacles to achieving this vision in Louise's way. For example, Louise believed it necessary to set up a coordinated management team, profit centers within the organization, and clear policies and guidelines so that everyone in the organization would understand where the company was going and support its direction of development:

We needed to set up systems for handling growth decisions about the direction of the company. We needed to implement the first strategic plan for the organization; we needed to start thinking long-term; and do a lot of client analysis; and set up a marketing team to go after more profitable types of clients.

At first, Georgia agreed that she wanted a growth-oriented policy. Louise took appropriate action by setting up profit centers, opening up the records to keep the managers informed of how they were doing, and working out job descriptions for everyone in the company so they all could work toward overall goals and objectives. But just as the program was starting to work, Georgia withdrew her support.

It was shortly after Louise, at Georgia's direction, had investigated some new product-related ideas that the company could sell along with its information processing and had found some people who were willing to back up the program that Georgia announced that she wasn't willing to extend the company any further into other areas. According to Louise, the crux of the problem was:

She talked a good line and said she wanted it to grow. But in reality, she didn't. She was afraid. I knew the potential, and she held it back.

Why? Louise described a situation which our research showed is often the case for women business owners, much less common for men. Women tend to involve themselves too closely in their own business ventures, so they are more personally at risk if something goes wrong. Then, instead of being guided by sound business rules that inform decision-making, they may react toward new opportunities out of fear, or they may be more erratic, as Georgia was, and respond to the ebb and flow of the current situation out of their feelings at the time. Louise described this classic problem in the light of Georgia's behavior:

She didn't want to do it, possibly because she was going through some personal problems at that point. She was so

financially tied to the company—which is another thing that
women managers do to themselves. They wrap themselves
up in their companies, and they become an extension of
themselves so that they get personally and financially involved where they become personally liable, whereas men
somehow don't. So, she'd get an idea, and that was the
idea of the moment: we had to charge ahead, work on
negotiations, and things always seemed to fall through. I
just finally got to the point where I got fed up with it—I
realized it was never going to change.

Was this situation really unethical or a problem with bad or
overly cautious management? In Louise's view, what made this
approach to business unethical was the fact that Georgia's
actions never matched her professed verbal intentions about the
future, so that spinning one's wheels became the norm. She
believed that Georgia had a hidden agenda based on private fears
and therefore wasn't dealing honestly with others. Perhaps she
didn't intend to be deceptive and devious—the fits and starts in
her business were the result of her inner fears—yet the results
were experienced as unethical by her supposed right hand—
Louise.

At a social gathering, Louise met Georgia's former partner,
who confirmed Louise's observations and experiences. She said
that Georgia was really only interested in "playing" at business,
not working. Louise finally left and started her own successful
company in the same field, using the principles that she had
attempted to implement at Georgia's company.

She commented further on this style of leadership, which she
considered both unethical and characteristic of many women:

How are women unethical? They let you think one thing,
their agenda is something else—but they don't ever let you
in on what that is. To me, that is unethical. If you are going
to have managers or people working for you, you deal
directly with them. You deal straight, you tell them what is
happening, what is going on, what the expectations are.
There were times when I felt she set me, as well as others,

up for failure. Georgia would jump on me for not making an accomplishment when I had no clue as to what the objective was. The agenda had changed, but I had never been informed of it . . . I think women are much more prone to doing this than men are.

Jef, another of the men we interviewed, believed that both men and women have a fairly good idea of what the rules are. The more sophisticated men are, the clearer the rules. He felt that anybody who had been working in the business world for more than a few years had a serious sense of how things operated: "Anyone knows whom you can talk about behind their backs, whom you can't, why you should and why you shouldn't, even how many pencils can be taken without getting into trouble." Rules—unwritten, but rules nonetheless. "I think women have not looked at the rules and figured them out, but looked at the rules and said 'Ah, this is like war. This is the same stupid man's game they have been playing for centuries. I am going to do it differently.' " Jef observed that the entire economic system with both its inertia and momentum is built on those rules—difficult but not impossible to alter.

Another factor, he added, is that a number of the top management people in large companies are former military men. Jef views this as almost a fact of life. The military is oriented toward a rewards-and-punishment system, and within that system those who follow the regulations are promoted. One of the problems he believed women encounter in their attempt to alter those rules was they don't know what form they want them to take.

Our research indicated that another way in which women may have trouble following the rules is when they seek to personalize situations. An attempt may be made to alter the rules that usually apply to everyone on the grounds that there is some special consideration due because of whom they are or their relationship to the person making the rules. Many of the men and women interviewed responded that if the rulemaker decides that he or she can't change the rules to treat someone differently, a woman was more likely to feel hurt, or become vindictive, whereas a man was more likely to see this as an attempt to influence which didn't work, view it as the breaks of the game, and go on to other things without getting stuck in feelings.

A prime example of this type of situation occurred when Kathie started her own crafts business and opened a shop in a major shopping center. In the course of running the shop for a year, she had three major unethical encounters—two with women, the other with a man—that led her to believe there was a key difference in the way men and women move outside the proper rules for doing business. Her experiences convinced her that whereas men are focused on the pragmatic advantages of what they are doing and more likely to simply lie or mislead to get what they want without injecting personal feelings into the situation, women are more likely to create lies or mislead when they feel a personal hurt and want revenge.

The first situation occurred when she moved into the shopping center. The men who owned the center promised that the center would not bring in an arts and crafts fair during the Christmas season as long as the center merchants' association didn't vote to do this. Based on these assurances, Kathie and her husband signed a ten-year lease, which gave the shopping center the right to cancel their lease if they didn't do at least five hundred thousand dollars per year in business. Even though the merchants' association didn't vote to support an arts and crafts fair, the management of the center brought one in anyway and it severely damaged Kathie's business. As a result, the business didn't make the five-hundred-thousand-dollar minimum, and the center cancelled their lease. Eventually, Kathie and her husband had their day in court, and the jury supported their claim for financial damages by the center.

The experience made Kathie cautious in future business dealings. Even though the financial loss was tremendous, it didn't compare with the feelings of anger, betrayal and bitterness which accompanied it.

While Kathie was first recruiting artists and craftspeople to be in her store, Rickie, a friend of hers from Southern California, moved to the area. They had worked together in the arts and crafts field before and Kathie encouraged her to come into the store. At first the arrangement seemed to work perfectly: Rickie did very well in selling her artwork, and, since it received commissions for all art sales, the store did well too. Since Kathie and Rickie had been good friends, they frequently lunched together.

Then Rickie began pushing for more—more time for lunch, a better place to sell in the store, a reduced rent, delayed rent, and more—just because she and Kathie were friends. When Kathie tried to stop the situation by appealing to the rules she used with everyone else, Rickie became angry and vindictive. "Soon she was spreading rumors in the art community about me and how tough I was to deal with, that I mistreated my artists and employees, and other things of this nature," Kathie said.

After several weeks of this, Kathie confronted Rickie about the problem. Kathie happened to see her at an arts fair, went over to her, and told her she was tired of the kind of treatment she had been experiencing and that she wanted to deal with her in the only way she felt ethical—treating her like everybody else without any preferential treatment. This only made the situation worse. During another arts and crafts fair, Kathie again tried to talk to Rickie. She thought maybe she had been too harsh on her before, so she said, "You know, I am really sorry that this happened from our friendship standpoint. I still feel very strongly that I had to react the way that I did and treat you the same as everyone else, because business is business and that is the way I handle it."

Although Kathie was almost apologizing for her earlier behavior in expressing some anger, Rickie didn't want to acknowledge that she might have behaved in any way inappropriately or unethically. Instead, as Kathie describes, "She wouldn't even speak to me. There was no talking about it. She turned away and acted like I wasn't there."

Kathie felt those two contrasting incidents sensitized her to some basic differences between the way women and men act unethically. Then another incident with a woman occurred that helped to reinforce this point of view.

By the following year, Kathie's business had grown so much that instead of having independent artists working for her she had to hire a manager to supervise about a dozen employees who sold artwork. She now had managers at a couple of stores. She believed one of her managers, Anne, was especially good. Kathie joked that she ran her store with the efficiency of a sergeant. And yet, though they worked closely together, Kathie had the idea that Anne didn't respect her very much. Perhaps this was because Kathie spent most of her time working with the artists and displays—the creative rather than the bottom-line side of the business. Kathie's husband was in charge of the accounting. Anne seemed to have a lot of respect for him.

Kathie couldn't quite put her finger on what was wrong: it was just a feeling she had based on the tone of Anne's voice when she answered a question, the glance in her eyes when she looked at her, the odd grimace she sometimes made when Kathie discussed something with her. Not wanting to upset her best manager, Kathie avoided calling Anne on what was going on. The feelings continued to simmer.

The issue came to a head when Kathie's husband noticed, as he checked their books, that the business was experiencing a decline. He and Kathie decided that they'd better cut back and therefore couldn't keep on the new employees that they had just hired for extra Christmas help. The employees who had been there prior to Christmas would keep their jobs for the time being, but perhaps further cuts would be made after the holidays.

Christmas is the highest-volume sales period in many retail businesses. Just before Thanksgiving, Kathie sent Anne a memo about the reduced sales. She also spoke with her at length about the possibility of cutting back the amount of employees after the holidays, a slow period. Kathie thought she had explained the situation quite well, and Anne seemed to acknowledge and support the company's position. But instead, as Kathie described it:

I got a phone call three days before Christmas that there was going to be a big walk-out, and the reason was because the manager had told these employees that had been with me for ages that they were not going to be able to work at the store anymore after Christmas. She convinced all of them to walk out on her word—the most crucial time when we need every person under the sun to be working.

Even though Kathie called her other employees to explain that Anne had misunderstood, that it was just temporary employees who would not be kept on, it did no good. The employees didn't come back. They had taken other jobs.

Why did Anne do this? All Kathie could think of was that the woman had carried some personal anger against her and had never been willing to talk it over with her, so the anger kept building, and finally she released it. In the end, the walk-out wasn't as financially damaging as Anne expected, since Kathie and her husband were able to recruit the office staff, plus a friend's teenagers who were off during the school holidays, to help out. The business ended up doing the same volume of sales as it had the previous year.

But the emotional trauma remains. A few weeks later, when Kathie sent Anne her final paycheck, she tried to talk to her, but Anne wouldn't talk. She also sent her a letter, but to no avail. "I wrote her how I felt that she had not only wronged me, but that she had wronged all of the employees, misrepresenting what I had asked her to do. I never received an answer, and I never saw her again," Kathie said.

We feel it is important to understand how men and women's business styles differ. It may appear on the surface that both sexes are playing the same game in the same way, but they are not. Knowing this can help us be more aware of what game *everyone* is playing. After all, a key to doing well in business is knowing and acknowledging the rules. If some people play by different rules, it becomes important to know that, too. The bottom line is to be in a better position to avoid some of the situations and disasters that some of these women experienced.

How? By knowing better what to expect and avoiding the situation. By being in a position to call people on their games and discuss the underlying feelings that may be leading toward conflict. And, finally, by solving the problem, smoothing over ruffled feelings, and bringing a potential crisis situation to a fruitful end.

Toward this goal, we need to develop a better understanding of what motivates some women to break rules and contracts.

Chapter 8

Ms. Match

EVEN IF
THE SHOE FITS,
YOU DON'T

"Over and over she writes she is my/ friend, . . .
Writes, too, that she will come to see me, writes/
again to put it off. . . ."

Mary to Fleming
Act Three

Keeping one's word is an important part of doing business
with anyone. People make an agreement and expect the
other person to follow through. But in many of the experiences
with other women, our interviewees revealed, this wasn't done.
A large number of women had led their business associates to
expect one thing but then did another—or nothing at all.

Men also make and break their words. But, again, our research suggests that there seems to be a difference in the way
women do it. Women working together often develop close
bonds that are based on expectations of trust and intimate
personal sharing, so a broken word goes beyond the loss of
monetary gain or personal advancement to a deep feeling of
betrayal.

A BROKEN PROMISE TO
REPAY

Virtually everyone in business has experiences with people who owe money, promise to repay, and don't. But when money is lent to someone on a personal basis in the spirit of helping in a temporary fix and the borrower takes advantage of the lender, a feeling of betrayal may set in.

And as we've indicated, the hurt feelings of the lender transcend the monetary loss. Marilyn experienced just such a situation twice—once when she loaned money and her car to one woman; the second time when she again loaned her car to another woman.

Marilyn, a sales representative, met Ruth at a business networking group. They quickly became friends. Many of Marilyn's friends had moved from the area. She travelled for her work a great deal and welcomed Ruth's friendship. When Ruth called her for help, she was pleased.

Ruth's car had broken down, and she didn't have a business credit card to obtain a rental. Marilyn offered to put the rental on her card, stressing that Ruth would be responsible if anything happened. Ruth agreed. The next day Ruth was in an accident. When Ruth told her she couldn't pay back the money owed for the rental, Marilyn felt used and angry.

Marilyn now admits that she should have taken this as a warning sign about Ruth, but she didn't. After her anger cooled down, she continued the friendship. A few weeks later Ruth approached her for a $450.00 loan. She wanted to take a class on how to get better results in her life. Marilyn agreed. She thought the class would be very positive: "It seemed like it was going to really help." Ruth gave Marilyn a written IOU, payable within thirty days.

Thirty days passed. Ruth didn't pay Marilyn back. At times she was spiteful toward Marilyn, as if she had no right to get her money back. Marilyn said:

She took the class, and then she got fired from her job. She was living in a residential hotel. I found out that she owed the hotel quite a bit of money, and I started calling her to get the money back. I asked, "When am I going to get the money?" She replied, "Get off my back. You're just afraid you are not going to get the money." She turned really awful. I never got the money from her and she treated me as though I wasn't entitled to it. I felt that she had been very unethical; she had lied to me and hadn't taken responsibility. It was really a painful lesson for me.

Marilyn's experience left her feeling bitter, bewildered, and betrayed. Although she had heard similar stories about men's lack of integrity and lack of responsibility when she told her own story to others, she felt there was an extra ingredient in her experience. Marilyn had been really touched by the other woman's needs. Her own desire for personal companionship clouded her warning system. The car incident should have sounded the alarm. It didn't. But Marilyn felt Ruth was a friend and Marilyn believed women should support each other. Marilyn admits that, in hindsight, she would not have made the loan. When Ruth didn't repay her, Marilyn felt her sense of trust and warmth toward Ruth torn.

A few years later Marilyn experienced a similar incident. She lent her car to Alice, a friend whose car was being repaired and who said she did not have the $600.00 to pay the garage until the following week. Marilyn was scheduled to be away on a business trip and wouldn't need her car for a week. She told Alice that she could use her car for the week with one condition: Alice had to have her insurance company cover Marilyn's car during the time Alice used it. Alice agreed. Before she left town, Marilyn asked Alice if she had called her insurance company to arrange coverage. "Yes, yes, I'm covered," Alice assured her. Marilyn went on her business trip, assuming everything was in order.

Alice was in an accident. And she hadn't obtained insurance coverage so the accident went against Marilyn's insurance. Her rates increased, and Alice never offered to pay the difference.

Marilyn's willingness to be helpful and trusting to a person in need was violated. As she describes the incident:

> I got back and there she was in her own car, and I wondered what happened to my car. She said, "Well, I have some bad news. I rear-ended your car on the Bay Bridge."
>
> It was $2,500.00 worth of damage, which practically totalled the car. I had just put a new engine in it, even though it was an old car. Alice said her insurance company wouldn't cover it and that she didn't know what to do. I found out that I was responsible and I tried to fight it.
>
> The bottom line: it ended up on my policy, and my insurance went up a tremendous amount. She didn't even offer to pay. I thought that she should. I had to switch insurance companies and my rates still went up. She still didn't offer to pay. I thought her behavior was unethical. If I had been the borrower, I would have paid the difference on the insurance claim.

A BROKEN PROMISE ABOUT A BUSINESS ARRANGEMENT

Modern business arrangements are based on contracts—agreements or promises to perform a service or task in exchange for something. Contracts keep the wheels of commerce turning. With greater profit potential or advantages somewhere else, there are always potential threats to any particular contract, and while this is as true for men as for women, our findings show that there does seem to be a difference in the way women break contracts as well as in their motives for breaking them.

Our research indicated that men tend to be more motivated by the practical or monetary advantages and women tend to be influenced more by feelings and relationships. Men tend to be more direct and open when they decide to break; women tend to be more indirect, making it unclear whether or not the contract or agreement is still in force. Comments and stories shared by both women and men seemed to reinforce these differences.

Gail had been an elementary school teacher after obtaining a degree in psychology. Later, she obtained the necessary licenses and worked as a counselor with a variety of psychotherapies—Gestalt, Transactional Analysis, Neuro-Linguistics, and Bioenergetics. Following her dream to work with people without problems, she took a position as a sales representative for a greeting card company. She was assigned a territory in the Bay Area of San Francisco by her manager, Darlene. Gail did very well and she felt she had the ideal job. Darlene complimented her progress and told her, "As long as you're doing well, you're going to get more."

A few months later Darlene informed Gail that one of her major accounts was to be assigned to another woman who "needed more territory." Gail was furious; she had been doing well and had been promised more territory. She felt she was being penalized in having to give up an account she had spent many months developing. And—she was the only representative who was to have an account pulled. It didn't make sense financially; there was no pragmatic justification for taking the account away. Gail considered the move highly unethical. She told Darlene she would be glad to give sales and follow-up service tips to the sales representative having problems. Darlene said that wasn't an option.

Gail stood up to her. She argued that she had taken the position with the clear understanding that she was to be given certain accounts. She stated firmly:

> My bottom line answer to her was, "Well, then I quit." Her answer to me was, "Don't threaten me." I said, "It is not a threat. I will not work that way. We made an agreement. This was our agreement, and I will not work that way. I am in business to make money. I need to make money."

As a result of this encounter, Darlene backed down. "I am really good at what I am doing," Gail stated. "If you are really okay about whom you are and where you are, it is harder for other people to treat you unethically. I just would not stand for it."

Darlene's attempt at changing Gail's agreement is illustrative of a frequent style or approach that our respondents reported many women have when they seek to break agreements. Darlene's reasons for changing the original terms of the agreement were not financial. Gail was doing quite well, and the woman to whom she was offering Gail's account was not doing well; in fact, she was in trouble. It appeared that Darlene's motivation for making the change was almost a social service, an altruistic gesture to help someone out. Darlene had told Gail she was sympathetic toward the other woman; she thought that Gail would be equally sympathetic and would contribute some of her accounts to the cause. In reviewing the experience, Gail said her boss's behavior didn't really surprise her. It had been her experience while in private practice, that her clientele of women tended to act from feelings rather than rationally when dealing with problems and finding solutions.

We learned in our study that men in business tend to not feel sorry for someone not making quota. They are typically hard-nosed and no-nonsense when it comes to sales. A person either makes it or he's out. A good performance is rewarded accordingly and a poor one reaps the consequences.

In most business there is an implied understanding that one will be loyal, at least outwardly, to one's own boss and to those above one in the organization. The basic rule is to work together as a team. The players normally support those in command. By joining the team, an unwritten promise is made to support the goals and plays of that team. However, our findings strongly suggested that many women either are unaware or don't adhere to these standards. In another situation, Gail worked under Toni. She discovered that Toni undermined the reputations and power of those above her by tearing them down to others:

> She was after power. Money was part of it. But it was really power. She took on much responsibility, but she was also

pushing other people who were above her out of the way. She did all she could to badmouth her superiors.

Gail described an instance where a high-level sales manager had recommended Toni for a higher position. When she was promoted, she immediately began to knock him to the company owner.

This strategy didn't work well. Others in the company noticed Toni stepping on others in her efforts to get ahead. Gail saw that Toni's future with the company was in jeopardy. Coworkers began excluding her from company "information" that was valuable to her position.

Our research disclosed that most men, in contrast, tended to be cagier in the battle for upward mobility in the office. They present a united front for the team, even though they may resent or desire the job of the person above them. Later, at a time when the person appears weak or vulnerable, men are more likely to seize the opportunity to openly strike and attempt to get the position. But until then the group appears solid.

The strategy Toni used—attempting to discredit and demean a person through a semi-secretive backhanded means while pretending to be part of the team—is employed by many women and few men. In most interviews we conducted, it was reported that this type of strategy is more likely to fail. The perpetrator is apt to be removed from the team as others become aware of his other unacceptable action. A strategy that breaks a basic promise of trust—that as long as one is on the team, one will support it and its leadership—can be a death warrant.

A BROKEN PROMISE
ABOUT LENDING
SUPPORT

A fertile area of unethical behavior is political infighting and power plays.

Politicking goes on all the time in an organization. Coalitions or groups of people form together around a particular policy or certain individuals involved in the infighting. Perhaps the most frequent problems in these situations is concern about support and loyalty. A person makes a commitment to support someone because he or she favors that person's position, then, at a critical juncture, pulls back that support. Why? To take advantage of a better offer, or perhaps because of fear for what might happen if continued support is perceived as being wrong or inappropriate by someone more powerful.

While these issues are not the exclusive domain of either men or women, our research indicated there seem to be key differences in the reasons that women and men choose to withdraw promised support. In general, men act to take advantage of the better offer; women act out of fear. This makes sense when one considers that men often are in a more powerful situation, so they have more opportunities to move ahead, whereas women are more likely to be blocked or have feelings of low self-esteem, which leads them to respond out of fear of loss.

A typical example of this occurred for Karen. Karen worked for a high-tech company in the area of research and development. A client in the military contacted her and asked a number of questions about a project over the phone. She agreed to meet with the client to give him a technical review. Normally, a salesperson would have handled the follow-up. Karen's new boss, Ben, was in charge of both the research and development and the marketing divisions. He was dubious about the military as a market for the new technology and questioned whether the technology was sufficiently developed for military use.

However, Karen was certain there was a market with the military and that the technology would work. The potential revenues to her company were high—approximately six hundred million dollars in sales. Before setting up the meeting, she spoke to Teresa, the company's director of employee relations. She wanted to make sure she should make the trip if a salesperson didn't accompany her, as regular policy would dictate. Since the marketing department showed little interest in pursuing the account, Teresa said it was all right for Karen to go alone. In fact, Teresa urged her to go.

Teresa reminded Karen of the company's principles that were designed to encourage employee initiative. She even quoted one: "Individuals in this company are rewarded for sticking their necks out and taking risks. If they know something is right or is going to be right, we will reward them for taking the risk and making the point." Based on that policy, Teresa told Karen, "Go do it. You know that the project will be successful. You know that it is going to go, so go do it."

Karen set up the meeting. The day before she left she still felt anxious about going, and again spoke to Teresa about her concerns. Again Teresa reassured her, offering her support if any problems occurred as a result of the meeting. Karen and Teresa quickly developed a rapport. They got into the habit of lunching together frequently.

Politics and egos exist in every office. Karen's was no exception. The salesperson was upset that she had gone into his territory, even though he ultimately would get the commissions on any sale which occurred. As a result, Ben told Karen he was going to fire her. When Karen went to Teresa about it, Teresa told Karen she would help write a letter to get her job back. The letter was written to Ben's boss, the division manager. At first, the matter seemed to disappear. The division manager reassured Karen she wasn't fired and that he would find her another job in the company. He did, though, explain he would place her in another division. Even though her action was potentially of great benefit to the company, she had stepped on the toes of her immediate boss and the salesman. Karen related that he said:

> "You are probably right. We have chosen the wrong technology; the products are out there, but you don't cross somebody politically, and I can't keep you in my division and hold my division together, so you are going to have to go, but I will find you another job."

In fact, he kept reassuring her that he was doing this with the assistance of Teresa during the next two weeks.

A slowdown of orders hit the company. Personnel laid off a few employees, and Karen was the first to go. The division manager was away on vacation. Teresa was unavailable to Karen.

Karen believed Teresa's actions were unethical. Teresa's encouragement and offer of future support had led her to make the trip which caused her dismissal. When pressure was on to reduce employees, Teresa feared for her own job. Karen felt sabotaged. Ethically, Teresa should have spoken out in defense of Karen. Out of fear of a possible loss, Teresa remained silent. "Her principle was to take care of herself," Karen stated. "I'm very much convinced of that."

Karen further personalized the incident. She felt she had developed a special closeness with Teresa, and the latter's failure to come through with the promised support hurt.

Whereas men develop an "old boy" network based on shared stories, hobbies, and work, Karen, like many other women, felt that with women this connecting went deeper, was more personal. Our respondents indicated that unlike most men, most women reveal intimate personal items to each other within a short time of initial contact. When Teresa didn't support her, Karen felt doubly hurt. Besides losing her job after Teresa had encouraged her actions, she lost a friend.

This personalized "hurt" was a recurrent theme heard from women, whatever the nature of the particular offense. The men in our survey reported that they didn't feel this way: when a promise was broken, their view was more philosophical—just one of those business things.

BROKEN PROMISES AND PERSONALITIES

Still another basis for women sabotaging each other, our respondents suggested, is a pure personality clash. A woman simply takes a dislike to another, possibly because the other woman appears to be a threat to her, or she just doesn't like the other woman's style. As a result, virtually anything can become an excuse to do something to harm her. And in these circumstances, the woman may make all kinds of promises to the other which she has no intention of keeping.

Julie worked as an administrator for the female associate dean of a department in a university. The dean, Barbara, was in charge of all the students in the department and was also responsible for the house staff.

From the time when Julie was first assigned to her there were some differences of personal style which set the two apart.

This was exacerbated by other factors. According to Julie, Barbara was under a great deal of strain because of all the responsibility she had. Then, too, Barbara experienced a certain degree of mistrust from the rest of the faculty, who felt that her credentials, teaching ability, and research skills were not particularly strong, although the students seemed to think well of her. Finally, Julie found that Barbara was a very rigid type of person, who was "very positive, very absolute about every opinion that she had. When she had formed an opinion of something, she didn't allow grounds for a general discussion: what she believed was the way she wanted things to be." Julie tended to be a more informal person; she was more flexible and yielding in her relationships with others.

It is not surprising that the two women didn't hit it off right away. But what is fairly unusual is the intensity with which Barbara showed her dislike.

Julie felt that Barbara had taken a strong dislike to her as soon as she had been assigned to her. She thought that part of the reason for this might have been because she had worked previously for someone whom Barbara didn't like.

Barbara would request certain items. If Julie or others in the department didn't drop whatever they were doing and obtain the items, she would literally yell and scream at the culprit. Or, as Julie described, "She would come into the office flailing her arms and throwing things down and screaming insults at the top of her lungs." Why? It seemed that the slightest incident in which she detected a lack of immediate responsiveness would trigger her off. For example, someone would send her a memo about something which she didn't like, or she would call Julie's office and when no one answered the phone right away, would become very angry. Julie felt her reactions were in the nature of a tantrum. Moreover, when Barbara was in moods like this, she would latch onto any minor mistake that someone had made and blow it up into a major issue.

In Julie's view, she was something of a lightning rod for Barbara's reaction. It was as if Barbara blamed her personally for whatever went wrong. As Julie recalled:

> It was generally over some minor piece of paper being sent to her or the dean as chairman [that would get her upset]. The memo would say to do this, or I would call or send her a memo asking her to do that, and she would, because *I* had asked her, absolutely fly off the handle.

Barbara's reactions created a major problem for Julie's department. Often Julie simply was passing on messages from the dean which asked Barbara, as associate dean, to do something. Barbara would respond that she wouldn't comply with the request. This would put Julie in a bind: Julie would tell the dean that something couldn't be done. Then, when the dean went to Barbara to ask her about the problem Julie had raised, Barbara was suddenly very cooperative. "I would look like an absolute idiot for raising the problem in the first place and not being able to get her to comply," Julie told us.

Things got worse when the university hired a new man, who was a close friend of Barbara's, into the department. Julie felt that Barbara stacked the cards against her by regaling him with stories of her incompetence.

As the months passed Julie tried to effect a reconciliation with Barbara, but she wouldn't listen. When Julie tried to offer an explanation by saying something like, "But you have to understand that . . ." Barbara would shoot back, "No, I don't have to understand anything," and proceed to verbally demean her in front of others.

She literally became Julie's nemesis. After a while, Julie just couldn't function:

So I was, over the course of eighteen months, under a constant barrage. It became increasingly difficult for me to function in my job. Things came to me from the chair in ways that would set me up to fail. They would put me in charge of a project where she was the major cause of the problem, and then she would not collaborate, and so the project would fail and then it would be blamed on me.

Eventually, this situation led to Julie's reassignment to a position with substantially less responsibility. A new departmental manager was hired to take her place, and they upgraded the position in order to be able to pay the new person, a man, more and give him a secretary and a staff. As a result, he soon had nineteen people under him, while Julie had only five. At the same time, she was given more routine duties, so she became in effect "a glorified secretary." And yet she stayed on. Barbara's treatment of her had completely undermined her confidence; the thought of doing anything else was terrifying. As Julie described her state at this point, "I was so bewildered and terrified that I could barely function . . . I could barely read a piece of paper."

Meanwhile, the new man was taking advantage of his new administrative position by breaking university rules. He was literally paying people under the table to redirect funds that were earmarked for something else. He was running the department she used to manage as a virtual fiefdom. He was promising people jobs in his department he was not certain he had and people were arranging to sell their homes to relocate for the promised jobs. Julie worried. Barbara either didn't seem to care or looked the other way. Barbara, he, and the dean appeared to be close. It was the last straw. Julie went to the chancellor to let him know what was going on—to get some help in her own struggle against Barbara's vendetta.

When the chancellor confronted Barbara, she immediately assumed Julie was behind it. Only one other person in Julie's department was willing to come forward to back up what she claimed was going on. She was moved into a small isolated office and given little to do. It was a dose of the same kind of treatment

Julie had been experiencing for months. Shortly, Julie was out of a job.

For Julie the whole situation was devastating. At first she was literally not able to work. After approximately six months of being out of work, she applied for disability. Only now is she healing as she collects her payments and begins going back to school at a large university to take courses leading towards a master's degree in public administration.

Why did Julie stay on as long as she did? Our research indicated that many women who get caught up in unethical employment situations sometimes stick it out because they feel emotionally trapped, much like the battered wives who can't leave their husbands. One reason is that the attacks against them wear them down: they undermine their confidence; they feel increasingly bad in the situations but also are increasingly powerless to leave it. In turn, whatever they do to change things doesn't work, and they end up feeling even more powerless to get out. While men don't seem to get stuck in this way, but tend to lash out more directly with their anger or feelings of hurt, women are more likely to keep that anger and hurt inside, so it doubles back on them, intensifies, and literally destroys them. This seems to be what happened to Julie. She knew what was happening; she knew her boss was engaging in a vendetta against her; and until the very end, when she reached out, like a drowning person, to the chancellor, she kept slipping further and further down into the mire. Her boss had beaten her down, and she let it prevent her from functioning. Julie, in effect, became a collaborator in her own destruction. She could have left earlier; she could have tried to speak to someone else earlier, but she did not. Her sense of powerlessness led her to act as if she had none, and the situation grew worse. As Julie lost power, her boss gained more and more of it, which enabled the boss to engage in more and more outrageous acts.

PROMISES, POLITICS, AND MALE-FEMALE DIFFERENCES

The discussion in this chapter on how women sabotage other women through broken promises and betrayals is not meant to suggest that men don't do the same thing to women or to other men in the corporate setting. They certainly do. But our findings substantiated the fact that there are distinct differences in styles. Most men are more direct and motivated by success concerns; most women are more apt to act covertly and respond out of jealousy and fear.

Pam's story is a classic example of this difference. She was sabotaged by both a man and a woman who ended up working together against her. Each chose to do it very differently.

Pam was working as a lab director in a large high-tech firm. Her background was engineering, not a common field for a woman, and she found a lot of resistance to her getting ahead in the company because of her sex. The time was the early 1980s. Pam had helped the company establish a research lab. Initially she ran the operation, although she didn't have the title of lab director until six years later, when the company underwent a reorganization. With the reorganization, the company promoted a number of other people who had been department heads to lab directors. All were men, leapfrogging over Pam into their positions, although she had effectively been directing the lab, after having set it up, for six years. When the company decided to make a more serious commitment to high technology, the men were appointed as lab directors first and given company cars as a reflection of their importance to the company. Four months after their promotions, Pam was made a lab director. But she felt a definite chill toward her. She was not a part of the male inner circle, and she was well aware of this. As she told us:

> After a few years as a lab director, it became apparent . . . that my career wasn't going to go anywhere else. It was just dead-ended in what I was doing.

Meanwhile, as lab director, one of her responsibilities was to hire and coach new engineers—all of them men. And as she did, these men would get promoted up to lab directors too, with the possibility of even further promotion in the company. As it happened, one of these men was the one who turned on her—apparently because he found this expedient for getting ahead in the company. He was very open and direct with her about what he was doing. There was no sneaking around corners or deception, as was the case in the stories of women sabotaging women our survey uncovered. He simply came right out and told her of his intentions. Pam shared her experience:

> I had hired and helped coach a number of men engineers, and they were just whizzing right on by me. When Alan, who really turned on me, became another lab director, he just sort of took a double barrel, aimed, and fired: essentially, he said, "I am not going to work with you, and you are not going to be successful because I refuse to work with you."

Why did he do that? One reason, according to Pam, is that he may have resented her as a woman, even though she had helped get him hired and had suggested he might want to consider a managerial position in the company. Once he got the position as a first-line manager for the engineering department, his relationship to Pam changed. Perhaps he sensed Pam's lack of power in the company and may have wanted to sever himself from a close connection with her so he would have a better chance of getting ahead. In fact, as Pam described his subsequent rise in the company, this seemed to be a clear pattern with him: he would get help from someone else, then, as he rose in the company and no longer needed that person, he would turn on him or her and even try to do him or her out of a job.

Pam had first noticed this pattern emerging when, as a first-line manager, Alan began to act secretively toward her and wouldn't let the engineers under him talk to her. She had been working with these men for years and had had a comfortable, informal relationship with them. He put up a barrier between

Pam and the other engineers, telling her she could "only talk to him and he would talk to his engineers." It was his way of reestablishing the traditional chain of command to show Pam what he thought her relationship to him and his department should be.

At the same time Alan began to systematically cultivate other executives higher up who could help him move ahead in the company. He became friendly with Pam's boss, who was duly impressed by him. "He just thought Alan walked on water," Pam said. After a couple of years, Pam's boss promoted Alan to a peer level with Pam as a lab director.

That was when Alan confronted Pam with his decision not to work with her. When he was promoted, his lab was supposed to work with Pam's lab. But he told her he didn't have to work with her. In fact, he warned her, "I am going to make your life miserable." His strategy seemed to work. Pam explained:

> He climbed up the ladder. As soon as he got there, he took aim at our boss, and within a year had knocked him out. And so then he was my boss. And six weeks later, he had pulled a political coup, because what he was really after was an even higher job and he had forced them to give him my boss's job, which they did, thinking he would stay. But instead he popped to another even higher position in the company. This guy really climbed. And at this point, he went after his next boss and it took him about a year or two to undo him and he took that one over.

Alan's actions toward Pam were made in a spirit of total pragmatism. He wanted to get ahead. He saw pulling away from her, despite her initial help, as the way to do it, and so he did. Everything was up front; he told her he simply didn't want to work with her anymore, and that was that.

One of the pooled secretaries, Carol, did some of the work for Alan while he was an engineer working for Pam. Pam suspected that Carol and Alan may have had a romantic attachment, although she wasn't sure whether this was just a mild flirtation or whether it had flowered into an affair. In either case,

she noticed that something was in the air when she returned
from three weeks' vacation over the Christmas holidays. Others
in the department said that Carol and Alan had been getting
together casually for hours on end, talking about going on a ski
trip, and other things having no connection with work. So
practically no work was done.

Pam tried to talk with Carol about mixing work with personal
time. Carol got very upset with her and didn't want to talk about
it. Soon after the confrontation, Pam noticed that Carol was no
longer producing work for her.

This went on for about two weeks, while Pam was trying to
decide what to do about the situation. Then Alan was promoted
to lab director and needed a secretary. Initially, he was assigned
an older woman. Pam approached him about swapping secretaries. She felt the older woman would work out better as a
secretary for herself and she did not want to be involved with
either Carol or Alan. It seemed like the ideal resolution.

After some discussion he agreed, and the swap was made.
Then Carol began a quiet undercover campaign to undermine
Pam in any way she could. She cut Pam out of the communica-
tions chain and then denied she did anything. Pam's explanation:

> Well, Carol went with him and then she helped him prevent
> me from getting any communication. I never got any of the
> memos that were distributed. She always saw to it that they
> were misdirected or whatever. And I would find out weeks
> later that the information had been passed around and I
> had just not gotten it. Sometimes I was just totally left off
> the distribution list and sometimes I was on it and never got
> the memo. And this was eighty percent of the time.

Pam questioned Carol about this, but Carol acted as though
she didn't understand. Pam continued:

> It was useless. I would ask her a couple of times. I would
> show her a memo that one of my guys would give me that I
> had not seen and she would say, "Well, I sent it out to you.
> I don't know why you didn't get it." And then there would

be others where my name was just totally left off and I would then confront Alan about that and he would say, "Well, these things happen. Don't worry about it. Don't feel bad." And then he would pat me on the head in a very patronizing way.

Pam wasn't sure whether Alan was in on it or whether he was simply supporting his secretary. In any case, the result was the same. Pam was increasingly isolated and rendered ineffective in performing her work.

At the same time, Carol extended her sabotage to isolating Pam's secretary. Soon after the non-delivered or misdirected memos situation started, Carol began talking about Pam's secretary to others, saying how badly she did all sorts of things. Eventually, Carol formed a clique of all the secretaries in the office, excluding Pam's. The end result was that it became increasingly difficult to get any work done. As Pam explained:

They would run around and have little groups and talk about things and all. And my secretary was absolutely shunned. It just made it a very difficult working environment. You know, you can't do anything if the people you have got to work with refuse to work with you.

The upshot was that Pam eventually left the firm. Both Alan and Carol had made it impossible for her to work effectively and isolated her by turning others in the lab against her. Note that they each went about the same process of isolating her in different ways: Alan was very direct about it, and his primary motive was undercutting Pam so he could get ahead. Carol acted deceptively, denying she was doing anything to undermine Pam while, in fact, she was. Her motivation may have been status or affiliation with a perceived winner. Presumably, she was angry when Pam had called her on the suspected fling with Alan and because Pam had exchanged her for another secretary. When Carol felt angry and hurt, she reacted by covert sabotage.

Pam indicated she was quite aware of the differences between

Alan's and Carol's styles and she believed they applied to men and women generally. She observed:

> Men are much more aggressive, very much competitive. I don't think women really work well in that arena. Men will negotiate a solution, but it has got to be the best for them individually. They have to come out of a negotiation having gotten the best of the other person.
>
> Women do things indirectly. Women don't really know what the rules are. I think women have some element of this tit-for-tat type of thing, but it is usually on a much smaller level than men. It is usually very much more petty. It's smaller things they get into. Men don't usually let the small things bother them. Women don't get beyond the small things.

PARTICULAR PEOPLE
OR PATTERNS

I noticed that in talking to numerous respondents about ethical behavior in corporations that the same themes came up again and again.

For instance, Diane worked in marketing and sales in a large Fortune 500 company. She suggested that a key reason for the difference in the motivations and styles of women and men in acting unethically was the greater emotional responsiveness of women. As she said, "I think I can safely say that women have a greater tendency to be more emotional or let their emotions play parts in decision-making more so than men."

In turn, our findings seem to indicate that this emotional orientation can be one reason that women tend to be more means-oriented than men, an observation Diane made and which we have heard from so many others. Conversely, our sources disclosed that men tend to be especially concerned with results, the bottom line.

How do such differences influence unethical behavior? Our

findings revealed that men are more likely to do something unethically for non-emotional reasons. Like Alan, they are apt to act unethically when that's the way to get ahead. Their emotions have nothing to do with it. It's more of an ego decision which is ends-oriented.

On the other hand, because they are more involved in what is happening emotionally, women are more concerned about the means or the process. The way things are done becomes more important; women can become more sensitive to everyday slights. Because their emotions are closer to the surface, and because they are more means-oriented, women can get hurt more. They are more likely to act unethically for emotional reasons because they are jealous and because they want to get back at someone they believe has done something to them.

This more emotional-means orientation of women seems to be a factor in the phenomena to which Diane pointed—that women can be especially trustworthy when they are loyal; they can be especially dangerous when they are not, because then, inspired by emotional factors, they may act in a vengeful manner. Or as Diane said:

> I feel the loyalty is much greater with women—if you can trust them. There is a fine line and you have to be a people person to know that, but I think they are more loyal. Now on the other side, if you can't trust them, God, they are the worst!

Victoria told us she usually preferred to give business to a woman-owned and operated firm. She was working with a television network, and the company gave her permission to subcontract with the artist of her choice. She chose a firm headed by a woman she had worked with before and, because she felt more trust toward a woman-operated firm, she didn't require everything to be in writing as she would have if she had been dealing with men.

In this case, the woman didn't come up with satisfactory artwork. Because nothing was in writing, she refused to make good on the verbal commitment. The result was that Victoria and the network were out $3,500.00. Victoria was extremely angry. She had trusted so much more because it was another woman. The broken promise hurt, and she felt betrayed. Victoria explained what happened:

> I realized afterward that there were two things involved, and one was blind trust. I did not insist that everything be specified in writing with the same kind of clarity and detail that I would have insisted on had it been men, because I would have been coming from a slightly different place and it would have been less trusting.
>
> But even more importantly, I was absolutely beside myself with fury. The reason I was so upset and angry was that I felt *very* betrayed, because it was bad enough to be screwed, but to be screwed by a woman! That was worse. That, to me, was even more outrageous, because I couldn't deal with it by saying "Well, what can you expect?" Which I probably would have said if it had been a man. I wouldn't have felt as morally outraged because I wouldn't have expected so much.

As we talked to her about this situation and her feelings about women in the workplace, Victoria reinforced what we heard from so many other women about the greater influence of emotions on women and their focus on means rather than ends. In Victoria's view, this orientation was reflected in the fact that women tend to be more likely to respond to the *disposition* or emotional feelings at the time, rather than to the *situation* or event. Women, in her opinion, are more attuned to the ongoing process, rather than the immediate results likely to be produced. In turn, when a woman acting in response to this orientation makes a mistake, others are more likely to blame her, since she acted because of her emotion rather than in response to a more dispassionate analysis of the situation. As Victoria said:

> If a woman falls, she falls much harder than any man, because her behavior is seen as dispositional rather than

situational. Her errant behavior supposedly comes from the beast in her.

Our findings revealed that this orientation toward emotions and means also disposes women to getting stuck in the intensity of a heated interchange that occurs in the course of doing business. It can take a long time for the negative or hostile feelings to dissipate, if they ever do—or these feelings can get expressed in acts of revenge. In contrast, reports indicated that men are more likely to put the incident aside and go on to something else, which drastically reduces the chances of retaliatory unethical actions. Victoria told us that she was working for a magazine at one time and attended a meeting where the officers of the magazine were working out the details of a large loan. In the middle of the negotiations, the magazine consultant, who earned hundreds of dollars an hour, became extremely aggravated and literally threw a tantrum. She reported, "He jumped up; he was all red in the face, he was sputtering; he walked out the door, slammed it behind him, and went home! I couldn't believe what I'd seen."

After about thirty seconds of silence, the meeting resumed as if nothing had happened. When the man came back the next day, everyone acted as though nothing had happened. No one raised the subject again and when Victoria asked some of the men why, they looked at her oddly, "as though I was nuts." They simply saw the incident as an anomaly; it was over and they wanted to let it pass and get on to doing business.

Our research indicated that had a woman done something like that, and other women observed her, the effects of the incident would hang on for a long time. "If a woman ever threw a tantrum like that in a meeting of that kind, she would never walk back into that room again. Ever," said Victoria. Why? Because of the emotional residue. The woman who did it would feel ashamed. She would feel she could never face the group again and the women who observed it would feel angry and upset. They would feel hostile toward the woman for creating a scene. But men, concerned more about the ends and results rather than the means and the process, would let it go in the interest of the benefit of the project.

This may help to explain why more and more women are going into business for themselves. Once a woman becomes her own boss, she possesses power. And her concern about losing it to another in the same organization is diminished significantly. But the ethical issues are no less significant—just different.

Chapter 9

Ms. Adventure

IT'S A JUNGLE OUT THERE, JANE

"Now, what an inexperienced queen you are/ To surround yourself with such taking bitches!"
Bothwell to Mary
Act One, Scene III

Our research revealed that many women who run their own businesses run into special ethical problems which women in the corporation or large organization don't face. In the high-pressure context of corporate politics, where ethical problems often involve getting ahead or feelings of resentment when others do, ethics become tied in with alignments and associations and changing coalitions of forces.

Our evidence indicated that when women run small companies, their ethical encounters often involve disloyal and resentful employees who take advantage of their leadership, or unethical suppliers and promoters who make promises to them which aren't fulfilled or who lie.

As more and more women run their own companies and frequently work with male suppliers, bankers, salesmen and other professionals, they are better able to contrast the ways in which women and men behave unethically toward them.

Many of the women to whom we spoke had unethical experiences with both women and men. Their reporting reinforces these observed characteristic differences in the styles of men and women: men tend to be more direct and ends-oriented when they do something unethically; women tend to be more indirect, devious, and means-oriented when they act unethically.

LYING, EGO-EXPANSIVE MEN: CHEATING, EGO-DEFENDING WOMEN

Susan has been involved in a number of successful entrepreneurial ventures, including heading up a marketing company, organizing a travel sales group, writing books, and designing toys. She reported that the men who acted unethically took advantage of her lack of knowledge when she was in the early stages of each new venture and somewhat naive about each particular field.

What she also noted was that the unethical encounters with men reflected what we came to see as the classic pattern: the men lied in order to build up their own egos and achieve greater success; they wanted to come across as being more successful and powerful than they really were or wanted to cut corners to make more money; ultimately, their shells unravelled, resulting in financial damages—to Susan as well as to themselves. However, she believed, the women who behaved unethically toward her did so not so much to make more money, but because of feelings of creative jealousy.

Susan's first major unethical experience with men occurred when she was seeking funding and partners to get involved in the management-administrative end of a game business. Her research showed that there was a need for a new category of games for adults which wasn't being marketed by other major companies, and that a good way to market it was through the direct sales, party plan approach, using game parties as a way to sell the games. Other very successful companies had been propelled by the same plan. However, at the time she had little experience in direct sales, needed funding for the venture, and didn't feel she had the experience in managing a growing company—and, in fact, preferred to concentrate on the creative end of things.

Several months after she had begun looking for partners, an associate in a weekly success and motivational group she attended recommended a man she knew in the financial community. Larson, she said, had "a genius for bringing people together." Susan was elated. Larson had a small financial planning business and had experience in funding small companies. He immediately became excited about Susan's idea and agreed there was a market for such games. (This was two years before the *Trivial Pursuit* craze swept the nation!) He told her he had the perfect partner, a former corporate vice-president in a large direct-sales company. If Elliot was interested in managing Susan's company, Larson would raise the money. He told her that he had several sources of private financing and all he had to do was tell them he had a good deal; within days the money would be there.

Susan met Elliot, and after much discussion he agreed to manage the company. Larson assured Susan the money would be there—that was all that was needed to write up a business plan. Elliot offered his assistance: he already had a draft for another company in which he was interested, and he felt he could simply plug in information on Susan's project with the list of other company products. Both men believed it all could be done within a week.

There was an immediate need to get prototypes in production to exhibit at a series of major toy and gift shows that were held at the beginning of the year. Susan explained this situation to Larson and Elliot, and both encouraged her to go ahead and make the commitments. After all, they said, money would be there in a matter of days. Besides, as Larson told her, she had partners now; she was no longer alone in her business efforts, so she should feel very secure.

Susan made the commitments. She borrowed a small amount of money from her family to make the necessary deposits to the artists and printers and to hold space for a trade ad. She also continued to work with her new partners to finalize the business plan. Nothing, though, was in writing. She went along on the basis of trust, since both men seemed honest and sincere and her associate had recommended Larson.

The day that Larson planned to get the money from his private sources, he discovered that his partner in the business had been embezzling from the firm. He went into shock and disappeared from view for two weeks, abandoning any plans to work on Susan's concept and company.

Without the money, there was no company. Overnight it fell apart. Susan owed money to the artists, printers, and ad agency. Elliot never returned her phone calls or answered her letters. She thought Larson was unethical. He had made certain claims about his own business expertise and connections that he could not fulfill; as a result, when his own business fell apart, he could not keep his commitment to Susan. She was not able to get the products on the market; she lost twenty thousand dollars. She was stunned.

Some years after this, Susan met Terrance while she was marketing books on sales techniques she had written and published. He sold sixty of her books at a trade show and then asked for about a dozen more. He was running a new, purportedly non-profit trade association in the sales industry. He had a reputation as someone who was going to clean up the industry. "He had the image of a kind of white knight, who was going to take on all the scam artists who were trying to take advantage of people seeking to start new sales businesses," Susan said. "He led people to trust him to do this, and he gave talks all over the place, supposedly to collect money for this association."

At the same time that Terrance was building a reputation for himself as a dedicated savior of the industry he was using the trade association as a cover to line his own pockets. No one suspected anything at first. An impressive board with highly visible sales leaders in the industry had been selected—although its members did very little but accrue the prestige of having their names affiliated with the association. Terrance had a free hand in managing the association; it was later learned that he had mingled the association funds with his own, exhausting them.

He never incorporated the association; he simply used it as a way to get consulting business.

He never paid Susan for the books he'd sold, although he promised that he would, and claimed that the association was having some financial difficulties and that others were showing their support by waiting a few months for payment of their bills. He continued to fly around the country doing publicity for the organization and participating in trade shows. Funds were generated through consulting, and he used his trade association connections to get into sales management consulting positions in various companies. He didn't have to do anything, just lend his name. In return, he would get bonuses for sales. In reality this created a conflict of interest, but at the time no one knew this.

Susan saw him from time to time. His story was always the same: he didn't have the money to pay her just yet, but he would soon. She felt guilty asking, because he said that while others were being sympathetic and supporting the organization, she was being petty in asking for her money. She said:

> He made me feel like the bad guy for asking, and I didn't put pressure on him besides asking at the time because I didn't want to embarrass the association. I believed his story about all the wonderful things he was trying to do to help the industry.

A year later it all began to come apart. Other people in similar situations began talking to each other. Newspaper columns appeared in industry papers about how Terrance was mismanaging the association and using it to further his own ends. Ultimately, members of the board discovered he had run up thousands of dollars in debt and that he had been pocketing funds. Eventually the association collapsed and he left the state.

Just prior to his abrupt departure, Susan concluded that the only way to get her money was to sue Terrance. By then, it was too late. Though she won, she has not been able to collect the judgment. "If I knew what I know now," Susan states, "I would have done it differently. I would have gone after him for the money right away and I wouldn't have been taken in by his stories of how he was doing all this sacrificing for the association.'' Susan believes that Terrance took advantage of her and other people's trust through the vehicle of the trade association.

In discussing the situations, Susan said she felt that they reflected a recurring pattern she experienced with unethical men in small businesses: these men wanted to seem more important and successful than they really were. They lied and induced others to act based on their false claims. In the first case only Susan was affected, but in the other, numerous people were hurt:

> It was a real ego thing with them. They wanted so desperately to be successful that they made claims that weren't so. Then they played the game as if they were the people they claimed to be. Their scams were totally results-oriented. They had a vision of being successful and getting ahead, so that's what they tried to do. They weren't trying to actively hurt anyone through revenge or jealousy or anything like that. But it just didn't matter to them if anyone was hurt. They played the game to win, whatever it took. And if someone got hurt—well, too bad.

Susan's experience with a woman who behaved unethically toward her was quite different.

Susan had designed some dolls and needed models. She found Randi's name in the phone book. Initially, Susan brought her some rough sketches of her idea. A fee arrangement was negotiated. Then, because she wanted to be really fair, Susan offered her the option that after she made the initial models, Randi would get a percentage of the royalties rather than simply getting paid to make the models:

> I thought it would be fair to do this because she was making a substantial contribution to making my idea a reality. If I paid only her fee, she would get a flat amount of one thousand dollars and I would own the items. However, after I sold them for a royalty, they might be worth much more

than this. I felt that if she was willing to take a risk with me, she should get more than the initial design payment.

Susan paid Randi to make the first two models. Randi then decided she did want to work on a percentage basis, so she made about a dozen other models this way. At first, Susan offered her twenty-five percent for her contribution, but as they continued to work together, she felt it would be fairer to make it a fifty-fifty split.

Everything seemed to be fine. Randi seemed excited about the arrangement and was very productive in creating models based on Susan's ideas.

Then Susan met Alice, who expressed some interest in managing a toy company based on her ideas, and Alice presented herself as a management and financial whiz. Susan put together a business plan with herself as the creative director and Randi as production director. After initially agreeing to the plan, Randi expressed her doubts privately to Alice. She didn't feel there would be enough for her to do in the company if Susan was the creative director. She also believed that the company should include many of the toy ideas she previously had turned into models. She even expressed doubts about some of the ideas Susan wanted to include. Finally, Alice spoke to Susan, telling her that she should be listed in the plan as marketing director—a function Susan didn't want—rather than the creative director. Susan finally agreed to do what the two other women wanted, though, because that was what it would take to put the company together.

Susan returned from a trip to New York with the news that a toy company wanted to license the line of toys they had created. It took another three months to nail down the contract. Shortly after it was signed, Randi offered to make a trip to New York to meet with the company in order to make sure they did a good job in turning the prototypes into production models. She said this would be an ideal time for her to meet personally with the production people in the company. Being short of funds, she asked for a loan to cover the plane fare for her trip.

Randi made good her promise to repay Susan. But otherwise, the trip proved the turning point in their relationship. Susan explained:

> Apparently what happened when she went to New York was that she met with the production people to work out the details; she also showed them some of my rough sketches for future ideas. But the person she met with told her they weren't interested in just ideas—they were interested in the finished model. She came away with the idea that they were buying her models only; my contribution to creating them and working out the details for the final model didn't matter. I just supplied the concept and that wasn't worth very much.

Randi didn't say this outright at the time, but she alluded to it when Susan objected to something else that happened on Randi's trip. She said that because the production people liked her work, she might be doing some other work for them. "Good," Susan replied, and mentioned their previously agreed-to arrangement in the preliminary business plan she had put together for Alice, that she would share a fifty-percent split on this work.

Randi became furious. She didn't think Susan was entitled to anything if she did further work with this company. When Susan pointed out that she had made the connection and that the going agenting fee in the industry, regardless of whether their business plan applied, was usually fifty-fifty, Randi would not hear of it. In fact, she snapped at Susan, "You should be satisfied to only get a few thousand in royalties for my work. They told me they're buying the project because they like my work."

Susan was extremely angry at the implications of Randi's remark that her own contribution wasn't valuable, but she felt that in the interest of the current contract it would be best to work out a compromise. She had further conversations with Randi about her future working arrangements with the company. Finally, they entered into what Susan thought was a compromise: Susan would get twenty-five percent of any of Randi's future earnings from the company, and in turn, if Susan was able to develop any spin-off products using the toy design, then Randi would get twenty-five percent for using the image. It seemed a fair solution, and both women continued to communicate about future developments for the toy project.

Without any apparent warning, Susan suddenly got a letter from Randi stating that she had never hired Susan as her agent and didn't expect to pay her anything for future work. She claimed that any future dealings with Susan would jeopardize all of her work, since Susan would claim a piece of everything. Not only did she send this letter to Susan, she sent it to the company that was planning on developing and marketing the toys.

Eventually an agreement was reached as to whether Susan would be entitled to a commission on future work. Susan felt she had smoothed things over with Randi, salvaging the current project. She also sent a letter detailing this new understanding to both Randi and the development company, stating their agreement to work together to make the current toy line a success.

The final chapter collapsed the entire project. Just before the toys were supposed to go into production, Susan met the publisher of a new children's book company. She told him that she had some stories based on her toys that were being manufactured, and he jumped on the idea of publishing one. "Unfortunately," Susan told me, "he proved to be unethical himself. He made it sound like he had the money and connections to bring out the book, when in fact, he did not."

Susan believed this self-styled publisher was one more example of the classic male style of behaving unethically. He tried to build himself up into something he was not, and then couldn't sustain the illusion.

What led to the ultimate demise of the project was Randi's teaming up with him. According to Susan:

> I let Randi know about this project and told her she would get twenty-five percent for the use of her images, as we had previously discussed, and she agreed. But then after I introduced her to David, things began to change. At first I

thought it was a good idea, because I thought we could all work together to make the project a success. I wasn't aware at the time that he lacked the money and expertise to pull it off. But initially, everything seemed fine. Randi seemed really enthusiastic about his interest, even smoothing our previous conflict over the commission arrangements.

When David made some suggestions about changing the look of the toys to match some of his publishing ideas, they seemed to be helpful and Randi jumped at his suggestions.

As it turned out, his ideas continued to change, creating a great deal of confusion for the toy company. He ran into problems with his first artist when he repeatedly changed his mind about the look of the toys and didn't have the money to pay the printer. He didn't tell Susan. Instead he convinced Randi that the printer had tried to steal his story and had a lawyer send the printer a threatening letter. Finally the two of them confronted Susan, claiming they needed to present a united front in dealing with the toy company so they didn't look ridiculous:

> It was incredible. It was my idea to begin with. The two of them came to me saying that he had rewritten my story so he could be considered a co-author, although he was still willing to grant me credit! He implied that with the changes he had suggested, the idea I had sold to the toy company was no longer mine. I had only supplied the concept. What they were really buying were Randi's models. The implied threat hung in the air. If I didn't go along with their decision to present a united front to the toy company, I would be out. He would publish the book with her images, using a modified concept; she could simply work directly with the company using her images, since the project was now based on a different concept.
>
> I had brought the two of them together. I had connected her with the company. And now she was working together with him to possibly push me out of the whole project. Adding insult to injury, she said she wanted to share equally

in any use of the images and she wanted full control over how they were expressed in any spin-off projects.

Susan felt helpless and furious, but she felt she had no choice. It seemed better at the time to be three-way partners on the book and let the doll project go ahead with the changes than to suddenly lose everything.

However, the publisher was unable to publish the book. David and Randi claimed they were going to deliver new artwork for the toys based on the book, but they didn't. Missing the deadline resulted in not getting into the toy company's catalog and the doll was ultimately dropped from their line.

In hindsight, Susan feels that if she had simply told the toy company that the book was not going to be published and to use the original toy models, the project could have been salvaged. Instead, it was scrapped.

When it became clear that the toys wouldn't be produced, Susan spoke to Randi about what happened:

> What was even more incredible was that she actually blamed me because I had introduced her to David in the first place. And then she proceeded to insult me and said that I shouldn't consider myself a toy designer; that I shouldn't write children's books; and that she felt she had a perfect right to make and sell toys on her own based on the models we had created together. When I said that I had originally come to her with the idea and paid her for the first models, she said I already had the original prototypes and that the money I had paid was for that and only that; that she could have dreamed up the concept herself in the first place, so she considered anything she created her own. Besides, I did so many other things, why did I have to try to cut in on her design field, too? I really couldn't believe it. Here the whole thing had started off as my idea, and now she was claiming ownership of the whole thing.

Susan hasn't spoken to Randi since, deciding not to contest her claimed rights to the toys. She feels certain that Randi was just expressing her own anger because the project collapsed and was really powerless to do anything about it:

> In that conversation it suddenly all came together for me. I realized what was going on and why she was so angry with me. She kept changing our agreement as the project developed and every time I introduced her to someone, I realize, she joined with them in this alliance. I think that a key reason for this is she must have felt a great deal of creative jealousy, because I do so many things successfully.
>
> She couldn't handle that I might contribute something in her field, too. She seemed to have a need to downplay my contribution because she was so insecure herself. So she did things behind my back to build herself up with the people I connected her with, and then tried to undermine what I had done with them so she could work with them directly. And she didn't want to acknowledge my contribution either as a creative designer who had the original concept or as an agent who had made a connection for her.

Qualitatively, Susan's experience with the woman who treated her unethically was extremely different from her experience with unethical men. Susan felt that all of the men acted as they did out of motivation to get ahead. They wanted to build up their egos, and they lied to do it—though ultimately none of them was able to follow through—and all the projects failed. She felt Randi's motivation was different from the men's. Susan believed Randi acted out of jealousy and because of her own insecurity, building herself up by putting Susan down.

When Randi remarked during her last conversation with Susan, "You have so many things, and I only have toys," Randi's underlying motivation became clear to Susan. "I suddenly recognized her jealousy at my creativity and her fear. That was why I feel she did what she did."

MEN DO IT FOR SELF-PROTECTION; WOMEN FOR REVENGE

Mary, another woman we interviewed, had similarly contrasting experiences with men and women who treated her unethically. And, like Susan, she felt there was a marked difference in their styles. Mary believed the men were motivated by pragmatic reasons, related to the desire to achieve or maintain an image of success; she thought the women were motivated by emotional reasons, particularly jealousy, and they assuaged these feelings in backstabbing and "revenge."

Mary ran a small advertising and public relations agency. The majority of her employees were women. Her name was on the door as the head of the agency; her employees did most of the work independent of Mary's direction, although various strategies were reviewed weekly. Mary devoted most of her time to outside speaking engagements and teaching workshops and classes. Through these efforts, she created widespread visibility for her firm and gained numerous clients.

Through these outside activities Mary met and hired a full-time accountant independent of her CPA firm and a manager to oversee the everyday operations. Routine functions were left to her trusted employees to handle largely on their own.

Several mistakes were made in doing the annual audit, and the wrong documents were filed with the IRS. In the ensuing investigation, negative publicity began appearing about the firm with Mary featured in the newspapers. She attempted to combat the charges, but the damage already was done. A PR firm getting bad PR, whether justified or not, creates a serious problem for that company, its owners, and its employees.

In the course of trying to offset this bad press, Mary discovered that one of her employees was actively fanning the flames by contacting the newspapers, the broadcast media, and even Mary's alma mater. Why? Mary sensed that Nancy had held a grudge against her for a long time. She had criticized Nancy's work several times and had told her she wasn't producing. Mary had come close to firing Nancy on several occasions but had kept her because she wanted to give Nancy a chance. Long before the fiasco with the IRS, one of the firm's clients had called Mary and had told her that Nancy was getting ready to start her own business, had approached several of the company's clients on the side, and had done some business outside the firm. When Mary confronted her, Nancy denied it. Mary believed that when the IRS investigation hit, Nancy saw it as a chance to retaliate.

Mary said that one of her greatest assets was that she was very trusting. It also proved to be one of her greatest liabilities. It took a while for Mary to learn exactly what Nancy was doing. When she did, she was shocked. Apparently, Nancy had taken Mary's files from the office and had called the editors of several newspapers in the area to make accusations. She charged that Mary took money from clients and then didn't provide them with any of the promised services. She also implied that Mary had failed to put funds which clients advanced for advertising into the trust account. The damage was done. When Mary realized the source and confronted her employee, Nancy left the firm, denying all accusations and saying, "You're always trying to put the blame on me. And you think you're so terrific. Well, you'll see. You think you've got it all, but you don't and you won't."

Eventually, some of the papers ran retractions, but buried them in the back pages.

Analyzing the situation later, Mary felt that Nancy was motivated by more than criticisms of her work. "This was not mere anger," Mary said, "I'm convinced she was deeply jealous and power oriented. She had a great need not to be wrong or to admit a mistake. When I confronted her about trying to start her own business and not working well with me, I think I triggered her anger. And then, because I was very successful, I think she felt badly about herself."

Nancy turned her anger and resentment into a one-woman crusade against Mary. Former clients made statements to the newspapers that they only dealt with Mary and they were dissatisfied with the services they received. What records remained showed that it was Nancy who had worked with these people.

Some time later, Mary discovered that Nancy had taken her list of clients and actively solicited them:

> But that wasn't all; not only was she trying to get new business, but she contacted several of my clients and suggested that they might have grounds to sue me because they didn't get the publicity expected. Realistically, it's understood that you can't guarantee the results of a PR campaign. You can only make your best efforts. In most cases, someone else in the firm was personally handling the account, not me. But she really seems to have wanted to get back at me. Friends in the business have called and said that she constantly talks about me, almost as if it's an obsession.
>
> Even today, if there's a story or an announcement that I will speak locally, the old newspaper articles are sent to the paper. Who does it, I don't know, but I can't help but wonder.

Mary's experience with another woman who tried to sabotage her was similar.

Carol specialized in advertising. Both women had been close friends for some time, and had frequently cross-referred. Through a mutual client Mary learned that Carol had been adding extra charges or had received deposits for work she didn't do. As a result, Mary lost some of her own clients, since she had made the referrals. Eventually, Carol declared bankruptcy. Meanwhile, some of the clients who experienced damages sued Mary, causing her to spend a significant amount defending herself in court. Ultimately, she won. Mary thought that Carol was angered by her success in extricating herself from the joint actions arising from Carol's sabotage and that Carol initiated a campaign against her. Carol's boyfriend called many of Mary's clients to complain about her work, claiming that he wanted to get some references to make a decision about hiring her to do some publicity. He even called Mary and threatened to call other clients and say that she had lied and cheated unless she supported Carol in these court actions:

> The whole thing was a big mess. Carol was doing about everything she could to get back at me when she was the one who screwed up in the first place. It's as though she wanted to bring me down with her. And then, when I succeeded in separating myself from her actions, she sought revenge, much as Nancy did. The major difference was that Carol got others to do her dirty work, while Nancy did it herself.

Carol's efforts to get back at Mary also continued for months. She would park in front of Mary's house and refused to return money Mary had previously loaned her, although a promissory note had been signed. She even slipped into Mary's office one night and destroyed some of her papers.

"What really distressed me," Mary said, "is the way she continued to put so much energy into getting back at me. She was really stuck in all that emotional baggage, and she kept acting out her hostility. She couldn't seem to let it go."

Mary's experience with a man was quite different. It occurred soon after all the negative publicity about Mary's company broke. She had known Harry, the director of a small seminar and educational business, for several years, and considered him a close friend. She gave some classes and seminars for him. She and her husband would occasionally go out socially with Harry and his wife. When the negative publicity hit, Harry suddenly didn't want to have anything to do with Mary. He and his wife dropped her and her husband, even calling and excluding them from a party at their home. He cancelled her classes for the next seminar catalog. Mary found that most of her other friends rallied while she went through her ordeal with the IRS. But Harry pulled away:

I was hurt. He was supposed to be a good friend. A close friend stands by you and supports you when the chips are down. Harry didn't. He was judgmental. I felt he had already tried and convicted me in his mind. And he not only dropped me, but he gave my classes to someone he had met through me, someone I had trained. When I ran into him at social functions, he studiously avoided me.

Mary was both amazed and upset at these actions. When she tried to confront Harry one day when she saw him at a political meeting, she said, he denied avoiding her, giving her a false excuse about dropping her classes:

He said he decided to do this, because "you can't teach here and teach for other organizations as well." His excuses were lame. I had been teaching at several other organizations for years; several of his other seminar leaders did plenty of freelancing, too. As I later heard from other friends, his reason was that he didn't want to be around anyone who seemed like she was failing. Or, as he put it to one person, he didn't want to have any cloud connected with his classes. He literally disconnected from me.

Since he had been a close friend, Mary saw his actions as a personal betrayal. "I feel that being a friend carries a responsibility. I guess Harry didn't share my opinion. I finally put my feelings in a letter to him. I never received a response."

For months she felt very angry about what he did. Mary's sense of personal betrayal was deep. Eventually, the bad publicity blew over, and Mary survived and continued her work. Her attempt to patch up her friendship with Harry failed. A few years later she ran into him at a benefit. Although he made no direct amends, he referred to things past being over.

But Mary no longer trusted him: he had betrayed her trust. Thinking about the situation later, she noted that the two women who tried to sabotage her had betrayed her trust, too. Yet, as did Susan, she felt there was a distinct difference between the styles of unethical women and men.

With the women, the triggers of their actions were personal; the vendettas against her were energetic and drawn out. However, with the man it was pragmatic: he didn't want to have his name linked to that of someone who was in legal or professional trouble. Any feelings of friendship didn't matter. As soon as Mary's problem subsided, he was back, ready to be friends again, totally oblivious to her own feelings of hurt and betrayal. He appeared willing to put every conflict between them aside. Mary felt the issue for him was keeping up appearances of success by having people around him who shared that image. It was in that frame of mind that he pushed Mary away. Harry treated others who experienced negative life situations similarly because he wanted to be around successful people and not affiliated with failure.

Whether in the corporation or self-employed, women can be the recipients of unethical behavior. But when that behavior originates from another woman, our respondents reported that it often involves revenge as a motive and deception as a tactic— deception that, camouflaged by a soft, feminine personality, can be a particularly deadly weapon.

Chapter 10

Ms. Cast

REVENGE IS
ITS OWN REWARD

*"My lord, my lord, it is hard to thrust a queen/
from her throne, but suppose a queen were led to
destroy herself, led carefully from one step to
another in a long/descent until at last she stood
condemned among her/own subjects, barren of
royalty, stripped of force . . ."*
                    Elizabeth to Burghley
                    Act One, Scene II

A s the women in our survey told their stories of unethical ex-employees, business associates, and partners, the evidence indicated that there was a kind of unexpected ruthlessness about many of the women perpetrators. On the surface, they seemed to the victims to be nice, friendly, helpful, vulnerable, even needy—someone one would trust. But then, beneath that seemingly supportive, calm exterior they plotted devious schemes that ultimately caused incredible pain. What made it even worse was that often the perpetrator had once appeared to be a friend.

What was significant about these stories—the victims seemed to agree—was the way many of the unethical women involved were able to disarm and mislead the victims. The great majority felt that if the perpetrators had been men, they would have been more wary. But they had felt that women would be more trustworthy.

When they were hit, then, the attack was more unexpected and deadly. It didn't seem to matter about the context—unethical women entrepreneurs, politicians, in corporations, in publishing, wherever—there was a ruthless, go-for-the-jugular quality. Their victims came out of the experience feeling devastated, betrayed, and shaken.

THE CLASSIC CON GAME

Sam, who ran a magazine publishing company, experienced one of the most dramatic examples of this kind of ruthless behavior.

It began innocently enough when Sam's friend, James, called to say he had met a woman who had an interesting business idea, and he wanted Sam to meet her. He invited Sam to spend a few days with him. Sam had known James for ten years. He trusted him and decided to fly to Palm Springs to hear more and meet the woman. As he told us:

> This is a guy who, on a personal level, I trust. He's a wheeler-dealer in real estate and things like that. I wouldn't want to be on the other end of some of his deals, but between the two of us, there's always been straight talk.

When Sam met Alexis, he was already primed to be receptive. She was an attractive, articulate woman in her mid-to-late thirties. She presented herself as vulnerable, needing his help to succeed in business. As Sam looked back, he felt she really was a master at appearing almost helpless.

Alexis explained her plight to him as they sat around the pool:

> "I just broke up a partnership. It was an unfortunate thing. The guy owes me a whole bunch of money, he is in trouble because of his ethics and tactics, and I heard he's in jail. So, I'm starting this thing now all by myself here. I need

some help. James says you have a merchant account for your business.''

She said she sold investment-quality coins and had lists of people and their phone numbers from all over the country to whom she sold the coins over the phone, along with an incentive trip to Mexico or Hawaii. The coins only cost her a few hundred dollars, as did the trip package. She would resell both for twenty-five hundred dollars. It sounded immensely profitable. But Alexis needed a merchant account so she could process each credit card purchase. If Sam would allow her to use his number, she was prepared to offer him a third of the receipts for each charge.

The project seemed foolproof to Sam. He wouldn't have to pay anything out to do this. There would be just a few minor administrative costs, and Alexis agreed to guarantee all the paper. As he explained:

> She was going to get all the authorizations, do all the work. All she had to do was run it through our account and we would then remit to her by wire transfer the same day. It seemed straight. So we worked up a contract and she signed it. All invoices were to be guaranteed by her. She would warrant that they were all valid, had been authorized, and so forth.

It sounded good. And she made her pitch so sincerely, even winsomely, that Sam threw his hat into the ring with her. Thinking he would be getting a windfall from a legitimate operation, he set up procedures for handling her orders as soon as he returned to his home in Northern California. Within days, they started coming in—a few at first, sometimes as many as five or seven a day. Using the authorization number Alexis had given him, he deposited the charge vouchers to his account, withheld thirty-three percent, and sent her the rest. As with all his charge customers, Sam sent out copies of the sales slips to the buyers to notify them that he had processed their orders.

Within another week Sam began to get phone calls from

surprised customers saying, "I never ordered the stuff"; "I don't know anything about this." When he called Alexis, she was completely cool. She had an easy explanation for what "must have" happened. "Oh, he must have gotten the bill and his wife didn't tell him"; "Oh, he must have ordered the stuff and didn't want his wife to know he's spending the money"; "The guy must have forgotten he ordered it"; or "We got him so absorbed in the trip to Mexico that he didn't realize he was ordering coins."

She seemed so sincere and believable. Sam accepted her explanation after she reassured him that she would take care of it and call anyone that questioned the charge. She even called him back to say she had resold the people who expressed some concern: "It's all taken care of." To avoid confusion in the future, she told Sam, she had hired a verifier, someone who would do nothing but call the customer back within twenty-four hours to verify the order.

However, complaints continued, and after about two months the whole deal began to fall apart. The total received amounted to approximately two-thirds of the original order. Shortly after Sam told Alexis he wanted to end the arrangement, the storm hit. "The bank terminated our merchant account and started charging back our accounts, far in excess of what we had in a reserve fund. Of course, we were liable, so the bank sued us. We are into the bank," Sam said. The total was $278,000.00— which represented the one hundred and five orders Alexis had run through his account.

Sam went to the police. They referred him to the FBI, which in turn decided to prosecute, recognizing that Sam was the victim of a scam, not a part of it. Alexis's fraud had triggered a domino effect. Not only did Sam's company go out of business, but the issuing bank went under. The bank trustees are suing his defunct company. Sam still has to defend himself in the pending suit.

So why did this particular scam happen? After all, scams are in the headlines daily. And what was so special about what this woman did? Sam felt that her vulnerable behavior was the key to his believing her in the first place and for letting things go on as long as they did. Initially, she seemed so open and upfront—and helpless. He said he didn't have the kind of initial suspicions or cautions he ordinarily would have had if he had been dealing with a man. Her femininity caught him off guard. And she used this facade to manipulate and control to achieve her criminal ends. Sam said:

> I think her approach was different in the sense that a man dealing with a man that he didn't know would have dealt in a more macho way, like "I got a real deal for you and this is what's in it for you and this is what's in it for me."
>
> She came into it with soft power. There was a real seductive quality to her. She's good. Oh, was she good! She could take the gold right out of your teeth. She didn't come on in a kittenish, seductive way but as a woman who really has her act together and who's got a couple of kids to support, who's separated, and who is really trying to make it with her resources and really do a good job. She would recruit support right away so that any of the doubts I had early on were resolved in her favor. And when she told me it was taken care of, I believed her. But if it had been a man, I think I would have asked for proof. Show me. Give me a delivery receipt. I think I would have been far more skeptical.

Alexis used her softness as a cover under which she was able to ruthlessly pursue her devious schemes. This unexpected ruthlessness appears to reflect a trait which some women have acquired as a kind of survival tool in the business world. "In fact, sometimes women have to be more masculine than men in order to survive the rough-and-tumble business world. They have to be hard, they have to be tough. They have to out-macho the macho," Sam observed.

Alexis certainly had this quality, although her scheme unravelled. As of this writing, she is in jail.

As for James, the man who introduced her to Sam—he also went to jail. Two months after his incarceration, he died of a heart attack. "I can't help thinking that his guilt was a factor," Sam noted.

BATTERY IN BUSINESS

Many women we interviewed felt that women with legitimate business goals in mind also can become extremely ruthless, especially when they are motivated by jealousy or revenge against a woman they resent, because she has become more successful than them. This happened to Mary Emily when she was starting her own business. Like Sam, she came out of the experience feeling shaken and devastated.

The incident occurred in the mid-1970s when Mary Emily was first getting into hairstyling. She was considering a fifty-fifty partnership with Carol, a woman in her fifties, who operated a facial salon. She was hesitant, though, since she had observed Carol being pushy and manipulative with others. They finally agreed to set up their businesses separately but side by side at the same location, sharing the rent; Mary Emily had a hair salon and Carol had a facial salon.

In the beginning everything was fine. Mary Emily wasn't making very much money, but the arrangement was beneficial for both women. Mary Emily brought in much of the new business. Women who had their hair done might subsequently arrange for Carol to do their facials, and vice versa.

Over the next five years Mary Emily began to get some television exposure, and her reputation grew. More and more people began to seek her out; and many clients thought she owned the whole business. While Mary Emily was gregarious and outgoing, Carol was quiet and even intimidated by others.

Mary Emily sensed Carol's anger toward her. As she told me, "About five and a half years down the line I could feel a lot of hostility toward me about my success; I had so much exposure, was getting better and better, making more and more money."

Then, when she planned to put on a seminar series about

beauty, Carol's anger bubbled over: she tried to stop it. Mary Emily recounts the experience:

> Once she found out that I was giving these seminars, she didn't like it at all. She felt that I was getting too powerful, that I was getting too far ahead of her, that I was getting too much publicity. And so she had her attorney draw up a contract to sue me so that I couldn't do the seminars. And there was no legal way she could stop me from doing them. It was just harassment on her part. She just wanted me out of the salon.

Mary Emily viewed Carol's objection as jealousy and hostility, pure and simple. Carol saw that Mary Emily was making at least as much money as she, with fewer employees, and she was jealous. "She felt that if she could squeeze me out, she would be able to take over the hairstyling and get that money. So she sued me."

But Mary Emily didn't leave—at least not then. They had a lease and she was determined that Carol wasn't going to push her out. There was one minor detail, though. She hadn't realized that Carol was going to step up her attacks, creating a climate of total hostility and fear for Mary Emily. Carol combined the silent treatment she had been giving Mary Emily with a series of rules and restrictions designed to hem in Mary Emily and her clients. At home, Mary Emily cried frequently because she felt so harassed. She said:

> For the whole eight or nine months I stayed on at the salon after she sued me, she never spoke to me once. It created such an incredible atmosphere that it made everyone else uncomfortable. It came to the point where I finally said, "Well, I am going to leave," and the last month I was there, she wouldn't let me use the bathrooms. I was forbidden to use certain parts of the salon. My clients couldn't wait in the main area. Well, you can imagine what kind of conflict that created for clients. They were very confused. It was very upsetting.

Then, in the last days she was there, Carol hired away one of the women Mary Emily had trained by offering her more money:

> She said, "I will give you twice what Mary Emily is paying if you'll work for me." So right then and there it was like a double whammy. The girl that I had sent to beauty college, the girl that I had trained, liked money more than she liked me and started working for Carol. So she just completely left me. Not only that, she had access to all the resources that I used. She got their names and addresses and started ordering the products that I had been carrying.

Mary Emily felt completely betrayed. As she explained:

> By the time I left it was just horrible, and I feel that it was because she just became jealous of me, of my popularity, of my being able to make good money, and she just couldn't take that competition any more, so she found a way to harass me. There was no legal way she could get me out, but she made it so unbearable to be there that of course I had to leave. I couldn't concentrate or do my work in such an atmosphere. I really feel it was a big sabotage.

Mary Emily later learned that Carol had been just as ruthless and vicious with some of her own employees. Carol literally sought to trap people into working and staying with her:

> She would get foreigners, people who hardly spoke English, and because she spoke their language, she would hire them and intimidate them so much that they were afraid to leave. As they told me later, she said that if they ever went out in their own businesses, she would make sure that they would go under in some way—she physically threatened them.

In the end, Carol's behavior backfired on her. Soon after Mary Emily left, six of Carol's key salon people also left. The remainder trickled away; several opened their own businesses. Eventually Carol's business went under. Meanwhile, Mary Emily thrived in her new location.

Mary Emily felt that Carol's hostile behavior was in part motivated by Carol's difficult childhood:

> She had to fight for everything she had. She had been persecuted as a child. So I think this was just a natural progression for her, to fight for this. She saw something being taken away from her when I happened to start making money. She felt threatened as she had when she was younger.

In any event, Carol's attacks on Mary Emily were personally devastating:

> When this happened, I was so shocked and so crushed that a person I had known for that many years would do this to me, I couldn't even approach her. I just wanted to get out. Once I realized her real hate for me, I didn't want to talk about it. I didn't even want to stay. And I knew she would drop the suit if I left, because basically that was all she wanted.

Past relationships, trust, fair business practices—none of that mattered. Carol was willing to do whatever she felt she had to to gain her ends.

Both Alexis and Carol showed the dark side of women learning to be assertive and aggressive to get what they want in the business world: a ruthlessness that does not care about its devastating effects on the victims.

POLITICS, POWER, AND PIRANHAS

Our research revealed that politics is another arena in which some women have encountered this tough-minded ruthlessness. Rachel had been involved in volunteer politics for years. She had just wound down a business when she ran into an old college friend who was also active in party politics. Heather had helped out in fund-raising and public relations for campaigns in the past. She suggested that Rachel run for office at the state level. Rachel related:

> It was Heather's idea. She talked me into doing the thing in the first place. I recall her saying, "Why don't you run for this office? You're in between one business and another, and it is absolutely the ideal time. You don't like this guy who's running now. So why don't you do it?"

Others in the party told Rachel her chances of winning were nil. Knowing the odds were against her, she still felt it would be a worthwhile experience. It would give her a forum to get some of the women's issues she endorsed on the table.

She accepted the challenge and unexpectedly won the primary. Then Heather appeared at her victory party and announced to everyone that she was going to be Rachel's campaign manager. Rachel was completely surprised by this announcement, since no formal arrangement had been made between the two.

A few days later Rachel sat down to breakfast with Heather to discuss the possibility. Heather was convincing. She said, "I'll advance the money and I'll take care of everything," and went on about her experience in the political arena.

Rachel had some qualms, yet she didn't say no. By default, Heather became *her* campaign manager; Rachel just let it happen. Day after day, the involvement grew. Neither took the ordinary precaution of writing down agreements or making it clear exactly who was responsible for what.

In hindsight, Rachel said that Heather eased herself in by buying her way into the campaign. She advanced all the money to get the campaign started and then, as Rachel described, "She considered it, in effect, her campaign." Initially, Rachel thought she would just go ahead and do what she had done in the primary, which was "work hard, do things, but continue to run on a shoestring." She had raised ten thousand dollars in the primary, and she intended to use the same strategy.

However, Heather's approach to winning the campaign was different. With her smooth and convincing style, she talked

Rachel into running a large-scale campaign and persuaded her that she could get money because she knew all the right people. Heather assured Rachel that she would advance the twelve thousand dollars to fund the campaign. Rachel's understanding was that with her fund-raising skills, Heather would raise the money to pay herself back. She clearly recalled Heather saying, "You will never have to pay anything in this campaign. I will see to that."

Looking back, Rachel realizes that certain things should have been spelled out. There should have been a written agreement. There should have been a written understanding about what would happen if monies weren't raised as expected. There should have been some limits placed on how much would be spent:

> She spent more money than we took in and her famous fund-raising skills did not turn out to be as advertised. I thought what was important were the issues and speaking up. But in retrospect what was important was the money and how the campaign finances were run. And it made me look like a hypocrite out there running around talking about good and ethical government when I found out later that her sense of ethics and mine were completely divorced from one another.

Rachel did not win the election. That was no surprise. The surprise came when she ended up with all the excess campaign debts. It had been Rachel's campaign in name only. Heather had kept her in the dark about the money. And the campaign was a financial disaster. After it was over, Heather assured Rachel that she would organize some fund-raisers to pay off the debt. Rachel was unaware of the extent of the debt:

> I still believed her. She said she was going to run all these fund-raisers. I didn't know what the debt was until January, two months after the election. She kept that away from me. She wouldn't allow me in my own campaign office, except to come in once in a while and shake hands with the staff.

She hired the staff. She informed me that it was her money; it was her campaign. I was supposed to do what I said I wanted to do, which was spend my time in the precinct giving speeches, writing articles, laying the issues out.

These assurances were not made in writing. And the fund-raisers scheduled were too little and too late. Then, when her fund-raising efforts didn't work, Heather turned around and sued Rachel to get back her original seed money:

> I ended up having to raise ten thousand dollars to pay off third-party debts, and then I paid thirty thousand dollars out because of the lawsuit. So thirty thousand dollars of my own money went down the tubes. It was a big lesson to me. I found out afterwards that when you run a campaign for public office, no matter what is done in your name and who takes responsibility, it is your responsibility because it is your campaign.

Rachel had trusted Heather blindly. "I guess she figured that I was just a pigeon," said Rachel sadly. "She wanted to build a track record. She had never been a full-fledged campaign manager. And she saw me as a way to do it. With my silent endorsement, she secured other campaign positions. Paying ones."

And so she did. She got some paying candidates, shelving many of the plans she had made for Rachel. When she sued Rachel to get back her money, she played even dirtier still. She made sure that people would back her up on her claims of having made no assurances to Rachel about never having to pay her back. How? By blackmail. Rachel said:

> I found out afterward that she had blackmailed enough officers and other elected officials by having information about their mistresses or lovers, or this or that, that there were a lot of people too scared to take her on.

In losing the campaign, Rachel lost thousands of dollars that she had never thought were at risk.

"But what if you had won?" we asked her. "Do you think Heather's piranha-like tactics might not have happened then?" Rachel replied:

> It would have been worse. She expected to get power in government through me. If I had won, she would have demanded to manage my Sacramento office, and she would have been a disaster. If I had denied her that, it would have been bitter, very bitter. And you know what? My little inner voice had told me, "Don't get involved with this woman, there is something wrong."

But Rachel didn't listen. Heather's offer seemed too good to refuse. In the end, Heather not only caused everything to fall apart because she couldn't live up to her promises, but she also attacked her victim. Rachel's money was gone; Heather's wasn't.

THE CORPORATE JUNGLE

Many other women and men in corporate businesses to whom we spoke had their own encounters with those they termed *incredibly vicious women* who they felt acted out of jealousy, greed, or anger.

When Hilary was promoted from secretary to administrator in a large company, the undercover attacks began. She was relatively new at the company but had been promoted because she took on some extra work and was going to school for management training. The other secretaries were outraged. They gossiped about her behind her back, and then acted as though she didn't exist when she was around. Hilary explained:

> There was such an uproar about that promotion that the women in the secretarial group totally ostracized me. They would not talk to me. They would not help me. There was tremendous resistance.

In fact, the secretaries nearly derailed her promotion. Her promotion papers were put on hold for a while, disappeared in official channels, and had to be redrawn. Eventually her boss went to the president of the company and got things moving again.

This was not the first time Hilary had experienced sabotage by a secretary. At one time she worked with Ward, a paralegal who travelled around the region taking depositions and writing wills. Sometimes they would be gone for whole days taking depositions and meeting with clients of the firm. At that time Ward was involved with Mona, his secretary. In fact, Ward was in the process of a divorce so that he and Mona could marry. Mona was not pleased that Hilary and Ward had to spend so much time together preparing for their cases.

Mona never voiced her anger, but bided her time until she saw her chance to "get back" at Hilary for spending so much time with her boss and lover. It came while Ward's wife's attorney was questioning Mona: she dropped the bomb that Hilary was also involved with Ward. The law firm's senior partner called Hilary in and asked if the accusation was true, and Hilary responded, "Of course not. No."

It didn't do any good. Mona's lie cost Hilary her job. She was implicated as a co-respondent in the divorce action. The partner told her, "Well, even if you're not involved, we certainly can't have you working for him while he's going through a messy divorce." She was asked to take a leave of absence, but she never went back. As it turned out, she was never called to court or named as co-respondent in any official papers. "But because the company didn't want to be implicated, I couldn't work for Ward anymore."

Subsequently, at another firm, Hilary met Fred, whom she later married. Fred, before dating Hilary, had been seeing Natalie, a secretary who worked for him.

Natalie never expressed her feelings to Fred or Hilary. Instead, she started an attack of quiet sabotage against Hilary. Hilary's career objective was to become a manager and she had shared that dream with Natalie during coffee breaks. Natalie took systematic steps to undermine Hilary's work. One technique was simply to take things Fred needed from Hilary's desk. Hilary commented, "There were things that disappeared from my desk. They were literally destroyed—memos, letters."

Another strategy was to drop comments that were unfavorable or degrading. The grand finale was when Hilary discovered a series of unfavorable letters and reviews in her file. And the discovery came about by accident! One of her friends had been asked to update and verify that all employee files were current. She mentioned to Hilary that she was surprised at the number of unfavorable references to Hilary's work in the file, all dated within the last few months. Hilary made arrangements to see the file.

Though Hilary was able to have the letters destroyed later, the extent of the damage done by the reports is unknown—anyone in management might have seen them. There was no way to tell, though there was no question that the charges in the letters were misleading and untrue. Signatures, including Fred's, had been forged on negative letters. A lot of time and thought had been put into completely discrediting Hilary.

Hilary could never prove that Natalie was behind these actions. However, Hilary was quite certain where the responsibility lay. She said:

> Although Fred had broken off with Natalie long before I went to work with the company, she still had to work for him and was just absolutely livid about the whole thing—there was a tremendous amount of slander and gossip.
>
> You can fire someone for putting false records in your file. But how could I prove it was her?
>
> Eventually, I confronted her with the accusation, saying it wasn't appropriate to say things about me at work or to do anything with my file, however angry she may feel about what happened with Fred. She never admitted writing the letters, but after that the harassment stopped.

Hilary felt Natalie's attack was spiteful and malicious. Natalie had nothing to gain by derailing Hilary's career; they worked in different departments, and Hilary and Fred already had made plans to marry. But Natalie must have felt that Hilary had wronged her. Her attack on Hilary was the only way Natalie felt she could get revenge—by defaming Hilary without revealing herself.

TWO WRITES MAKE A WRONG

Lana found herself at the receiving end of a vendetta with a woman who began by helping her out but then turned that help into a quagmire of legal threats. Again, there was an innocent, unsuspecting start and an uproar of a vicious attack at the end.

While visiting with a friend in New England, Lana met Helene, a casual acquaintance of her hostess. Lana happened to mention that she wanted to write a book. Helene's eyes lighted up—she said she was a terrific researcher and loved to write. She offered to help Lana write it, saying she could go to Lana's Florida home to help her do it. All Lana had to do was provide her with a place to stay for a few days. She would review the material, and then take it from there. The proposal sounded ideal. Lana felt she worked better when she had someone with whom to share ideas.

After some correspondence in which Lana explained the extensive research already completed, a financial agreement was agreed upon and Helene made plane reservations.

Lana showed Helene her personal notes, the latest abstracts, the complete research of the literature and her collection of books and articles on the topic. She took several hours to explain her ideas and feelings about the book. Helene took extensive notes. They talked for an additional three hours on tape about some of the directions Lana wanted to take. She was to transcribe the material and forward it to Helene.

However, after Helene left, Lana evaluated their session and came to a sobering conclusion: Helene wasn't in a position to provide the creative input Lana had expected. She immediately wrote to Helene saying that perhaps they might get together on another project when she needed some solid editing—something she felt Helene was good at—but she felt she needed to work on her own at the moment.

That's when the battle began. Helene called and asked for Lana's notes and the tapes. Initially, Lana had said she would have the tapes transcribed, but that the notes were her personal property. Thinking about it later, she felt Helene's request was inappropriate. After all, she explained, "It was stuff from the work I had done. She had brought nothing down with her."

Two nights later, a Friday night, she got a call from Helene's attorney, who announced that he was making arrangements to have the notes and tapes picked up. Lana brushed him off, laughing, "You've got to be kidding. Call me Monday morning." And she thought that would be the end of it.

The attorney called back. Lana had turned her answering machine on and was flabbergasted the following morning when she listened to his message:

> He said he was instructed to take action on Monday morning at 10:00 a.m. if I did not give him the notes and tapes, and that things would come out in litigation that would be detrimental to my professional as well as my personal life.

Early Saturday morning, she got another threatening call on her machine saying she would have to pay all legal fees, of about five to six thousand dollars each for the tapes and the notes if she didn't respond:

> The whole situation was incredible. The woman was threatening to sue and expose me if I didn't turn over my own material to her. It was nuts. She had spent a few hours contributing nothing of value to my work. And what made it even more painful was that when she was staying with me, I had revealed some information, very personal information. My marriage was ending. I had just taken a lover— it was not information that I wanted to get out.

So I guess she thought she could intimidate me and that she could blackmail me.

Lana turned the whole thing over to an attorney. She never did send Helene the notes and tapes; she gave them to her attorney instead, with instructions to countersue if necessary. At this point, it is unlikely that the matter will ever go to court. Helene's own actions and those of the attorney acting on her behalf stepped over the border between permissible requests and outright extortion. Lana was advised that one of Helene's attorney's letters, citing the cases he had won in court and threatening her if she didn't settle, might be enough to get him disbarred.

The experience has been a costly one for Lana, both in terms of emotional pain and the financial expense of hiring an attorney. It had all occurred because of a few pages of notes and three hours of taped conversation on her own material. And that's what seemed so strange. There was little Helene could do with Lana's material. And yet, for those few scraps, Helene had hired an attorney to intimidate Lana. The amount in dispute was minimal. Helene threatened Lana with financial loss, personal embarrassment, and professional exposure. She was ready to use blackmail, extortion—whatever it took—to attain her ends.

MAGAZINE
MALEVOLENCE

Like Lana, Joy entered into a writing venture with the best of intentions. Joy was the editor. She was inspired by the vision of Vicky, who wanted to create a magazine appealing to the new liberated career woman. Joy was excited to be involved. She had been a writer for many years, working for newspapers and book publishers, doing a little public relations here and there. She had known Vicky for several years and they had often talked over the possibility of creating a magazine, but nothing seemed to click. Each idea had some drawback; for instance, the editorial content might sound great, but there didn't seem to be an advertising appeal. Or the magazine was marketable, but it didn't interest Vicky.

Then an idea hit. Joy jumped on it. She told Vicky, who was looking for people to write or edit the publication for free, "You've got yourself an editor if you want her, but offer me part of it. I can do things for free to an extent, but offer me part of the business." Joy said, "So it was agreed. I would work the first six months for nothing, putting together the editorial package. I would bring people I knew into the business. I would get photographers and typesetters and different people who cared about the topic involved, and in exchange, I would have the opportunity to buy in, to be an owner and profit."

At first, the formula worked well. After the first six months, the magazine offered her a small income—fifteen hundred dollars an issue—with the understanding that this amount would go up as subscriptions increased and the advertising rates went up.

Feeling everything was fine, Joy continued to pour heart and soul into the enterprise for about two years. As she put it:

> I really worked hard, very, very hard. Maybe one hundred to one hundred twenty hours a month for the magazine, plus bringing in other people who could get money and get good articles going. So I was able to help the magazine in a number of areas and put Vicky in contact with the right people. This was besides my regular job.

Soon, Vicky and her husband put Joy on the board and she began buying stock. Meanwhile, she concentrated on what she considered her role in the magazine—creating good articles with good illustrations, plus interacting with the writers, artists, and photographers "to try to get them to continue working for no money, or very little."

However, Joy was very isolated from the business side, and when she started to pay attention to this and the public relations side, she noticed some things she didn't like. As she explained:

It seemed to me that Vicky was using people, using them up and complaining that they didn't give more. One evening it occurred to me that whenever I was invited as editor to speak to groups, I would include Vicky as the publisher; I thought it was good to see the publisher and editor together. But I realized that when she was asked to speak, she didn't include me. My feelings got hurt over that.

Another time, she debated with Vicky about all the people who were working for free, hoping to get something for their labor. So far, Vicky had only led them on, giving them nothing. At the same time, Vicky complained that these people weren't giving enough:

> I told her, "Well, you know, Vicky, they are working for free, volunteering, and it is your dream, not theirs. If you want it to be their dream, so that they give as much as you, you have to offer them ownership in it. You have to give them a piece of the pie like you have with me."

Joy thought that Vicky realized this problem, even acknowledged it. But from that day on, she sensed hostility on Vicky's part—as though Vicky resented her for bringing the issue up.

Then, after a few more issues of the magazine, the fifteen-hundred-dollar payments stopped. Joy knew that cash was tight, and yet she knew she was working very hard. Confronting Vicky, she told her, "I can't work for free; you are piling up quite an amount of money owed to me."

Joy suggested a number of possibilities: Vicky could pay her half the amount twice a month or she could pay part in cash and the rest in some kind of trade-off, possibly eating in restaurants in trade for advertising in the magazine. She was also open to ideas from Vicky. When none of the ideas proved to Vicky's liking, Joy suggested that Vicky trade her ownership. Vicky said no. "She said that was not possible. They couldn't trade me ownership, because I had to buy ownership."

Meanwhile, Joy was becoming more and more resentful. "I felt I was giving all this time for nothing in return, and I was feeling really angry about it." On top of that, Vicky raised the price of a share in the magazine to over double the amount that Joy had previously paid.

The situation was becoming more and more intolerable. Joy was on the board, but had little information as to what was going on. She didn't know exactly how many shares were issued, what they cost, or how many she owned. It was as if she had been stumbling along in the dark for more than two years, trusting Vicky to do what was fair, so she could concentrate on turning out a good editorial product. Now that she was finally paying attention to the business side, she felt Vicky had been exploiting and taking advantage of her good will and faith.

Joy again confronted her. And this time Vicky backed down somewhat after the discussion. She would consider giving Joy a greater ownership interest. She would give Joy more money. It would take some time to work out the details. But she seemed sincere, and Joy left the meeting feeling fairly good.

However, Joy felt tired and wanted to take a vacation. She decided to go to Europe for two months. At first, Vicky resisted. "How can you go away?" she asked. Joy answered that she would work twice as hard before she left to complete two extra issues. Vicky would be covered for four months. Vicky agreed. She promised to put the money she would owe Joy in her bank account while she was gone. When she returned, Joy would plunge in, refreshed, to work on the magazine:

> She said OK. I went away feeling good and I gave her deposit slips for my account. She had a key to my post office box. I felt my old self emerging, ready for a new adventure.

As it turned out, Vicky did nothing. Joy called a few times from Europe, but never was able to speak to her. The person who answered assured her everything was fine, and they were looking forward to her return. But when she got back, Vicky fired her. She refused to pay the money she owed. Though Joy took the matter to court and got a judgment in her favor, she never saw any money.

SO WHO'S RUTHLESS
NOW?

These victims reported a certain ferocity of attack by the women who treated them unethically. Their reports indicated the motivations for the attacks appeared similar—a deep-seated anger, jealousy, resentment, or passion for revenge. Often it was masked by an unprincipled woman biding her time or lying in wait until the appropriate moment to strike. When she did, the all-out nature of the attack was devastating.

One greedy woman set up a man to take the fall in a credit card scam. Another envious woman tried to derail a woman associate's business with lawsuits. A third power-hungry woman tried to take over a woman's political campaign, and when it didn't work, she squirmed out of the mountain of debts she had piled up. A fourth tried to sabotage a former coworker when she got promoted or had a personal relationship with a former lover; one unscrupulous woman tried the tactics of extortion to get some written material to which she had no right; while another exploited a writer/editor for years with empty promises about money, participation, and ownership, and then took it all away without warning.

There was a common theme of viciousness, ruthlessness, and pure revenge. In each case, they wreaked havoc which lasted for some time. Afterwards, most of their victims bounced back; the perpetrators, ironically, often ended up victims of their own viciousness. The woman who engineered the credit card scam is now in jail. The one who tried to derail the associate's business went into bankruptcy. The political campaigner lost her power. The coworkers either found themselves out of a job or mired in the lower reaches of the corporate hierarchy. The woman who tried extortion never got the materials she wanted and ended up with large legal bills—her own. And the magazine publisher who exploited the writer/editor lost her magazine a few months later.

Thus, in a sense, many of these unethical women got their just desserts for their efforts to shatter others' lives. Their subsequent defeats aren't, of course, much solace to their victims, who have had to pull their own lives and emotions back together. Yet it does make one think about unethical behavior.

Although there is no doubt that unethical men in the marketplace can be just as, or even more, ruthless and calculating than the women cited in these cases, in reviewing these stories of women's unethical business behavior with the victims and others, there was general agreement that there was something uniquely feminine about these actions. In some cases, the women covered up their ruthlessness with a soft quality that belied the cold calculation and maliciousness going on underneath (as in the case of the credit card scammer). Or in others, the woman acted out of a deep-seated, festering desire for revenge due to her own insecurities and low self-esteem (as in the case of the facial salon owner). Or from feelings of intense personal jealousy (as in the case of the secretary). All these women acted more out of feelings and emotions than pragmatic concerns.

This is not to say that some men might not cover up their unethical actions with a veneer of friendship and good feelings, or that men might not attack due to their own emotional reactions. But, based on my own observations and the reactions of hundreds of people with whom I have spoken about the actions of unethical women in the marketplace, certain qualities are more characteristic of unethical women than unethical men.

Unethical behavior, victims, tactics, historical and societal factors, game-playing, rules, insecurity, jealousy, politics, deception, sabotage. What does it all mean? It means that the issue of women who behave unethically is complex to say the least. Where does it all lead? Back to power and what it is, what it demands, how and where to get it, what to do with it, how to keep it, and how to use it—ethically.

Chapter 11

Ms. Sion

ANSWERS, SOLUTIONS, AND CLUES

"I think I see truer, And that this may be someone to whom I can reach a hand And feel a clasp, and trust it. A woman's hand, . . . willing to help."

Mary to Elizabeth
Act Three

Mary's words are, in retrospect, ironic and tragic. Modern-day Elizabeths—vicious, deceitful, and conniving—strike out against their sisters through sabotage, subterfuge, and rumor. Theirs is the dark side of woman moving ahead in the business world.

Woman to Woman has closely explored the roots of this unethical behavior among women and has found that in many instances it is not deliberate. Rather, it is an unconscious reaction to and result of low self-esteem developed in childhood—low self-esteem that has caused us to feel inferior to men, anxious and doubtful about our abilities, fearful of female competition, and envious of female success and power.

Inferiority, anxiety, doubt, fear, envy—play important and damaging roles in women treating other women unethically. But, ironically, they are clues to the transition from sabotage to support.

There are, I believe, three major steps in effecting this transition. The first is awareness, the second is commitment, the third is action.

To deal with and solve the problem of women's unethical behavior toward one another, we must be aware of a number of things. First, we must be aware that there is in fact a problem: at worst many women are, and at best many women are perceived to be unethical in dealings with other women. Second, we must be aware that, intentionally or not, we have contributed to and are responsible for this actual or perceived behavior. Third, we must be aware of the roots of this behavior. Fourth, we must be aware that unethical actions are not genetic but behavioral and therefore can be changed.

Next, we must commit ourselves to work toward that change. We must reinforce our awareness with sufficient amounts of conviction, energy, passion, determination, perserverance, and stamina. Then we must take action. We must act to enhance our self-esteem and that of our sisters; we must act to develop the concept of a professional relationship; we must act to learn the "rules of the game" and communicate them to others; we must act to become more direct in our business dealings; and we must act to deal with unethical behavior when and where it occurs.

SELF-ESTEEM

What does "enhance our self-esteem and that of our sisters" mean and how is it done? It means overcoming the early childhood programming that teaches us that we are inferior, that our sisters are rivals, that women in business are an "every woman for herself" endeavor. It involves learning and practicing "overt support" with other women—developing a sense of team play, reinforcing old alliances, and creating new ones.

Self-esteem is perhaps the single most important requirement for success. But it's not that easy for women to achieve. It is simply a fact that in most of the world's societies, women hold at best a second place position to men and consequently do not develop a strong sense of self-worth. And this lack of self-esteem does not stop with our view of ourselves, but necessarily extends to our view of our sisters. We have seen the results of this second-rate attitude displayed time and time again in examples cited in this book.

Anne Wilson Schaef, in her book, *Women's Reality,* points out that, "When women say 'I do not like or trust other women,' what we are really saying is 'I don't like myself.' And this, in turn, can be expanded to 'I don't like femaleness.' " She goes on to say that women believe that being born female means "to be born innately inferior, damaged. That there is something innately wrong with us."[1]

This feeling of innate inferiority can be traced to childhood and can be credited with helping to create the stereotypes that women have been fighting for centuries. The female stereotype, indeed a reflection of other people's and of society's standards, works against women in two ways.

First, it tells us that women are passive, weak, emotional, fearful, jealous, and conniving—unadmirable qualities. Those of us who buy into this stereotype have no choice but to hold ourselves and other women in low esteem.

Second, what about those of us who do not accept the stereotype but see ourselves as strong, brave, independent, confident, and straightforward? We also suffer an attack on our self-esteem because society places a particularly low value on women who "behave like men." Does this mean that the situation is hopeless? Hardly.

In *Women Managers: Travelers in a Male World,* Judi Marshall[2] points out that "sex role stereotypes are essentially social creations," and that since we created them, we can also change them. "If attitudes in women changed," she says, "their views of themselves and their behavior would change too." How? Since our self-esteem, or lack of it, has its roots in childhood, perhaps we should start there.

One's self-concept begins in the home and is perpetuated by

and through the educational system. As we have already discovered, boys and girls are raised differently. We have discussed the fact that most boys are involved in team play and learn team work, risk taking, aggressive behavior, and rules. Most girls, on the other hand, play house, turn-taking, and other safe games. She is told to "be careful." He is told to "get in there and fight." He is paid for work, she is thanked and smiled at. We have observed the results of these differences on individual self-esteem as well as on performance in the business world. But what can we do to change it? Not all of us are parents, but all of us can make some positive efforts toward improving the environment for children.

Prominent educator Maria Montessori emphasized the importance of the environment in a child's development. She believed that all adults, not just the parents, must be consciously aware of their influence on a child at all times. Their attitudes must be worthy of imitation because eventually those attitudes will be reflected, for good or for bad, in the attitudes of the child.

In *Women and Self Esteem,* Linda Tschirhart Sanford and Mary Ellen Donovan address the importance of early childhood in the development of self-esteem:

> We learn not only by listening, but also by watching. As children we were probably extremely attuned to the behavior of others, particularly our parents or surrogate parents. We watched them closely, intensely, carefully because they were so frequently around, because they had tremendous power over us, and because by pleasing them we secured our place within their hearts and ensured our survival. We also watched them because we hoped they could provide us with an inkling of what it meant to be a "big person," something we some day would be and in the process of observing our parents', or surrogate parents', clothing, manner, speech, and general behavior, we learned how to behave ourselves . . . The process by which we learned this is called role modelling and it continues far beyond childhood. As women we identify role models in adolescence,

in young adulthood, and well into maturity. And the models we choose strongly influence our feelings not only about ourselves, but about our "sisters."[3]

Our research for *Woman to Woman* has indicated that one deterrent to a woman's self-esteem, and thus another possible explanation for her unethical behavior, has been the lack of good role models.

RosaBeth Moss Kanter[4] identifies four role models that trap women—mother, seductress, pet, and iron maiden. The first three put women in nurturing, subservient, and dependent categories, and, according to research, do not generally produce ambitious or successful businesswomen. Those women deemed successful in roles other than Kanter's first three typically identified their fathers as their role models.

The last role model, the iron maiden, identifies woman as strong enough to be unattractive and definitely dangerous. Elizabeth Tudor attests to the power, longevity, and wickedness of this model and displays all its characteristics. She is unable and unwilling to share power with another woman. She chooses covert means to thrust a queen from her throne. She is motivated by fear, jealousy, uncertainty, and insecurity, and worse yet, her behavior is easily recognized and accepted today.

We would probably all agree that none of these models is accurate or acceptable, but can we do anything to change them? Yes, and the first step is awareness.

We must be aware that we are role models to each other and to our children. We must be alert to the image we project, particularly to the younger or less powerful, and take overt action in being a role model. When we were children, this was called "showing a good example."

Part of this awareness is being conscious of the feelings or attitudes that have proved supportive of the stereotypes and destructive of women. Step back and examine anger, jealousy, feelings of insecurity, uncertainty, and fear when they arise—in you or in another woman. Ask yourself from where the feeling comes. Is it the logical, rational result of the situation at hand?

Or does it stem from low self-esteem? Could giving in to this feeling be destructive to an individual or to the collective goals of women? If the answer to either of the last two questions, is yes or maybe, then take action to minimize the feeling and its effects.

One such feeling that has proved supportive of female stereotypes and destructive of women is envy. In her book, *The Snow White Syndrome—All About Envy,*[5] Berkeley psychotherapist Betsy Cohen examines envy and its harmful effects on both the "envious" and the "envied." Cohen found that women have a particular problem with envy. She points out that most men have been taught to deal with their envy by being competitive, but most women are taught that competition is unfeminine. Cohen believes that, despite this, women can deal with their envy once they become aware of it. If you are the recipient of envy, she suggests, look on it as a compliment and think of yourself as a role model for others. If you are envious, learn to compete with yourself, not with others. Recognize that you are doing the best you can. Try to develop compensating qualities. You can't have everything in life, so concentrate on your good points. Trade envies—you may find that each of us envies something about the other. Talk it over.

Examining destructive feelings and attitudes may not only minimizes their ill effects, but can also improve us as role models. In our interview with her, entertainer and talk show host Mariette Hartley stressed women's importance and power as role models to our daughters. She believes that many women grew up listening to the voice that said "you can't" which eroded their confidence and made them fearful of taking risks. Hartley said:

> This is all purely subjective now, but I think that a lot of us are raised by women who have not dared to risk and have also been told by their mothers that we cannot do this, we cannot do that.

But now, in this new generation, she and other women believe that we can take steps to change that early mind-set. We have to act to overcome that early fear, to have more confidence in ourselves and in our power. "Our legacy," Hartley says, "is to pass to our daughters an attitude of can-do and support."

In addition to awareness of ourselves as role models, we must also be aware of other women as role models.

Identify people who are good role models and watch them. If we came to view ourselves as weak, dependent, and insecure by watching and ultimately imitating weak role models, then we can become supportive and ethical—and possibly increase our self-esteem in the process—by watching and imitating strong role models. Also, identify people who are bad role models. You can learn as much from a failure as you can from a success.

Formal schooling has a tremendous impact on the development of our self-esteem. Sanford and Donovan point out that "most of us spent a major portion of our time during our formative years in school, and schools today are among the most powerful of influences. The primary purpose of formal schooling, they say, is to socialize children, to give them the skills to function as productive citizens, and to teach them the larger cultures values. "Schools shape our most fundamental beliefs about our purpose and possibilities in this world."[6]

The authors point out that when most females began school, at the age of five or six, we were in no position to resist being sent there. And were we unable to challenge what we learned once we got there. Schools and teachers, they point out, wielded great authority and we were relatively powerless. So rather than analyzing what we were taught or questioning its truth, we more than likely just believed it.[7]

This passivity was particularly unfortunate for females, since so much of what we were taught in school "impeded the development of our self-esteem."[8]

Research shows that male narcissism was long prevalent in the text books, the language, and the attitudes of our major educational institutions and, to a great extent, these stereotypes and attitudes have influenced the future success levels and behaviors of those exposed to them.

Sanford and Donovan also point out that the further we went in school the less were our chances of having experiences that would boost our self-esteem. Why? Because as we got into the higher grades and went on to college, our teachers were more and more likely to be males rather than females. In what they call "Blueprints for Change," they suggest ways of counteracting the impact of schooling on women's self-esteem. They suggest examining how schooling contributed to or diminished our sense of significance, power, competence, community, individuality, reality, values, and ethics. They ask us to "identify what was negative and inaccurate, then throw it out and replace it with something "more positive, accurate, and up-to-date."[9] They further urge that women think about the specific things they were taught in school and evaluate their truths:

> In addition to questioning what we were taught, it is often helpful to our sense of selves to expand our knowledge. The American school system gives the impression that once people graduate from high school or college, they cease to learn. But adult education is a viable option in many communities and it exists for people who want to expand their knowledge. Community colleges, recreation departments, continuing educations departments of colleges and universities, some women's organizations and the like offer courses and sometimes they are inexpensive or offer scholarships. Many women specifically feel they "miss something" in the particular areas of physical education, shop and auto mechanics, math and sciences. Adult education can help us to fill in some of the gaps. For others, continuing education is an extension of interest developed in school. It is also a way to connect with our community. Remember, no one knows everything and no one is ever too old to keep on learning.[10]

The authors further encourage women to "look at shaming and ridicule as inhumane and to begin to question any sense of inferiority you grew up with as a result of these methods. The problem is with the methods—not with you."[11]

They address the teachers of children today and urge them to consider their impact on children's developing self-concepts. They encourage teachers to question the use of "problematic methods of teaching" and to replace them with more humane methods. They also urge teachers to act in their own classrooms to counteract any detrimental effects they might have had. Sanford and Donovan then pose the challenging question, "How are you a role model for your students?"[12]

Women & Self Esteem points out that as parents we can be aware of what is taught in our children's schools and of how it is being taught. We must take whatever time and effort is required to be active in parent/teacher association, to observe our children's classes, and to react against teaching styles that diminish our children's self-esteem. Reading over their textbooks for demeaning stereotypes of people is one means of doing this.

Every bit as important as self-esteem is the esteem we have for other women. If we are to move from sabotage to support, we must overcome women's negative programming, regardless of its origin, which has taught us to see each other as rivals, as enemies, as obstacles to each other's success. I believe that the only way we can do this is to engage in what I call "overt support."

I spoke earlier about the need for women to become more overt in their business dealings but it is equally important, perhaps more so, for them to become overt in their support of each other. I believe a critical element in achieving this is the development of a sense of team play.

The "sense of team play" is a concept referenced often in our research and interviews. No one defined it precisely, but most seemed to agree that whatever it is, women don't have it. Why? It seems that most women were not taught this concept as children. But it is an important one for business relationships and can be acquired.

As Betty Lehan Harragan pointed out in *Games Mother Never Taught You,*[13] "Cooperative teamwork is a human relationship; it cannot be learned out of books but has to be practiced in action."

For the purposes of this discussion, let me define what I mean by team and team play. "Team" is two or more people working together toward a common goal. "Team play" refers to the dynamics within that team—namely that each member has a defined job and that the successful completion of each job will lead to the achievement of the common goal and to a reward that will be shared—not necessarily equally—by all.

Then there are also rules of team play—not to be confused with "the rules of the game." Using a football game as a point of reference, the team rules are those that regulate the behavior and relationship between individual members on the same team. The rules of the game are those that regulate the behavior and conduct of the members of both teams toward each other, the referees, and the fans. The game rules then are always the same for both teams. The team rules, however, may occasionally differ—from team to team, coach to coach, or game to game.

There are also what might be called general team rules that arise from the nature of teams. Any time you have two or more people, you will have differentiated skills. In the case of teams, members are chosen on the basis that their individual skills in combination will result in the best chance for achieving the common goal. It is also important to recognize that these individual skills *alone* probably have little or no value or ability in achieving that common goal; therefore, it is necessary that there be cooperation between these individuals and their skills.

Once we have two or more people with differentiated skills who theoretically recognize the need for cooperation among them, we need someone to manage those people and those skills. And this manager must be powerful and effective. We ensure this power and effectiveness in part, certainly, by choosing the right personality for the job, but also by making rules for the other team members to follow in relation to him. Rules like Betty Lehan Harragan's "Don't talk back to the coach." Harragan points out that "organized team sports also teach boys indelible lessons about authority relationships. . . . It soon becomes clear that every team needs a leader, a decision maker, an arbiter . . . the coach or the captain is the ultimate authority and the motivator. He evaluates skills, assigns positions, decides who plays in the first line up, who gets benched, who is substituted, and his authority is unquestioned.''

Individual team members with individual skills and a common goal give rise to other rules of team play:

"Do your job to the best of your ability."

"Be aware of how you and your performance affect the other team members."

"Follow the game plan and help others to do so."

"Encourage your teammates."

"Remember that the *other* team is the enemy."[14]

There are also, I have observed, certain components of team play that are close to rules in their power and importance. One is the overwhelming sense of victory and joy that occurs when one team member is successful. Although all teams consist of two or more people, it is almost always the case that only one of them can actually score the points. But if you have ever watched team sports, you will note that the player who opens up the opportunity for the scoring player is just as thrilled as the one who makes the points. This attitude is absolutely crucial to the concept of team play—and overt support.

One of our interviewees who stressed the importance of learning team play is Laurie Harp, currently president of Aplex Corporation, and who previously ran a major microcomputer company. She supports the position that women should learn from men how to be team players:

> I think men are the ultimate game players, and women are the ultimate game players' square. These go back to traditional roles. Men are taught as boys to play games—all the team sports. Boys were always in these game roles, but never really went about telling each other how they felt. If somebody had not done a good job, they wouldn't tell him that. Somehow they always disguise it. It's a group setting. In meetings, you always hear a team lingo. It's amazing. Men are game players.

In contrast, she suggested, women don't always understand these rules; they weren't brought up this way, and as a result they have a hard time struggling up the corporate ladder, often having to make it on their own. And often viewing other women as competitors rather than potential teammates.

Like many other women entrepreneurs we interviewed, Harp believes women have to work on acquiring this team-playing skill. And they should watch men to see how they do it, since men already know the rules and feel comfortable in this role.

The importance of being a team player and political strategist is also stressed in an article by Mary Jean Parson on how to handle a situation where a colleague does something that seems unethical.[15] She stresses that one should not suddenly confront or expose the person so as to cause an uproar or crisis situation. It is important to be diplomatic and work things out in a graceful way so as to preserve your own principles and yet be part of a team, if it is in your best interest to keep the job or the business.

For example, Parson describes a hypothetical situation where an assistant to the president in the company wants to unethically feed some information about a bid to his friend, so that the friend will have a leg up on getting the project. Not only do you, as someone involved closely in coordinating the project, disapprove, but the president's assistant wants you to deliver the information to the friend.

According to Parson, the wrong approach is to refuse directly when someone in power wants you to do something a certain way. That's a sure way either to lose your job immediately or to find yourself out of the channels of power in the company, since others no longer trust you as a team player. Instead, you should finesse a refusal.

In this hypothetical situation, you shouldn't act as a messenger when you clearly think that delivering the message is unethical. But you can stall for time to decide how to go about not doing this in an amicable, non-threatening way. You might mention having an appointment that would prevent you from doing this to make it clear, without actually saying so, that you are not a messenger. Possibly, too, you might find a diplomatic way to present your side of the story to the boss—in this case, the company president—without directly making the other person look bad and setting up a supervisor-employee conflict which the supervisor almost always wins. You could put together some figures on the pros and cons of why the company should make the choice and lay out the arguments which would support a good business-sense decision. Then it is up to the president to decide.

The advantage of this kind of strategy is that the individual can avoid unethical behavior without creating an enemy of a colleague in the process. Or, as Parson puts it: "Single, lonely whistle-blowers usually cannot change a company, or if they do, they generally wreck their own careers in the process."[16]

A person lower down in the business hierarchy needs to respect the hierarchy and the relationships with colleagues which cross-cut it. Unethical behavior may be encountered at times. If the whole company is unethical, it may be time to leave. But if the behavior of a powerful colleague is an aberration, it is usually best to work around the problem and not create an enemy by a head-on confrontation which would embarrass the other side. By thinking like a team player, you can express your own point of view to those who count, but you take into consideration the political dynamics of the situation and the kind of diplomacy needed to stay on the team.

Another crucial aspect of team play is the understanding that we are "all in this together." In *Women's Reality*, Anne Wilson Schaef points out that "We have become isolated from one another and this has blinded us to the commonality of our experience."[17] We have lost sight of, or perhaps have never seen, that one woman's struggle toward success is a joint, not an individual, effort. I believe part of the problem is that we have dwelt too long on discovering why we never developed this sense of oneness, this feeling of cooperation, this commitment to support. It is time to begin developing it. I suggest we begin by reexamining and revitalizing some old, but not outdated, weapons.

Networking is one of those "old alliances" that I mentioned earlier. It has been around for a long time. We need to take a fresh look at it, approach it with some fresh attitudes and ideas, and breathe new life into it.

Networking has typically been viewed as a means of getting something. "I can acquire more contacts, I can be seen, I can promote myself." But many women who have already made some progress up the corporate ladder feel that they don't need the particular benefits it offers. To them I say, do it in order to promote others, to offer something to other women who need active, overt support.

Networking is a prime example of the team play concept I mentioned earlier. Think of it as a way of learning the team play you didn't learn as a child. It is individuals working together toward a common goal—opening up opportunities for their peers and rejoicing and feeling victorious when only one of them is successful. And remember that ideally the best network will consist of women in all phases and levels of business and will include peers who support each other's goals as well as women on the power rungs of the career ladder who can give more than they can get from a networking situation, accept it, and hopefully even seek it out.

There is another type of networking that I would encourage. I call it personal networking. And the need for it arises out of women's low self-esteem.

Coreen Cordova, a successful business owner and television personality, commented, "I do think that a lot of things that happen between women that are negative are because of jealousy. They are jealous and they are not confident enough in themselves. I think when women lack confidence in what they do, they are unable to support other women."

Cordova noted that the women who were successful were not afraid of giving praise. She believes that women have to take an active part in creating their own confidence in themselves and carefully select the people surrounding them to be part of a supportive network.

Mariette Hartley echoed this belief when she said, "Women

have to be kinder to other women . . . have a loving group around you who will be honest with you but not cruelly honest." Leadership trainer Marjorie Blanchard reinforces and supports both Cordova and Hartley and adds, "Women need to vocally praise other women . . . the 'atta girl' in front of others, not behind the scenes."

In the work environment it is next to impossible to choose the people with whom you interact. You can, of course, make a conscious effort to be overtly supportive of those around you, but you can do little to ensure that they will do the same in return. In our personal lives, however, the options are far greater and I believe we should take advantage of them. We should surround ourselves with people we know to be supportive, honest, and ethical. We should share with them—experiences, ideas, successes, failures, and, most importantly, support.

Let me go one step further. There is a need for professional networking where we meet regularly with people who may or may not be personal friends; the purpose of such networking is to reinforce us professionally and to aid each other in achieving our career goals. There is also a need for personal networking, which essentially performs the same function but on a more personal, friendly level. I believe, however, that networking need not necessarily refer only to such defined groups. I think we can effectively network with strangers, and evidence indicates that this is already beginning to happen. We can recognize that "we are all in this together" and see all women as comprising the ultimate network, worthy of support. How do we interact with these unknown women? In much the same way as members of a team interact in a game—by recognizing our common goals.

One of our interviewees, venture capitalist Lois Stone, believes that she has seen this happening already. "I see more and more support from other women which was very difficult to get at one point in time. I have seen this within the last few years," She described that in the past when she made "cold calls" to get through to a senior executive, the executive's secretary would usually give her the "once over." "Who is this? Why do you want to call my boss?" But now, she has found, her reception is much warmer. In fact, she reports, "very often it is the secretary who goes to the boss and is my intermediary whereas before she would be an obstruction."

In her view, the reason this has changed is that women are starting to value themselves more and are therefore coming to place more value on other women. We can encourage and accelerate this change by being aware of our common goals and by espousing and overtly supporting the concept of "networking with strangers." In the network of all women there are no strangers, there are only sisters we haven't met. I believe that if we recognize and internalize this attitude, we will begin to see more and more examples like the ones cited by Lois Stone.

The overt support exemplified by networking becomes more specific in the concept of mentoring. Much attention has been given to the importance of mentors in a woman's movement to the top. But what we most often hear is the importance of having a mentor, and since more women have been rising to higher corporate levels in recent years, I suggest the importance of mentoring increases. Those of us who have succeeded in moving up the ladder must, if we truly wish to end the sabotaging of women, take overt action to help pull others up also.

Studies show that women at lower organization levels need more reinforcement and encouragement than their male counterparts. We must actively reinforce and encourage their progress. Research also indicates that women at higher levels must devote more effort to promoting their protégés.

Of prime importance in mentoring is sharing. Share your experiences, your successes, and, definitely, your failures. Give your protégé the opportunity to learn from them—as well as from her own. And pay attention to your protégé's career goals, progress, and needs. Overt support requires a high level of consciousness. Constantly ask yourself, "What can I do to promote this woman? To encourage her? To increase her awareness of herself and her goals?" Be sensitive to her needs: She may be uncomfortable asking for answers, support, or advice, so you may have to ask her what she needs and then respond.

Recommend her for additional job responsibilities and special assignments. Express your confidence in her to others and give her the opportunity to prove you right. You will both look good.

Even if you are not in a position to become a full-fledged mentor, or if you haven't reached that requisite level of power to mentor, there are still things you can do for other women in the workplace. You can encourage them. If you are in a management position, encourage the women in your department to advance into executive status. This process can begin by their actively seeking—with your help—to improve their situations; by their attempting to seek out new responsibilities. And encourage women to encourage other women.

Offer feedback. Be aware of the actions of other women and give them positive feedback whenever possible and appropriate. I say "appropriate," because undeserved praise never truly helped anyone. The feedback must be honest and constructive. Then publicize the successes and strong points of other women whenever possible. If you are in a position to do so, communicate their ideas to management.

In addressing women's development, author Judi Marshall says that there are two critical factors in the process of change. They are that the numbers must grow and that "the individuals concerned should act 'as if they make a difference,' thus influencing the sphere in which they operate." The point I am trying to make is that it all gets back to teamwork, which is another word for support, which just might be another word for success.

In addition to building self-esteem, a sense of team play, and overt support, we can, I believe, go a long way toward eliminating women's unethical behavior by confronting the issue of women's business relationships. I believe the issue of women's sabotage of each other often stems from a basic confusion between professional and personal relationships in business. During my interview with Barbara Mackoff, mentioned in Chapter Seven, she made the point that women often run into difficulties with each other because they typically seek a personal rather than—or in addition to—a professional connection with other women in business. When a woman establishes a personal relationship with a woman associate, she may feel upset, even betrayed, when that woman ultimately makes decisions that are primarily professional in nature. Mackoff explained the dynamics this way:

> Women, when they meet each other in the business sense, have a tendency to want to look for some compatibility, something to like, a sense of belonging or co-membership with another woman. Men don't do that. Rather, men tend to look at bottom line results such as how will this affect the product or service or whatever they are trying to sell, or how they can impress particular people in order to move along this line of the corporate ladder. But women are always trying to make that personal connection.

As a result, Mackoff thinks, women have developed conventions of socializing, meeting, and greeting each other that create an impression of closeness that isn't really there or shouldn't be there in a business relationship—at least not initially. The problem with such intimacy is that it creates the expectation that somehow this other woman will stand up for you. That you can trust her. That she won't betray you. Unfortunately, the business world doesn't always operate that way because people commonly make decisions on pragmatic not personal bases. When the woman with whom personal and friendly information has been shared makes a business decision for practical reasons, it can appear to be unethical or an act of betrayal.

Another drawback to the personalizing of a business relationship is that when a woman reveals intimate information to others it puts her in a vulnerable position—as happened in Ginny Foat's situation.

As a general rule, remember that if you *relate* personally in a business situation, you will tend to *react* personally in that business situation. This applies not only to how we react to business associates' decisions and behavior, but also to how and why we make decisions affecting them. If women can depersonalize business relationships they can avoid allowing personalities and misplaced loyalties to sway them in their business decisions. Mackoff said:

> I have heard women say about a colleague, "Well, I just don't like the guy. I didn't want to spend any time with him." And I say "But you know he is one of your colleagues and those relationships are going to propel you through that work situation." It is as if there is something righteous about saying "I don't spend time with people I don't like." That is appropriate when you are dating and marrying and in friendships outside of work. But it is really inappropriate on the job.

Another aspect of the professional versus personal business relationship issue is contracts. Many people, and women in particular, shy away from written agreements when dealing with family and friends. This can be particularly dangerous for a woman who makes her business associates into friends.

Management consultant Christopher Hegarty points out that business transactions can run into major problems if the participants do not clarify exactly what an agreement entails. Since each participant is inclined to interpret an agreement—written or verbal—in the light most favorable to himself or herself, two people can have two very different perceptions of what has been agreed upon. Secondly, with no precise definition of the relationship, it is easy for the parties to behave or be perceived to behave unethically.

Women are particularly vulnerable to this trap, since they often feel uncomfortable writing it all down in a formal contract, because somehow they feel it is an insult to the other person's integrity or to their own. They may feel that a formal contract shows a lack of trust in one another and fail to put all the fine points in writing. Then, over time, opinions about the original agreement may change, or perhaps one partner really does try to take advantage of the other.

Personalizing business relationships can also mean using emotions rather than research in entering into business relationships or transactions. Many of the women in our survey said that when they got all excited about ideas they usually went by their gut level feelings about people and deals and did not research— or check up on—either. These feelings can be important. They can work as storm warnings when there is a problem with a person or a deal. Or they can give an all-clear signal to a business relationship. But sometimes they can be wrong. It is important to balance intuition with a healthy dose of caution and analysis.

By urging women to depersonalize business relationships I am not encouraging women to depersonalize themselves, or to divest themselves of all emotion. I think one of the big myths we have accepted over time is that women "should be more like men." I do not believe that the answer to women's success in business lies in their effectively "becoming men." On the contrary, as I have already said, I believe that we can achieve a level of power in the business world comparable to men's by becoming aware, committed, and active—not by disavowing or eliminating all our female traits. In fact, I believe that we can enhance our power and success by using the very characteristics that have historically been cited as signs of our weakness: compassion, vulnerability, protectiveness, and nurturing.

These are labels that have long been applied to women in order to explain why we could not be effective or successful in the business world. Instead of allowing them to be used against us, instead of seeing them as "yet another example of women's emotional rather than professional nature," let's make them business assets, business advantages that we, as women, have over men. And let's express them positively. Instead of saying, "She is vulnerable," let's say, "She is approachable. She is open to suggestions, to creative thought, to seeing the human side of the argument." And if she is protective and nurturing, let's say, "She is a manager who supports her people. She trains them, encourages them, and helps them to grow."

Evidence indicates that this is already happening. Felice N. Schwartz, president of a New York research firm on corporate women, states in an article in *Business Week* "Women today feel free to express what we have seen as male qualities: goal orientation, competitiveness, the ability to conceptualize, the aggressive pursuit of responsibility.'' She points out that ''women are being promoted because they bring new management styles to the corporations. Experts say that female personality traits such as an ability to build consensus and encourage participation are in demand today.''[19]

All this suggests that we do not have to ''become men.'' That we can keep ourselves whole. That we can enhance the workplace and make ourselves more successful.

This talk about the characteristics necessary for success ties in directly with the issue of rules in business because both are misconstrued as gender-related.

As this book has shown, there is a prevalent attitude among both men and women that ''men operate by the rules,'' ''men made the rules'' and/or ''women don't know how to operate by the rules.'' Sheila Murray Bethel, speaker and author specializing in leadership, said when we interviewed her for our survey, ''The men know the rules better than women. They know the secret ones and they go and live by them. We don't even know all the rules yet.''

But how do we learn them? In much the same way that men did—by observing, by trial and error. I don't think men actually made the rules as much as they simply discovered them. So, with few exceptions, I don't think the rules are ''men's rules'' at all: they are business rules. And if that is true, these rules are not gender-related, and we can learn them and use them as successfully as men have. We can begin by the simple act of observation.

Some of our unfortunate experiences should suggest that Rule Number One is probably ''Don't act out.'' Murray Bethel says,

> Women are more open to talking and saying, ''Hey, that is unethical.'' Men are not. One of the unwritten rules is ''You don't discuss it out loud and you don't make a scene.'' If it is unethical, maybe you don't do business with that person any more, or you ignore them. Or you discuss it privately. You are not supposed to lay things out on the

table for all to see. You go quietly behind the scenes and finesse it. That is called politics.

This kind of "behind the scenes" finessing, however, is not to be confused with being covert or clandestine. We must be direct in addressing unethical behavior without being under-handed, and it is important to know the difference. Women must recognize the value of solving problems behind the scenes, without publicly disrupting business relationships.

A related rule could be stated as "Confront it, then forget it." This is the rule that often applies immediately after Rule Number One. Having directly addressed someone's behavior without making a scene, let go of it and carry on business as usual.

Murray Bethel points out that men have their blow-ups, usually in private, then, recognizing this as part of the business game, they put hostile feelings aside and continue the relation-ship as colleagues who will still work together. As she describes,

> The men go and have their silent confrontation, or they go to court and sue each other for millions of dollars, which I have seen personally a couple of times, then they go out and play golf the next day. Now, not all men can do that but the big boys do. You don't get to be a big boy unless you understand how to do that. Many women don't have the training, the background, the ability, or understand yet that is the way the game is played.

Having stressed that these "rules of business" are not gender-related, I now suggest—no, I demand—that we create one that is. The Last Rule: Communicate the Rules.

In discussing women's relationship with each other, Judi Marshall admits that she is "disappointed because experiences and gained understandings remained unshared. Each individual must start afresh with his or her own quest and may feel alone and unique because unaware of and unguided by other travel-lers."[20]

Women, as I have pointed out in earlier chapters, are often reluctant to share their business experiences with other women, particularly those younger and less powerful, who would find such experiences enlightening and helpful. Why? Perhaps it is the risk factor again. But sharing one's knowledge of the rules with professional peers or superiors is not terribly threatening. After all, you're not telling them anything they don't probably already know and haven't already used. You are merely discussing, not giving away secrets. But to offer an "underling" hints for success and advancement might allow another woman to move up and further crowd that already too-small room at the top. Worse yet, the other woman might use help and advice to actually take your spot. Take the risk. Communicate the rules. It is one more component in overt support.

The word "overt," when applied to support, is relatively nonthreatening. It has connotations of strength, power, something obvious, something you can see and depend on.

By definition (overt: not hidden), being overt is not a negative or unethical activity. And management consultant Jef Blum, one of our interviewees, believes that it should not be viewed as such. He believes that in order to achieve their goals women need to become more direct in the way they interact and communicate with others. Being overt simply gets the job done better. People understand what you want and do it. It produces results, and there is less resentment in the end.

Our research has shown us that women become covert when they are taught that being overt is unfeminine and unattractive. But women's reputation for covert behavior has seriously undermined their rise to power and therefore must be counteracted—overtly.

Covert actions can breed a climate of distrust and resentment. Women tend to be more covert in the way they interact and use power because they feel less sure of having that power to use. But now it is time for them to learn to take that power and use it. Jef Blum said:

> Women had to get their jobs done in a world that said women can't do anything. So what they developed was the capability of manipulating the situation covertly. Men have

been able to go at it fairly straightforwardly. And women resent this. Anybody would resent having to manipulate or be covert in order to get the job done. It is extra difficult. It takes a great deal more thought. You rarely get the kind of definitive results that you want. You get something near, but not exactly, what you are looking for. So, there has always been this resentment or this building resentment. Women have learned to manipulate covertly and men have learned to manipulate overtly and men have built this game called "business" around overt manipulation.

According to Blum, women feel uncomfortable being overt because they feel unsure in this role. At the same time, they particularly resent other women when they act in an overt way: they seemed to have stepped out of the more traditional, feminine, nurturing role:

> Women have really come to resent having to act covertly so they act vehemently against the overt. They hate the overt for having forced them to be a certain way.
>
> A woman doesn't like to have to be overt because that exposes her. Being overt is a very neck-on-the-block experience.
>
> Once she has spoken her opinion, once she has stood in a business meeting, and there are a bunch of people there, some of whom she relies on, some who rely on her, and she voices her opinion, she has stated overtly where she is.
>
> Now I think part of the really serious problem lies in the fact that women resent overt women more than they resent overt men. Because they are women who have learned to play the game and they may view them as less feminine and therefore less likeable. So that contributes to their resentment. I also think that women, generally speaking, think less of themselves for having been placed in this covert role.

Direct dealing in business situations should also extend, many believe, to feelings and emotions. By directly expressing emotions, like anger or frustration, women will avoid the trap of letting these feelings build up inside and letting them manifest themselves in unconscious, covert, and often harmful ways. Mackoff explained, "Women have a tendency to think that they can sit on their anger or frustration. They tell themselves that they don't want to express this—that they don't want to seem like hysterical women—and so they sit on it. They think they can handle it. But what happens is the poison starts to seep out through the cracks. It translates itself into actions that are expressions of anger, like lateness, errors, a sarcastic tone, or the inability to look someone in the eye for prolonged periods of time."

And while the woman may think she has kept her anger or frustration hidden, she hasn't, according to Mackoff. Instead, she has simply communicated it in an indirect way which is not very clearly understood. It is much better for everyone concerned if she is direct, so the problem can be dealt with and handled.

By letting these feelings out more directly, women are in a position to get it out and move on rather than getting hung up in hurt, angry feelings. Mackoff continues:

> If something has evoked a really strong response in you, it is going to come out. Your response is going to come out in some way or another. Somehow men learn to let that response out. It is like yelling at each other during softball. When they were boys, they would go out for a soft drink and a snow cone afterwards; as men, it is a beer. Men are really practiced at getting it out and moving on. Women don't have enough practice doing that.

This ability to express feelings and then move on is particularly helpful in the final step of my "overt action" plan for change—dealing with unethical behavior when and where it occurs.

When you observe unethical behavior, whether directed at you or somewhere else, be conscious of it. Be aware that unethical behavior contributes to destructive role modelling. Ask yourself, "Is this an objectively unethical act? Or am I merely letting my low self-esteem perceive a slight where it may not actually exist?" If you determine that there has actually been unethical behavior, take overt action—immediately. Deal with the situation when it arises and work toward destroying unethical behavior as a model. By acting affirmatively and immediately you are also putting others on notice that you aren't willing to tolerate unethical behavior. This means speaking diplomatically to the person about the problem in ways that produce solutions, not battlegrounds.

Psychologist Alan Leavens, who also participated in our survey, offered advice on how to confront unethical behavior. He points that even the shy person must speak up in such a circumstance. If one says nothing, Leavens says, the negative behavior is reinforced.

Suppose you become aware that another woman has been backstabbing or gossiping about you. Consider approaching her and saying that you are aware of what has been happening; that you are hurt, disappointed, and angry; that you would like to change the situation; and would like to work with her to effect a solution. This enables her to feel receptive, not defensive, about the situation, and she may be more inclined to seek a positive way to change. If the woman claims no knowledge of the behavior you describe, then explain exactly what happened. Tell her what actions were done and how they had a negative impact on you. Such a process should help raise the woman's level of awareness. And your diplomacy may be a critical factor in the behavioral change you are seeking. She may truly be unconscious of what she is doing; she may be acting out of fear or an inner desire to get ahead, and may be behaving unethically in order to achieve that goal without realizing the impact of her actions on you or others.

As Leavens puts it:

> Even if I know the person is being an asshole, I want to be diplomatic and I want to give him the benefit of the doubt.

We do certain things that are born out of unconscious desires to get ahead, and sometimes we say things without realizing that we are saying them.

It is important to let the other person know you are aware he or she is acting in this unconscious, destructive way. By making him or her conscious, you hope he or she will be more aware in the future, and will want to change. Use remarks such as the following to make this point:

Maybe you don't realize that what you have been saying about me might hurt me. But it does, and I am hoping that now that I have told you this, you will be more aware when you are talking to anyone about me. I would hope that you would ask yourself, "Can this possibly affect anyone negatively?" Or ask yourself, "Even if it is positive, should I be the one to be talking about this?"

Many of the psychologists we interviewed reported good results with people responding positively to personal interaction. The key to success in using such an approach, however, is in not causing the other person to become defensive. Avoid saying, "You did this," or "You did that," which comes across like an accusation. Preface your comments with an "I" statement, in which you express your own feelings and indicate how you felt in response to what you perceive someone did. An "I" statement softens the impact of your claims about another's behavior. It emphasizes your feelings about the situation rather than what the person did. In touching on dynamics, Leavens adds:

You do not cause the person to become defensive. The simplest example I can think of is if you walk up to somebody and say "You did something," that person is immediately going to think "Oh, oh, what did I do?"

But if I come up to you and say, "I am really hurt by what you have done," or "I am really hurt by something you said," it lessens the impact of the statement a little bit, because I am saying I am hurt. I'm not saying, "You screwed up." It is an "I" statement. I am stating my feelings.

It doesn't put the other person on the defensive, as would "You did such and such." You can say, "I am aware of something that has occurred that is bothering me and I want to talk to you about it." Again, I might be more willing to hear that than somebody coming up to me and saying, "Boy, you really screwed up."

In many cases a person will be receptive to change if he or she is presented, in a nonthreatening way, with the information that he or she is hurting someone. Most people don't intentionally want to hurt others, so they will be willing to change their behavior, as long as they don't feel they are being accused of behaving badly, which causes them to feel threatened. Leavens suggests you soften your approach:

> You put me on the defensive, and I am not going to hear what you have to say very clearly. But if you come up and say, "I am finding that I am really angry with you. You are not even aware why I am angry, and I thought that I would like to talk to you about it," I am going to feel sorry you are angry, unless I know I am purposely doing something terrible to you. I am going to feel sorry that you are hurt and I am going to be very amenable to hearing what it is that I have done, because you have approached me so nicely, diplomatically, and unaccusingly. My years of practice have validated this with most people. If one is not accused of wrongdoing, then one is more willing to look at the wrongdoing than when they are called by a name.

What if this nonthreatening, diplomatic approach to resolve the problem doesn't work? Depending on your position in the organization and whether the person causing the problem is a coworker or an employer, there are two options.

First, if he or she is a coworker, do everything you can to resolve it directly with him or her, and then talk about taking it to a higher level; say you feel you have to see a supervisor about the problem if you can't work it out between yourselves. If your suggestion does not motivate the other person to change, then it might be appropriate to seek assistance from someone in a higher position. Leavens says:

> So, approach him or her and invite him or her to lunch or to a walk, or whatever, and then finally, just appeal: "I don't know what else to do. I have tried everything to contact you about this problem that I feel we are having together. Do you have any suggestions for what I might do?" If that absolutely fails, then the only thing left to do is to say, "Look, I really don't want to have to go to the supervisor, but this is affecting my work tremendously. I had hoped to work it out with you, but we don't seem to be getting anywhere. I don't want to bring in so and so. Would you prefer that I do, or do you have any suggestions on how we might work it out?" At this point you have tried maybe three or four times and it hasn't worked. As a final attempt, you are saying that you're willing to try one more time before calling in a referee.

The other option, finally, is to leave the organization, which may be necessary if the person causing the problem is above you. If a supervisor has been made aware of the problem and continues to act in a way that hurts you, it may not be possible to change the situation. Going higher in the organization might make it more difficult for you under other circumstances if the higher-level manager supports your supervisor.

The working environment could become even worse if you complain and your supervisor knows that you have. If you choose to dig in your heels and stay despite being the target of unethical behavior, you are likely to get more upset and hostile. This can lead you to react vengefully yourself, which can result in worse problems, such as being fired and getting a bad recommendation. If you recognize that the situation won't get any better and you leave, the odds are that you can find a new and much better working environment.

If you leave because of an uncomfortable situation, it's crucial that you leave gracefully. Keep the doors open for the future, because you may find you are involved in working with someone who previously treated you unethically; or that that person perhaps is in power over something you want. If you've burned your bridges behind you by staging a nasty or public confrontation, you may undercut your opportunities in the future. If you've been as diplomatic as possible under the circumstances, future possibilities are left open.

People and circumstances change, and you may want to establish contact again. As long as you leave smoothly, you can. Otherwise, it may be difficult, if not impossible. At all costs, avoid parting shots. It makes good business sense to avoid making enemies and to leave the doors open for future business together. It's like playing a game. You may wallop your opponent; but at the end, you shake hands and make up. Then you're ready to play again.

By metaphorically shaking hands when you leave a job you keep the doors open and the bridges up. Then, there is always that opening to do business again when the opportunity arises. It may feel good to get out the explosion of anger and resentment, but in the long run, you pay. After all, that's what the business game is all about: making money, in an ethical way, and keeping the channels open in order to do it.

Chapter 12

Ms. Sive

A FINAL
WORD

The challenge of turning women's sabotage of each other into support is one to which all women must respond. We must be aware of the problem, of our part in it, of its roots, and of the possibility for change.We must commit ourselves to work toward positive change. We must take action to accomplish that change.

If the problem begins with low self-esteem, the solution must begin there also. By building up our self-esteem and that of our sisters, we can reverse the attitude that we are inferior and that other women are our natural enemies. And we can develop and use team play as a means of increasing our support of one another. By grasping the concept of a professional versus personal business relationship, we can reduce the chances of viewing our sisters as unethical and deceitful when they are merely acting in a professional manner. By observing and sharing we can help each other to recognize the rules of the game and use them to our advantage. By becoming more direct in our business dealings, we can counteract the covert and underhanded stereotypes by which women have suffered for so long. And, by acting against unethical behavior when and where it occurs, we can spread the word that we are not willing to tolerate such behavior in *our* workplace.

I believe that by succeeding in these efforts, we will make

incredible strides in the journey from sabotage to support. I am committed and am inviting you to commit to these efforts and to the goal of eventually lending truth and credence to Elizabeth's words:

"It seemed if I saw you near, and we talked as sisters over these poor realms of ours, some light might break that we'd never see apart."

Will you join me?

Notes

CHAPTER TWO

1. Daniel Yankelovitch, *New Rules: Searching For Self Fulfillments in A World Turned Upside Down* (New York: Random House, 1981).
2. Karen Pennar and Edward Mervosh, "Women at Work," *Business Week* (January 28, 1985), p. 80.
3. *Ibid.*
4. S. J. Diamond, "Women on the Job: Surge Widely Felt," *Los Angeles Times,* (1984), p. 9.
5. Phyllis Chesler, *Mothers on Trial: The Battle For Children and Custody* (New York: McGraw Hill, 1986).
6. Diamond, *op. cit.*
7. Doris Byron Fuller, "Working Women Reshaping Economy," *Los Angeles Times* (September 12, 1984), pp. 1, 6.
8. Karen Tumulty, "Wage Gap: Women Still the Second Sex," *Los Angeles Times* (September 13, 1984), p. 7.
9. *Ibid.,* p. 6.
10. Kathleen Hendrix, "Women Executives: Is It a Doll or a Bear Market?" *Los Angeles Times* (September 14, 1984), pp. 1, 18.
11. Helen Rogan, "Women Executives Feel that Men Both Aid and Hinder Their Careers." *The Wall Street Journal* (October 29, 1984), p. 31.
12. Peter Berger, "Battered Pillars of the American System, *Fortune* (April 1975), pp. 133–50.
13. R. H. Maslow, *The Farther Reaches of Human Nature* (New York: Viking Press, 1971).
14. Thomas J. Hayes, "Ethics in Business: Problem Identification and Potential Solutions," *Hospital Material Management Quarterly* (May 1983), pp. 37–38.
15. Harold L. Johnson, "Ethics and the Executive," *Business Horizons,* Vol. 24, No. 2 (May–June 1981), p. 56.
16. David F. Linowes, "International Business and Morality," Delivered to the Center for International Education, Urbana-Champaign, Illinois, March 25, 1977. *Vital Speeches of the Day,* Vol. 43, No. 15 (May 15, 1977), pp. 475–478.

17. Mary Cunningham "Productivity: Does Business Need Values? *Across the Board* (December 1981), p. 8.

18. Terence E. Deal and Allan A. Kennedy, *Corporate Cultures* (Menlo Park, California: Addison-Wesley Publishing Company, 1982), p. 27.

19. *Ibid.,* p. 151.

20. Rosabeth Moss Kanter, *Men and Women of the Corporation* (New York: Basic Books, 1977), pp. 77, 82.

21. *Ibid.,* p. 134.

22. *Ibid.,* p. 134.

23. *Ibid.,* p. 147.

24. *Ibid.* p., 151.

25. *Ibid.,* p. 158.

26. *Ibid.,* pp. 186–7.

27. Kevin McDermott, "New Players, New Rules," *D&B Reports* (September/Octorber 1985), p. 20.

28. Carol Gilligan, *In a Different Voice,* (Cambridge, Mass.: Harvard University Press, 1982), p. 10.

29. *Ibid.,* p. 10.

30. Judith Trotsky, "Must Women Executives Be Such Barracudas?" *The Wall Street Journal* (November 9, 1981), p. 24.

31. Garda W. Bowman, N. Beatrice Worthy, Stephen A. Greyser, "Are Women Executives People?" *Harvard Business Review: Problems in Review,* 1965.

32. Henry Weill, "A New Study Reveals Some Surprising Findings About the Fatal Flaws of Top Managers," *Savvy* (January 1984), p. 39.

33. Carol Ann Beauvais, "The Family and the Work Group: Dilemmas for Women in Authority, *Dissertation Abstracts International,* Vol. 37 (7B) (January 1977), p. 3595-B.

34. V. E. O'Leary, *Some Attitudinal Barriers to Occupational Aspirations in Women Beyond Sex-role Stereotypes* (Cambridge, Mass.: Little Brown and Company, 1976).

35. Abigail C. Nichols, "Women and Leadership, Strategies for Social Workers and Clients," Based on a paper presented at the First Annual South Central Women's Studies Conference, Fort Worth, Texas, June 1978. Graduate School of Social Work, University of Texas at Arlington, pp. 814–823.

36. Helen Rogan, "Executive Women Find It Difficult to Balance Demands on Job, Home," *The Wall Street Journal* (October 30, 1984), p. 33.

37. Jennifer S. Macleod, "The Double Standard in Qualifications," *Employment Relations Today,* Vol. 10, No. 2 (Summer 1983), pp. 153–7.

38. Susan Fraker, "Why Women Aren't Getting to the Top," *Fortune* (April 16, 1984), pp. 40–44.

39. Anonymous, "Living in a Man's World . . . and Not Turning Into a Man," *Vogue* (August 1983), pp. 301, 380.

40. Helen Rogan, "Top Women Executives Find Path to Power is Strewn with Hurdles," *The Wall Street Journal* (October 25, 1985), p. 4.

41. Decker and Yoshihara, "Most Women Place Family Before Job," *Los Angeles Times* (September 10, 1984), p. 8.

42. *Ibid.,* p. 17.

43. *Ibid.*, pp. 18–20.

44. Charlotte Decker Sutton and Kris K. Moore, "Executive Women—Twenty Years Later," *Harvard Business Review* (September–October 1985), p. 2.

45.. *Ibid.*, p. 4.

CHAPTER THREE

1. Ellen B.Dickstein, "Biological and Cognitive Bases of Moral Functioning," *Human Development*, Volume 22, (1979).

3. Augusto Blasi, "Bridging Moral Cognition and Moral Action: A Critical Review of the Literature," *Psychological Bulletin*, Vol. 88, No. 1 (July 1980), p. 27.

4. *Ibid.*, p. 28.

5. Dickstein, *op. cit.*, p. 55.

6. *Ibid.*

7. Jean Baker Miller, *Toward A New Psychology of Women* (Boston: Beacon Press, 1976).

8. Rosabeth Moss Kanter, *Men and Women of the Corporation* (New York: Basic Books, 1977.).

9. Miriam Frances Eiseman, "Interrelationships Among Psychological Androgeny, Moral Judgment and Ego Development in an Adult Population," Ph.D. Dissertation, University of Kentucky, 1978. *Dissertation Abstracts International*, Vol. 40 (3-B) (September 1979), pp. 1361-2–B.

10. Lore Ellen Kantrowitz, "Sex Role Development and Intellectual and Ethical Development in Young Adults," Ed. D. Dissertation, Boston University School of Education, *Dissertation Abstracts International*, Vol. 41 (5-B) (November 1980), p. 1942–B.

11. Miller, *op. cit.*, 11–12.

12. *Ibid.*, pp. 49, 142.

13. Anne Wilson Schaef, *Women's Reality: An Emerging Female System in a White Male Society* (Minneapolis, Minnesota: Winston Press, 1985), pp. 28–29.

14. *Ibid.*, p. 40.

15. Carol Gilligan, *In A Different Voice* (Cambridge, Mass: Harvard University Press, 1982).

16. *Ibid.*, pp. 10–11.

17. Gilligan, *op. cit.*, p. 66.

18. *Ibid.*, p. 69.

19. *Ibid.*, p. 105.

20. *Ibid.*, p. 138.

21. Eileen McDonagh, "Social Exchange and Moral Development: Dimensions of Self, Self-Image, and Identity," in *Human Relations*, Vol. 35., No. 8, (1982).

22. Mary Zey-Ferrell and O. C. Ferrell, "Role-Set Configuration and Opportunity as Predicators of Unethical Behavior in Organizations," *Human Relations*, Vol. 35, No. 7, (1982), pp. 587–604; Mary Zey-Ferrell, K. Mark

Weaver, O. C. Ferrell, "Predicting Unethical Behavior Among Marketing Practitioners," *Human Behavior*, Vol. 32, No. 7 (1979), pp. 557–569.

23. *Ibid.*

24. McDonagh, *op. cit.*, pp. 659–674.

25. Richard L. Gorsuch, "R. B. Cattell: An Integration of Psychology and Ethics," *Multivariate Behavioral Research*, Vol. 19 (April/July 1984), p. 209.

26.. Richard Christie and Florence L. Geis, *Studies in Machiavellianism*, (New York: Academic Press, 1970).

27. Shelby D. Hunt and Lawrence B. Chonko, "Marketing and Machiavellianism," *Journal of Marketing*, Vol. 48 (Summer 1984), p. 31.

28. Karen Van Wagner and Cheryl Swanson, "From Machiavelli to Ms: Differences in Male-Female Power Styles," *Public Administration Review*, Vol. 39, No. 1 (January/February 1979), pp. 66–72.

29. *Ibid.*, p. 69.

30. *Ibid.*,

31. Paul John Lavrakas, "Human Differences in the Ability to Differentiate Spoken Lies from Spoken Truths," Ph.D. Dissertation, Loyola University, 1977, *Dissertation Abstracts International* Vol. 37, 12–B, Part I (June 1977), pp. 6406-B–6407-B.

32. William R. Pope, Components of Moral Evaluation: Actors and the Accounts They Provide for Lies," Ph. D. Dissertation, Virginia Commonwealth University, *Dissertation Abstracts International*, Vol. 42, 11-B (May 1982), p. 4622-B.

33. Bella M. DePaulo and Robert Rosenthal, "Telling Lies," *Journal of Personality and Social Psychology*, Vol. 37, No. 10 (1979), p. 1719.

34. Virginia E. Schein, Examining an Illusion: The Role of Deceptive Behaviors in Organizations," *Human Relations*, Vol. 32, No. 4 (1979), p. 292.

35. W. Harvey Hegarty and Henry P. Sims, Jr., "Some Determinants of Unethical Decision Behavior: An Experiment," *Journal of Applied Psychology*, Vol. 63, No. 4 (1978), pp. 451–2.

36. *Ibid.*, pp. 451–7.

37. "Social Conditioning and Competition," *The Executive Female*, (November/December, 1981), p. 27.

38. Sheila K. Collins, "A Comparison of Top and Middle-Level Women Administrators in Social Work, Nursing and Education: Career Supports and Barriers," *Administration in Social Work*, Vol. 8, No. 2 (Summer 1984), pp. 25–34.

39. E. Aronson and D. R. Mettes, "Dishonest Behavior as a Function of Differential Levels of Induced Self-Esteem," *Journal of Personal and Social Psychology*," Vol. 9 (1968), pp. 121–27.

40. Richard G. Graf, "Induced Self-Esteem as a Determinant of Behavior," *The Journal of Social Psychology*, Vol. 85 (1971), pp. 213–17.

41. Carolyn B. Reed, "Professional Women Today: The Relationship of Their Sex-Role Identities to Anxiety, Depression, Hostility, and Selected Demographic Variables," Ph. D. Dissertation, University of Florida, 1979, *Dissertation Abstracts International*, Vol. 40, 4-A (October 1979), p. 1883-A.

42. Paula Johnson, "Women and Power: Toward a Theory of Effectiveness,: *Journal of Social Issues*, Vol. 32, No. 3 (1976), p. 99.

43. Arlie Russell Hochschild, "A Review of Sex Role Research," *American Journal of Sociology*, Vol. 78, No. 4 (January 1973), pp. 1011–1029.

44. Maury Silver and Daniel Geller, "On the Irrelevance of Evil: The Organization and Individual Action," *Journal of Social Issues*, Vol. 34, No. 4 (1978), pp. 125–136.

45. Arthur Selwyn Miller, "Business Morality: Some Unanswered (and Perhaps Unanswerable) Questions," *The Annals of the American Academy of Political and Social Science*, No. 363 (January 1966), pp.95–101.

46. Louise Bernikow, "We're Dancing as Fast as We Can," *Savvy* (April 1984), p. 43.

47. Mary Glenn Wiley and Arlene Eskilson, "The Interaction of Sex and Power Base on Perceptions of Managerial Effectiveness," *Academy of Management Journal*, No. 3, (November 25, 1982), pp. 671–77.

48. Natasha Josefowitz, "Management Men and Women: Closed vs. Open Doors," *Harvard Business Review* (September–October 1980), pp. 4–6.

49. Penny H. Baron, "Self-Esteem, Ingratiation, and Evaluation of Unknown Others," *Journal of Personality and Social Psychology*, Vol. 30, No. 1 (July 1974), p. 104––09.

50. Milton Layden, "Whipping Your Worst Enemy on the Job: Hostility," *Nation's Business* (October 1978), pp. 87–90.

51. Martin Symonds, "Psychodynamics of Aggression in Women," *The American Journal of Psychoanalysis*, Vol. 36, No. 3 (1976), pp. 195–203.

52. Ray S. Greenburg, "Discussion of The Psychodynamics of Aggression in Woman," *The American Journal of Psychoanalysis*, Vol. 36, No. 3, pp. 205–06.

53 Michael Ballard Quanty, "An Experimental Evaluation of the Aggression Catharsis Hypothesis," Ph.D. Dissertation, University of Missouri, *Dissertation Abstracts International*, Vol. 39, 10-B (April 1979), p. 5149-B.

54. Paul E. Spector, "Relations of Organizational Frustration with Reported Behavioral Reactions of Employees," *Journal of Applied Psychology*, Vol. 60, No. 5 (1975), pp. 635–7.

55. *Ibid.*

56. John Francis Kremer, "The Effect of Level of Provocation and Attributions About the Provoker on Aggression and Anger," Ph.D. Dissertation, Loyola University of Chicago, 1976, *Dissertation Abstracts International*, Vol. 36, 11-B (May 1976), pp. 5800-B–5801-B.

57. Paul Richard Bleda, "Affect, Attraction, and Group Member Responsiveness to an Intergroup Transgression," Ph. D. Dissertation, Purdue University, *Dissertation Abstracts International*, Vol. 36 3-B (March 1976), p. 4460-B.

58. Janice Zeedyk-Ryan and Gene F. Smith, "The Effects of Crowding on Hostility, Anxiety, and Desire for Social Interaction," *The Journal of Social Psychology*, Vol. 120 (1983), pp. 245–252.

59. Suzanne Gordon, "Anger, Power,and Women's Sense of Self," *Ms.* (July 1985), pp. 42–3.

60. Robert F. Bales, "The Equilibrium Problem in Small Groups," in Talcott Parsons, Robert F. Bales and Edward A. Shils, *Working Papers in the Theory of Action* (New York: The Free Press, 1953), pp. 111–161.

61. Louise Tutelian, "Bendix Redux," *Savvy* (April 1984), p. 17.

Chapter 5

1. Carol Gilligan, *In A Different Voice* (Cambridge, Mass: Harvard University Press, 1982).
Jean Baker Miller, *Toward A New Psychology of Women* (Boston, Mass: Beacon Press, 1976).

Chapter Eleven

1. Anne Wilson Schaef, *Women's Reality; An Emerging Female System in a White Male Society* (Minneapolis, Minnesota:: Winston Press, 1985), p. 24.
2. Judi Marshall, *Women Managers: Travelers in a Male World* (New York: John Wiley & Sons Inc., 1984), pp. 24, 26
3. Linda Tschirhart Sanford and Mary Ellen Donovan, *Women & Self Esteem* (New York: Penguin Books, 1984), P. 65
4. Rosabeth Moss Kanter, *Men and Women of the Corporation* (New York: Basic Books, 1977).
5. Betsy Cohen, *The Snow White Syndrome* (New York: The Macmillan Company, 1986).
6. Sanford and Donovan, *op. cit,* p. 177
7. *Ibid.,* p. 180.
8. *Ibid.*
9. *Ibid.,* p. 191–193.
10. *Ibid.,* p. 195.
11. *Ibid.*
12. *Ibid.,* p. 196.
13. Betty Lehan Harragan, *Games Mother Never Taught You* (New York: Rawson Associates, 1977), p. 51.
14. *Ibid.,* p. 51.
15. Mary Jean Parson, "When A Colleague Doesn't Play Fair," *Savvy* (December 1986), pp. 14–15.
16. *Ibid.*
17. Schaef, *op. cit.*
18. Marshall, *op. cit.,* pp. 220–221.
19. Felice N. Schwartz, "Corporate Women: What It Takes to Get to the Top," *Businessweek* (June 22, 1987).
20. Marshall, *op. cit.*

Bibliography

Abels, S.L., Abels, P., & Richmond, S.A. "Ethics Shock: Technology, Life Styles and Future Practice." *Proceedings of the National Conference on Social Welfare Annual Forum,* May 28, 1973) 145–146.

Anon. "A Lady Living in a Man's World . . . and Not Turning into a Man." *Vogue,* August, 1983. pp. 301–380.

Anon. "Dear Betty Harragan: Although I am Co-owner and Corporate Officer of Our Company, I Had a Disturbing Experience with Some Male Associates." *Working Woman,* (March, 1985) p. 33.

Armstrong, A. Mc. "The Relationship Among Need for Power, Sex of Subject, Career Choice, and the Social and Psychological Barriers that Limit Leadership Opportunities for Women." (The Fielding Institute, 1978). *Dissertation Abstracts International, 39,* (1979): 6188B.

Aronson, E., and Mettee, D.R. "Dishonest Behavior as a Function of Differential Levels of Induced Self-esteem." *Journal of Personal and Social Psychology, 9,* (1968): 121–127.

Bales, R.F. *The Equilibrium Problem in Small Groups, in Talcott Parsons, Robert F. Bales and Edward A. Shils: Working Papers in the Theory of Action.* New York: The Free Press, 1953.

Baron, P.H. "Self-esteem, Ingratiation, and Evaluation of Unknown Others." *Journal of Personality and Social Psychology, 30,* (1), (July, 1974): 104–109.

Bayes, M., and Newton, P.M. "Women in Authority: A Sociopsychological Analysis." *Journal of Applied Behavioral Science, 14* (1), (January, 1978): 9120.

Beauvais, C. "The Family and the Work Group: Dilemmas for Women in Authority." *Dissertation Abstracts International, 37* (7B), (January 1977): 3595B.

Berger, P. "Battered Pillars of the American System." *Fortune,* April 1975, 130–150.

Bernard, J. *The Female World*. New York: Free Press, 1981.

Bernikow, L. "We're Dancing as Fast as We Can." *Savvy*, April 1984, 43.

Blasi, A. "Bridging Moral Cognition and Moral Action: A Critical Review of the Literature." *Psychological Bulletin, 88* (1), July 1980, pp. 27–28, 37.

Bleda, P.R. "Affect, Attraction and Group Member Responsiveness to an Intergroup Transgression," (Doctoral dissertation, Purdue University). *Dissertation Abstracts International, 36,* (3-B), (March, 1976): 4660B.

Bok, S. *Lying: Moral choice in public life*. New York: Pantheon Books, 1978.

Bowman, G.W., Worthy, N.B., and Greyser, S.A. "Are Women Executives People?" *The Harvard Business Review: Problems in review,* (July/August 1965): 95–101.

Boyers, R. "Observations on Lying and Liars." *Review of Existential Psychology and Psychiatry, 13,* (2), (January/March 1974): 150.

Braginsky, D.D. "Machiavellianism and Manipulative Interpersonal Behavior in Children." *Journal of Experimental Psychology, 6,* (1970): 77–99.

Bray, R. "The New Economy of Women Wage-earners." *Ms.* July 1985, 104.

Burck, C.G. "The Intricate Politics of the Corporation." *Fortune,* April 1975, pp. 110, 190.

Burke, P.J. "Scapegoating: An Alternative to Role Differentiation." *Sociometry, 32,* (2), (June 1969): 159–168.

Chesler, P. *Mothers On Trial: The Battle for Children and Custody*. New York: McGraw-Hill Book. Co., 1986.

Christie, R. & Geis, F.L. *Studies in Machiavellianism*. New York: Academic Press, 1970.

Cohen, B. *The Snow White Syndrome*. New York: The Macmillan Publishing Company, 1986.

Collins, S.K. "A Comparison of Top and Middle Level Women Administrators in Social Work, Nursing, and Education: Career Supports and Barriers." *Administration in Social Work, 8,* (2) (Summer 1984): 25–34.

Comadena, M.E. "Examinations of the Deception Attribution Process of Friends and Intimates." (Doctoral dissertation, Purdue University, 1981). *Dissertation Abstracts International, 42,* (8-B), (February 1982): 3491B.

Connelly, A.A. "Communication and Group Cohesiveness in the Organizational Work Group." (Doctoral dissertation, Michigan

State University). *Dissertation Abstracts International, 34,* (6-B),/ (December 1973): 2986B.

Cunningham, M. "Productivity: Does Business Need Values? *Across the Board.* December 1981, 8–9.

Deal, T.E., and Kennedy, A.A., *Corporate Cultures,* Menlo Park, CA: Addison-Wesley, 1982.

Decker, C. and Yoshihara, N. "Most Women Place Family Before Job." *Los Angeles Times* September 10, 1984, 1, 8.

DePaulo, B.M., & Rosenthal, R. Telling Lies. *Journal of Personality and Social Psychology, 37,* (10) (1979), 1713, 1719.

Diamond, S.J. "Women on the Job: Surge Widely Felt." *Los Angeles Times,* September 9, 1984, 1,8.

Dickstein, E.B., "Biological and Cognitive Bases of Moral Functioning." *Human Development 22,* (1979): 38–55.

Eiseman, M.F. "Interrelationships Among Psychological Androgeny, Moral Judgment and Ego Development in an Adult Population." (Doctoral dissertation, University of Kentucky, 1978). *Dissertation Abstracts International, 40* (3B), (September 1979): 1361B-1362B.

Farrington, D.P., and Kidd, R.F. "Is Financial Dishonesty a Rational Decision?" *British Journal of Social and Clinical Psychology, 16,* (1977): 135–146.

Feldman, R.S. "Nonverbal Disclosure of Deception and Interpersonal Affect." (Doctoral dissertation, University of Wisconsin-Madison, 1974). *Dissertation Abstracts International, 35,* (9-B), (March 1976): 4706B.

Forsyth, D.R."Moral Attribution and the Evaluation of Action." (Doctoral dissertation, University of Florida, 1978). *Dissertation Abstracts International, 39,* (10-B), (1979): 5134B.

Fortino, D. "Office Troublemakers: Ways to Beat Them at Their Own Game." *Harper's Bazaar,* August 1980, 89.

Fraker, S. "Why Women Aren't Getting to the Top." *Fortune,* April 16, 1984, 40–44.

Fried, L. "Hostility in Organization Change." *Journal of Systems Management* (June 1972) 15.

Fuller, D.B. "Working Women Reshaping Economy." *Los Angeles Times,* September 12, 1984, 1–6.

Garland, A.W. "The Surprising Boom of Women Entrepreneurs." *Ms.* July 1985, 94.

Geisler, J.R. "The Relationship of Self-esteem to Face-saving Behavior." (Doctoral dissertation, California School of Professional Psychology). *Dissertation Abstracts International, 38,* (9-B), (March 1978): 4455B–4456B.

Gilligan, C. *In a Different Voice*. Cambridge, MA: Harvard University Press, 1982.

Gordon, S. "Anger, Power, and Women's Sense of Self. *Ms.* July 1985, 42.

Gorsuch, R.L. "R.B. Cattell. An Integration of Psychology and Ethics." *Multivariate Behavioral Research, 19,* (April/July 1984): 209–211.

Graf, R.G. "Induced Self-Esteem as a Determinant of Behavior." *The Journal of Social Psychology, 85,* (1971): 213–217.

Gratch, A. "Are you a Tamed Rebel?" *The Executive Female,* May/June 1985, 21–22.

Greenburg, R.S. "Discussion of the Psychodynamics of Aggression in Women." *The American Journal of Psychoanalysis, 36,* (3), (Fall 1976): 205–206.

Harragan, B.L. *Games Mother Never Taught You*. New York: Rawson Associates, 1977.

Harris, G.T. "Godfathers and Gossips." *Industry Week, 207,* (2) (October, 1972): 32–37.

Hayes, T.J. "Ethics in Business: Problem Identification and Potential Solutions." *Hospital Material Management Quarterly,* (May 1983): 37–38.

Hegarty, W.H., & Sims, H.P., Jr., Some Determinants of Unethical Decision Behavior: An Experiment. *Journal of Applied Psychology, 63,* (4), (1978): 451–457.

Hendrix, K. "Influx of Women Changing Workplace." *Los Angeles Times,* /September 14, 1984, 1, 18, 31.

Hochschild, A. "The American Woman: Another Idol of Social Science." *Transaction,* December 1970, 14.

Hochschild, A.R. "A Review of Sex-role Research." *American Journal of Sociology, 78,* (4), (1973): 1011–1029.

Hoffman, M.L. "Personality and Social Development." *American Review of Psychology 28,* (1977): 295–321.

Hunt, S.D. and Chonko, L.B. "Marketing and Machiavellianism." *Journal of Marketing, 48,* (Summer 1984): 31–40.

Johnson, H.L. "Ethics and the Executive." *Business Horizons, 24,* (2), (May/June 1981): 53–59.

Johnson, P. "Women and Power: Toward a Theory of Effectiveness." *Journal of Social Issues, 32,* (3) (1976): 99–110.

Josefowitz, N. "Management Men and Women: Closed vs. Open Doors." *Harvard Business Review,* (September/October 1980): 4–6.

Kanter, R.M. *Men and Women of the Corporation,* New York: Basic Books, (1977).

Kantrowitz, L.E. "Sex Role Development and Intellectual and Ethical Development in Young Adults." (Doctoral dissertation, Boston University School of Education). *Dissertation Abstracts International, 41*(5B), (November 1980): 1942B.

Katz, J. "Cover-up and Collective Integrity: On the Natural Antagonisms of Authority Internal and External to Organizations." *Social Problems, 25,* (1) (October 1977).

Kiechel, W., III., "Facing up to Executive Anger." *Fortune,* November 1981, 205–208.

Kremer, J.F. "The Effect of Level of Provocation and Attributions About the Provoker on Aggression and Anger." (Doctoral dissertation, Loyola University of Chicago). *Dissertation Abstracts International, 36,* (3-B), (May 1976): 5800B-5801B.

Lasden, M. "The Check is in the Mail: The Fine Art of Corporate Lying." *Computer Decisions, 16,* (2) (February 1984): 83,90.

Lavrakas, P.J. "Human Differences in the Ability to Differentiate Spoken Lies from Spoken Truths." (Doctoral dissertation, Loyola University). *Dissertation Abstracts International, 37,* (12-B, part 1), (June 1977): 6406B–6407B.

Layden, M. "Whipping Your Worst Enemy on the Job: Hostility." *Nations's Business,* October 1978, 87–90.

Lever, J. "Sex Differences in the Games Children Play." *Social Problems, 23,* (1976): 478–487.

Light, H.K. "Differences in Employed Women's Anxiety, Depression, and Hostility Levels According to Their Career and Family Role Commitment." *Psychological Reports, 55,* (1984): 290.

Linowes, D.F. "International Business and Morality." *Vital speeches of the day,* Vol. 43, No. 15, (March 25, 1977): 475–478.

Macleod, J.S. "The Double Standard in Qualifications." *Employment Relations Today, 10,* No. 2 (Summer 1983): 153–157.

McDermott, K., "New Players, New Rules." *D&B Reports,* (September/October 1985), 20–22.

McDonagh, E.L. "Social Exchange and Moral Development: Dimensions of Self, Self Image and Identity." *Human Relations, 35,* (8) (1982): 659–674.

Marshall, J. *Women Managers: Travelers in a Male World.* New York: John Wiley & Sons, Inc., 1984.

Maslow, R.H. *The Farther Reaches of Human Nature.* New York: Viking Press, 1971.

Miller, A.S. "Business Morality: Some Unanswered (and Perhaps Unanswerable) Questions." *The Annals of the American Academy of Political and Social Science,* (363), (January 1966): 95–101.

Miller, J.B. *Toward a New Psychology of Women*. Boston: Beacon Press, 1976.

Miranker, C.W. "Women Struggle to Climb Valley's High Tech Ladder." *San Francisco Examiner*, September 11, 1985, D1, 7.

Nichols, A. "Women and Leadership: Strategies for Social Workers and Clients." *Proceedings of the First Annual South Central Women's Studies Conference*, Fort Worth, TX, (June 1978): 814–823.

Nieters, J.L. "The Differential Role of Facial and Body Cues in the Recognition of Disguised Emotional Responses." (Doctoral dissertation, Saint Louis University, 1975). *Dissertation Abstracts International, 42*, (8-B), (1976): 3491B.

O'Leary, V.E. *Some Attitudinal Barriers to Occupational Aspirations in Women in Beyond Sex-role Stereotypes*, Boston, MA: Little Brown and Company, 1976.

Orth, C.D., and Jacobs, F. "Women in Managment: Pattern for Change." *Harvard Business Review*, (July/August 1971): 140, 145, 146.

Parker, T.C. "Actual Control, Perception of Control and Personal Versus Universal Helplessness." (Doctoral dissertation, Syracuse University, 1980). *Dissertation Abstracts International, 42*, (1-A), (1981): 138A.

Parson, M.J. "When A Colleague Doesn't Play Fair." *Savvy*, December 1986, 14–15.

Pennar, K. & Mervosh, E. "Women at Work." *Business Week*, January 1985, 80.

Perlman, L. "The Management of Hostility in Female Led vs. Male Led Self Study Groups: The fear of Women." *Dissertation Abstracts International, 38* (3-B) (1977): 1414B–1415B.

Pope, W.R. "Components of Moral Evaluation: Actors and the Accounts They Provide for Lies." (Doctoral dissertation, Virginia Commonwealth University). *Dissertation Abstracts International, 42*, (11-B) (May 1982): 4622B.

Quanty, M.B. "An Experimental Evaluation of the Aggression Catharsis Hypothesis." (Doctoral dissertation, University of Missouri). *Dissertation Abstracts International, 39*, (10-B) (April 1979): 5149B.

Reed, C.B. "Professional Women Today: The Relationship of Their Sex-role Identities to Anxiety, Depression, Hostility and Selected Demographic Variables." (Doctoral dissertation, University of Florida). *Dissertation Abstracts International, 40*, (4-A) (October 1979): 1883A.

Rogan, H. 'Young Executive Women Advance Farther, Faster Than Predecessors." *The Wall Street Journal*, October 26, 1984, 13, 52.

———. "Women Executives Feel That Men Both Aid and Hinder Their Careers." *The Wall Street Journal,* October 29, 1984, 31.

———. "Executive Women Still Find it Difficult to Balance Demands of Home, Job." *The Wall Street Journal,* October 30, 1984, 33.

———. "Top Women Executives Find Path to Power is Strewn With Hurdles." *The Wall Street Journal,* October 25, 1985, Section 2:4.

Rosen, B. and Jerdee, T.H. "Sex Stereotyping in the Executive Suite." *The Harvard Business Review: Problems in Review* (March/April 1974): 51–53.

Russo, N.P. "Overview in Sex-roles, Fertility, and the Motherhood Mandate." *Psychology of Women Quarterly, 4,* (1979): 7–15.

Sakai, J.D. "Nonverbal Communication in the Detection of Deception Among Women and Men." (Doctoral dissertation, University of California, Davis). *Dissertation Abstracts International, 37,* (12-B, part 1) (June 1982): 6406B–6407B.

Sanford, L.T. and Donovan, M.E. *Women & Self Esteem.* New York: Penguin Books, 1984.

Schaef, A.W. *Women's Reality: An Emerging Female System in a White Male Society.* Minneapolis, Minnesota: Winston Press, 1985.

Schein, V.E. "Examining and Illusion: The Role of Deceptive Behaviors in Organizations." *Human Relations, 32,* (4) (1979): 287–295.

Schwartz, F.N. "Corporate Women: What It Takes to Get to the Top." *Businessweek.* June 22, 1987.

Sherlock, P. "Women in Business Management." Paper presented for Psychology 662 class, University of Santa Clara June 23, 1977.

Silver, M., and Geller, D. "On the Irrelevance of Evil. The Organization and Individual Action." *Journal of Social Issues, 34,* (4) (1978): 125–136.

"Social Conditioning and Competition." *The Executive Female,* November/December 1981, 27.

Solodky, M.L. "Objective Self-awareness, Standards of Evaluation, Levels of Incentive and Moral Behavior." (Doctoral dissertation, Illinois Institute of Technology). *Dissertation Abstracts International, 40.* (8-B) (1980): 4033B-4034B.

"Speaking out About the Workplace: Survey Results." *The Executive Female,* November/December 1981, 6–8.

Spector, P.E. "Relationships of Organizational Frustration with Reported Behavioral Reactions of Employees." *Journal of Applied Psychology, 60,* (5) (1975) 635–637.

Stark, N.R. "The Career Counselor." *The Executive Female,* May/June 1985, 33.

Sutton, C.D., and Moore, K.K. "Executive Women—Twenty Years Later." *Harvard Business Review,* (September/October 1985): 2–7.

Symonds, M. "Psychodynamics of Aggression in Women." *The American Journal of Psychoanalysis, 36,* (3) (1976): 195–203.

Trafford, A., et al., "She's Come a Long Way—or Has She?" *U.S. News and World Report,* August 6, 1985, 45.

Trotsky, J. "Must Women Executives be Such Barracudas?" *The Wall Street Journal,* November, 1981, 24.

Tumulty, K. "Wage Gap: Women Still the Second Sex." *Los Angeles Times,* September 13, 1984, 6,7,.

Tutelian, L. "Bendix Redux." *Savvy.* (April, 1984). 17.

Vaden, R.E., and Lynn, N.B. "The Administrative Person: Will Women Bring a Differing Morality to Management?" *University of Michigan Business Review,* Vol. 31, No. 2 (March 1979): 22–25.

Van Wagner, K., and Swanson, C. "From Machiavelli to Ms: Differences in Male-Female Power Styles." *Public Administration Review 39* (1) (January/February 1979): 66–72.

Wallace, D., & Rothaus, P. "Communication, Group Loyalty, and Trust in the PD Game." *Conflict Resolution, 13,* (3) (September 1969): 370–380.

Weil, H. "A New Study Reveals Some Surprising Findings About the Fatal Flaws of Top Managers." *Savvy,* January 1984, 39.

Wiley, M.G., and Eskilson, A. "The Interaction of Sex and Power Base on Perceptions of Managerial Effectiveness." *Academy of Management Journal,* (3) (November 25, 1982): 671–677.

Wilkes, R.E. "Fraudulent Behavior by Consumers." *Journal of Marketing, 42,* (4) (October 1978): 67–75.

Wilson, G.T. "Solving Ethical Problems and Saving Your Career." *Business Horizons,* (November/December, 1983) 16–20.

Wright, D. "Piaget's Theory of Practical Morality." *British Journal of Psychology, 73* (1982): 279–280, 282.

Yankelovich, D. *New Rules: Searching for Self-Fulfillment in a World Turned Upside-Down.* New York: Random House, Inc., 1981.

Zeedyk-Ryan, J., and Smith, G.F. "The Effects of Crowding on Hostility, Anxiety, and Desire for Social Interaction." *The Journal of Social Psychology, 120,* (1983): 245–252.

Zey-Ferrell, M., and Ferrell, O.C. "Role-set Configuration and Opportunity as Predictors of Unethical Behavior in Organizations." *Human Relations, 35,* (7) (1982): 587–604.

Zey-Ferrell, M., Weaver, K.M., and Ferrell, O.C. "Predicting Unethical Behavior among Marketing Practitioners." *Human Behavior, 32,* (7) 557–569.